Brothers, buses, pirates and belles

The Thomas Bros. story

by Phil Trotter

First published in Great Britain in 2023
by Bryngold Books Ltd.,
100 Brynau Wood, Cimla,
Neath, South Wales SA11 3YQ.

www.bryngoldbooks.com

**Typesetting, layout,
editing and design
by Bryngold Books**

Copyright © Phil Trotter & David Roberts 2023

All rights reserved. No part of this publication may be reproduced, stored in a retrieval system, or transmitted in any form, or by any means, electronic, mechanical, photocopying, recording, or otherwise without the prior permission, in writing, of the copyright holder, nor be otherwise circulated in any form or binding or cover other than that in which it is published and without a similar condition being imposed on the subsequent publisher.

ISBN 978-1-905900-57-2

www.bryngoldbooks.com

To work rest and play

Brothers, Buses, Pirates and Belles is dedicated to those who kept the wheels turning at Thomas Bros. (Port Talbot) Ltd. as well as those who used the company's buses for travel to and from school, work, to the cinema, the shops or for a plethora of other reasons. Among them, those whose journeys were filled with joyful anticipation of a sunny summer's day at Aberavon Beach and others whose use of the services might have been for more mundane reasons. This book also remembers all those no longer with us who contributed to the success of the proud company and its predecessors.

Itinerary for

Author and his quest to fill transport history gap	6
Bus company with an eventful back story	7
Buses arrived amid steam, slag and sand	8
Trials and tragedy of the troubled twenties	16
Charabanc dream often became a nightmare	26
Rivalry that brought piracy to valley roads	28
Transport legislation that changed the bus industry	36
Dark clouds broke to reveal a silver lining	44
When Bedfords ruled the road	48
Austerity to affluence via the positive route	56
Routes that tested the best	60
The electrifying financial idea that was BET	74
Was that colour Thomas Bros. blue or green?	78

the journey

82	**New freedoms, but state control was looming**
86	The topless belles of 'Bravon
96	Routes around town and up the valley
102	A crusader, highwayman and the maid . . .
118	**Hard working road staff kept the wheels turning**
128	Memories in miniature
132	**Modern premises that made life easier for staff**
138	Scattered survivors
142	**A change of colour and what might have been**
146	Firms in the Thomas Bros. genealogy
148	A day in the life of buses and drivers
152	**Facts and Figures about the fleet**
170	**The Dragon that ran a bus fleet of its own**
175	Bibliography
176	A big thank you!

Author and his quest to fill transport history gap

Phil Trotter spent nearly 40 years in the bus industry, retiring as Marketing Manager for First Cymru Buses, which was formerly South Wales Transport, in 2019. Over the years he witnessed at first hand the transition from being part of a nationalised industry to a locally owned management buy-out and subsequently to becoming part of a large multi-national transport group.

Deregulation of bus and coach services came in the 1980s and brought with it a return to some of the competitive cut and thrust which would have been familiar to those working in the industry in the 1920s. Some of that activity took place at Port Talbot, an area for which Phil produced passenger transport publicity material for many years.

Born and brought up in Swansea at a time when his parents, like many others had yet to purchase a car, Phil soon got to know and love the local transport network, with its hard-working AEC buses, the Mumbles Railway and at the same time the open toppers operated at Aberavon Beach during the summer months by Thomas Bros.

There was a minor blip to proceedings linked to any thoughts of perhaps a career in the transport industry during the 1970s while Phil trained as a teacher in Wrexham and as is often the case at that age, other distractions were given priority!

A subsequent full time role with a students' union, however, proved to be an excellent training ground for business. But even then, the vintage vehicles of M.A.Evans & Son of Wrexham were at the centre of college life.

One of these in particular, was a petrol engined Bedford SB, registration number

Phil Trotter — a man who set off on a mission to preserve the history of Port Talbot's main bus company, but discoverd a whole lot more besides as he dug deep into the town's passenger transport past.

TUN 548. Phil remembers fondly how this favourite of the time managed to blow smoke rings when idling.

After two less than happy years teaching where the only highlight of each day was a ride on an ex-Merthyr Leyland double decker, he soon broke free from the chalk face and joined South Wales Transport.

As a lifetime transport enthusiast Phil has travelled extensively throughout Europe photographing numerous transport systems. He has also been very active in the bus and railway preservation movement.

More recently, as a member of Mensa, Phil has become a confirmed advocate of digital media as a method by which transport operators can quickly monitor services and communicate with their customers.

Bus company with an eventful back story

Brothers, buses, pirates and belles came into being following a realisation that when it came to the publication of the story of the four companies which merged to form the enlarged South Wales Transport organisation at the end of the 1960s, Thomas Bros. (Port Talbot) Ltd. had largely been overlooked.

Early research soon revealed that there was an eventful back story to the company and an initial plan to take the easy route and investigate only the years from 1950 to 1970 was quickly abandoned.

The result is that not only has the story of Thomas Bros. (Port Talbot) Ltd., been told for the first time, but uniquely alongside it and immensley fascinating, that of the pre-Second World War local bus operators in and around the town has been given the kind of airing it has for so long deserved.

To understand exactly why and how the bus companies at Port Talbot evolved and led to the eventual formation of Thomas Bros. it is important to take into account the political, social and economic changes which took place in the town over the years and which had an effect on bus services in the borough. Clearly, the massive steelworks was and still is at the heart of the community.

In the 1960s Aberavon Beach was an important leisure destination for the people of South Wales with the local authority harbouring aspirations for it to become the Blackpool of South Wales. To a degree they succeeded, attracting as many as 120,000 visitors during peak weekends. Although the availability of low priced holidays in sunny southern Europe soon eclipsed their efforts, recent events have shown that there may still be a market for what these days are popularly referred to as 'staycations'.

It is easy to get carried away examining the detail of different bus types. As someone whose career was spent attempting to show the positive, human side of a large bus operator, part of which succeeded Thomas Bros. at Port Talbot, I have long believed that people are and always will be, at the heart of every bus operator, whether they are the company's drivers, conductors, engineers, managers or — and most importantly of course — the paying passengers.

Some of the buildings used by Thomas Bros. are also touched on, for seemingly innocuous structures, including an early days ramshackle collection, can often hold a wealth of memories for those people who used them or even lived close by.

There can be little doubt that Brothers, buses, pirates and belles is about much more than a bus company. If reading it brings back memories or if you have any photographs which you'd like to share, why not add them to the Thomas Bros. Facebook page? Search 'Thomas Bros. (Port Talbot) Ltd., Memories'. It would further help to keep the memory of the company alive.

Phil Trotter, 2023

> 'By day the valley was filled with clouds of steam and smoke. By night it was dazzled by the glare of furnaces.'

The Afan Valley today is a magnet for anyone from far and wide seeking fresh air recreation. Winding its way north east from the urban centre of Port Talbot it boasts an extensive forest park offering glorious views, leafy woodland walks and some of the world's best mountain bike trails.

This is set against the tranquil backdrop of steep sided hills, the constant call of songbirds and an abundance of greenery. Communities such as Cwmavon, Pontrhydyfen, Tonmawr, Cymmer and Glyncorrwg all focus on Port Talbot as their nearest centre for business and leisure. Rewind just over a century and this environment would have been much different.

The Afan Valley forms part of the South Wales Coalfield. In the upper valley there were several deep pits, plus many small drift mines driven into the hillsides. In the lower valley around Cwmavon, where it widened t, a metal industry grew. Here there was room for blast furnaces, rail and bar mills, coke ovens and tinplate works. In the daytime clouds of steam and smoke enveloped the valley, while at night the glare of the furnaces lit up the streets and hillsides.

This 14-seater 1928 Bean vehicle, KO 8824, was obtained by Thomas Bros. from East Surrey Traction in 1932 and remained in the fleet until 1940.

Buses arrived amid steam, slag and sand

A horse-drawn brake operated by Mr. E. John of Taibach in 1911, typical of transport in pre-motorised times.

Oliver Fenton, one of the first car owners in Port Talbot, at the wheel of a steam powered vehicle. He later became a key player in early bus operation in the town.

A typical early 20th Century Port Talbot skyline scene — all chimney stacks and smoke.

The air would have been laden with toxic fumes which poisoned the flora and fauna and led to farmers taking court action in search of a remedy. For much of the 19th Century and well into the 20th, the River Afan and its tributaries were severely polluted.

By the start of the 20th century the iron and copper producers of the Afan Valley were finding the transport costs of imported foreign ores excessive. As a result, industries were being relocated nearer the coast to reduce costs. As the ports developed, copper production in the Lower Swansea Valley soon eclipsed that at Cwmavon.

The industrialisation around Cwmavon and on the coast meant that the existing dock facility at Aberavon needed upgrading to handle the increasing traffic of raw materials and finished products. There was severe competition from docks at Swansea and Cardiff at this time.

Welsh landowner, industrialist and Liberal Party politician, Christopher Rice Mansel Talbot MP, whose family home was Margam Castle, realised that his land was a resource to be exploited both for his personal wealth and for the benefit of the region. Talbot could see that improved transport links would oil the wheels of industry, securing further growth. In 1834 and 1836 he introduced a Bill in Parliament to expand the old dock at Aberavon. The revitalised dock became known as Port Talbot in his honour, a name which later came to encompass the whole town. It took a further 85 years however before the Borough of Port Talbot was formally established, in 1921.

As each industry developed, workers were attracted into the area and settlements were established in the valley to house them with their families. Those communities which had built up in the Afan Valley had a daily need to move workers from home to their place of employment and a requirement to bring in the much needed additional workforce from further afield. For example, the population of Glyncorrwg increased from 600 in 1861 to over 6000 in 1901. Clearly, in order to move the raw materials and products to and from the ports, as well as workers to and from industry, transport became an essential requirement.

Christopher Rice Mansel Talbot.

The histories of the railways of the Afan Valley have been documented elsewhere, but it is worth noting that the passenger facilities they offered were quite rudimentary and unable to provide the door to door service offered by road transport. For those living any distance from the railway, the day might begin and end with a long walk to the nearest station. In any case, the railways were more concerned with the high volume and value freight movements, leaving opportunities for bus owners in the 20th century.

Four railway companies had been established in the previous century. Again, Talbot played an important role in the development of railways through his chairmanship of the South Wales Railway which in 1863 became part of the Great Western Railway, at which time he joined their board.

■ **The South Wales Mineral Railway:**
Built between 1856-65 this linked Glyncorrwg, Cymmer via the Gyfylchi tunnel with Briton Ferry docks. It also carried coal from the mines. The SWMR was never a financial success and was worked by the GWR from 1908, this arrangement being consolidated in the railway grouping of 1923. The line saw a public passenger service for a relativelyt short time, lasting only until September 1930.

■ **The Llynfi and Ogmore Railway:**
In 1878 this linked with Cymmer via a tunnel from the Llynfi Valley near Caerau and later up the valley to Abergwynfi. The line linked the Afan Valley with the towns of Bridgend, Porthcawl and Cardiff.

- **The Rhondda and Swansea Bay Railway:** This was incorporated in 1882 to connect the upper end of the Rhondda Fawr with Swansea via Blaengwynfi, Cymmer and Cwmavon to transport coal and other minerals to Swansea Docks. At Port Talbot, there were two stations, Aberavon Town and Aberavon Seaside. Significantly, the line crossed the main road (Station Road) through Port Talbot via a level crossing and continued towards Briton Ferry along what is now the B4286, Afan Way. A passenger service of seven trains a day ran between Treherbert and Swansea, with two on Sundays. The line closed in December 1962.

- **The Port Talbot Railway and Dock Company:** This latecomer, opened in 1898, linked the Pelenna Valley, Pontryhydyfen and Glyncorrwg to Port Talbot Docks. A passenger service of four trains a day was augmented with an extra Saturday afternoon trip and a return evening trip. The passenger service between Port Talbot and Maesteg was withdrawn from September 1933.

Christopher Talbot had died in January 1890 aged 86; his only son, Theodore, had pre-deceased him after a riding accident in 1876. Therefore, his unmarried daughter, Emily Charlotte, then 39 and by all accounts a force to be reckoned with inherited his wealth of around £6 million. She continued her father's interest in industrial growth and was the principal shareholder in the P.T.R.&D. When she in turn died in 1918 she was described as one of the UK's wealthiest women and an eminent philanthropist.

The origins of the principal industry which still defines the town of Port Talbot stretched back as far as 1253 when the monks of Margam Abbey began extracting iron and lead ores. A more sophisticated start was made in 1902 by the Port Talbot Iron and Steel Company on a site near Port Talbot Dock on land leased from Emily Talbot and the Margam Estate. A miscalculation of the building costs and technical problems meant that steelmaking there never really achieved the owners' aspirations and production ceased with 250 redundancies in 1903. Had it lasted a little longer the steel company would have benefited from the increasing demand for its products between 1910 and 1918 with the advent of the First World War.

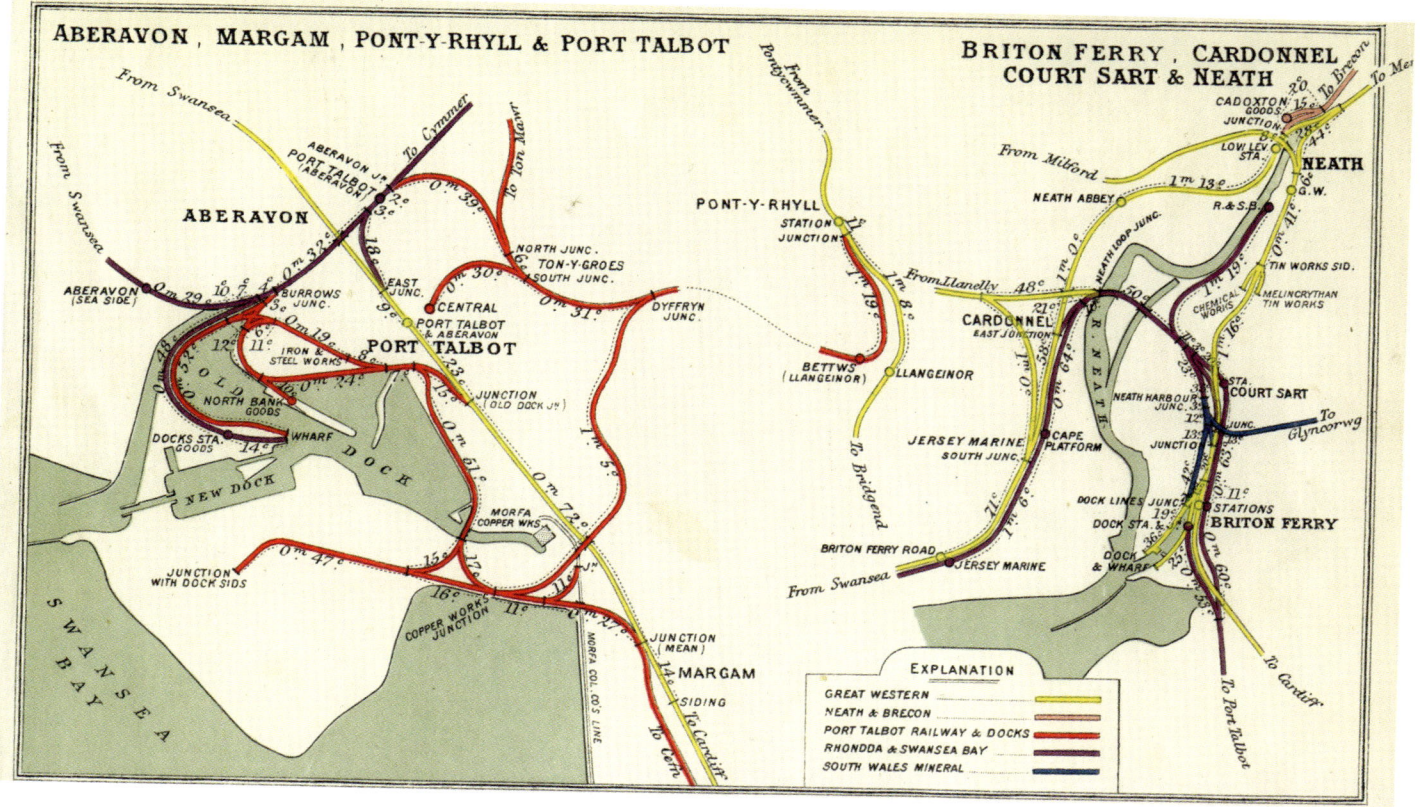

A Railway Clearing House junction map showing railways in Port Talbot and Neath in 1920. The RCH was responsible for allocating revenue to the various companies.

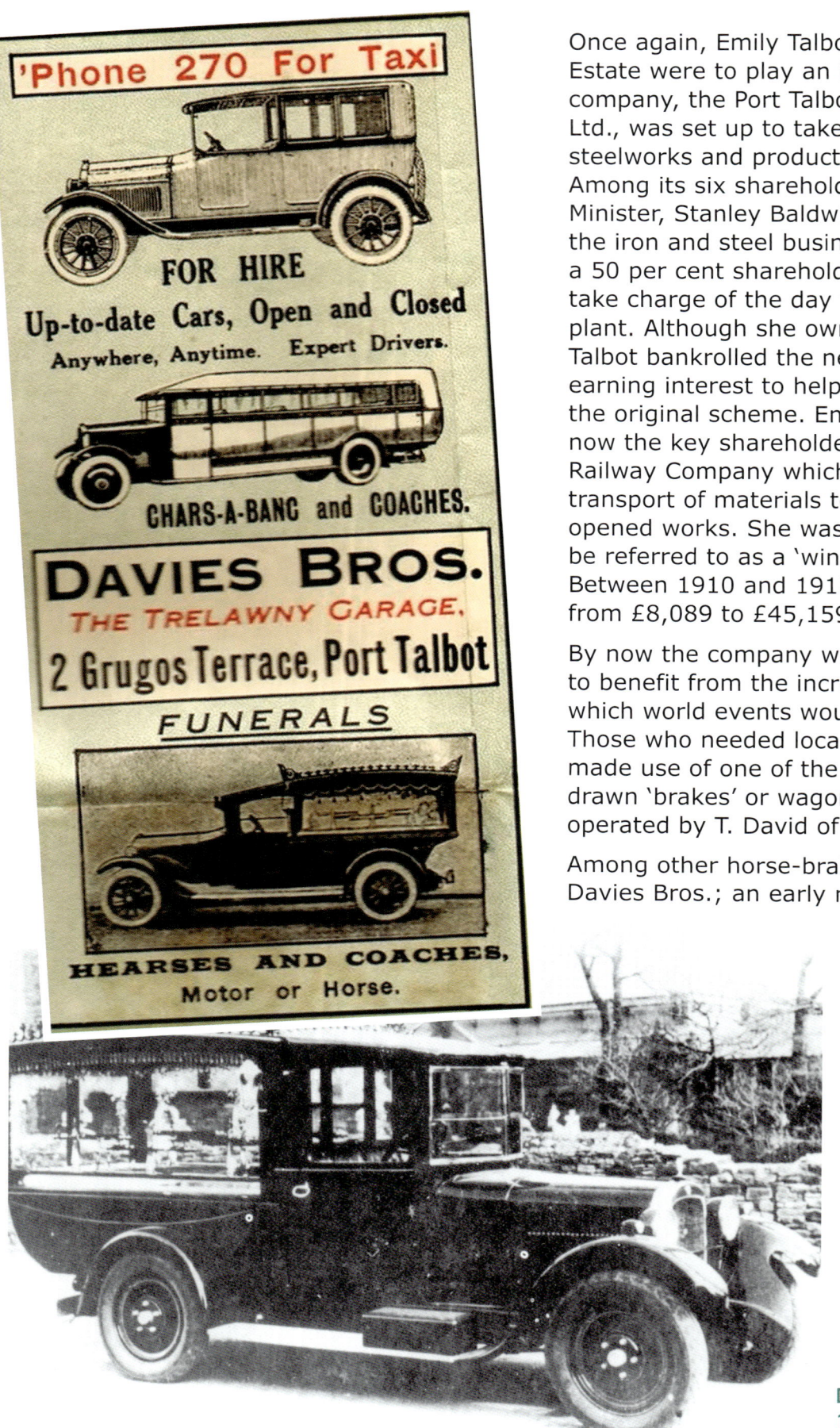

Once again, Emily Talbot and the Margam Estate were to play an important role. A new company, the Port Talbot Steel Company Ltd., was set up to take over the old steelworks and production restarted in 1908. Among its six shareholders was future Prime Minister, Stanley Baldwin whose family ran the iron and steel business which as a 50 per cent shareholder was persuaded to take charge of the day to day running of the plant. Although she owned no shares, Emily Talbot bankrolled the new organisation, earning interest to help cover her losses on the original scheme. Emily, of course, was now the key shareholder in the Port Talbot Railway Company which benefitted from the transport of materials to and from the re-opened works. She was in what today would be referred to as a 'win-win' situation. Between 1910 and 1912 the PTSC profit rose from £8,089 to £45,159.

By now the company was in a good position to benefit from the increase in steel demand which world events would soon require. Those who needed local transport could have made use of one of the area's several horse drawn 'brakes' or wagonettes, such as those operated by T. David of Cwmavon.

Among other horse-brake operators were the Davies Bros.; an early manifestation of operator Davies Bros. Ltd. of Port Talbot which turned to motor buses in 1923. Hitherto Davies Bros. had run taxis and hearses in the area. This enterprise was overseen by the very astute Dick Davies. Another of the brake operators was oil dealer Evan Thomas, who lived at 1, Alfred

Davies Bros. ran this 1926 Dodge hearse, registered TX 402.

Street, Aberavon. His family included wife Margaret, daughter Sarah and significantly, sons Thomas Gwyn and Evan Stanley. In the 1911 census, Thomas was described as a brake driver and Evan as an oilman. The business was carried out from a large outbuilding at the rear of the family home.

During August 1901 it was reported that a Swansea motor wagonette visited Aberavon and took public dignitaries for a run to the beach. This was believed to have been the first occasion on which a motor vehicle had been seen there and crowds thronged Aberavon to witness what was then a novel spectacle.

In 1901 there was also a proposal from Glamorgan County Council to build a tramway from Briton Ferry to Taibach, but this was turned down by Margam Council. In 1905 the Aberavon District Tramways Syndicate, Ltd., a company registered in Newport, was given powers to build three and three quarter miles of tramway from Aberavon town through Port Talbot to Margam. Again, this was never progressed, but might have been if the huge steelworks had been present at the time. Equally enticing is the thought that the Briton Ferry to Taibach scheme could have met the Neath & District Tramway and formed the basis of an interurban tram route between Port Talbot and neighbouring Neath.

In May 1906, it was reported that a London syndicate planned to run motor buses between Taibach, Port Talbot, Cwmavon and Aberavon Beach. Four were to enter service in June with the fleet being expanded to 15 if it became a success.

Emily Charlotte Talbot

Commercial Motor and the Western Mail newspaper reported on 10th October 1907 that a public meeting had been held at the Central Restaurant, Aberavon under the chairmanship of Captain Oliver Felton along with Harry Arthur Burgess JP of Pentyla, Mrs. Charlotte Arnold of Aberavon and David Jones of the Angel public house.

Aberavon Town Council granted running powers to the company around the same time. The business side of the proposition was in the hands of Mr. David W. Drummond, a Port Talbot solicitor, who submitted a draft prospectus. In November the London & Port Talbot Motor Company was registered with an authorised capital of £10,000 in £1 shares. Its registered office was given as Bank Chambers, Aberavon and its aims included the construction and sale of passenger vehicles. The new company announced that it was in the market to buy single deck buses suitable for carrying 12 passengers as well as luggage. It was estimated that the annual takings per vehicle would be about £1,065, and that there would be a working profit of about £500 per vehicle per annum. Commercial Motor magazine observed that these figures seemed rather optimistic, but was generally supportive of the scheme, bearing in mind the needs of Aberavon, Cwmavon and Taibach if 'careful

One of the earliest photographs of a Port Talbot passenger carrier is this one of 1922 Guy Charabanc, NY 1826, operated by Mason of Cwmavon at the time.

The 'Thomas Bros.' family and many of the facts about it, as recorded in 1911 census of England and Wales.

management' ensued. All this appears to have been a little premature for on 9th January 1908 Commercial Motor reported that: 'We understand that the formation of the London and Port Talbot Motor Company, Limited, has not yet been completed'.

The inclusion of London in the title was probably done to include Messrs. S. Broad and A. Haswell whose addresses were given as 'in the City.' The company disappeared after 1907 and it seems that the later Aberavon & District Motor Co., of 20 High Street, Aberavon was the same operation under a different name. Indeed, David Jones and Oliver Felton were named as managing it.

Among the company's early buses in 1907 were a 40hp Bussing-Straker Squire single decker and a chain driven Lacoste & Battmann double decker from London where the type had been found to suffer from frequent breakdowns. More than likely this came from the Arrow Omnibus Company which had amalgamated with the Provincial Omnibus Company and was seeking to dispose of these unreliable buses. Colonel Frank Searle, assistant engineer with Provincial, related later that "Everything that could go wrong with the vehicles went wrong," and that the senior engineer "was up day and night attending to their varied and sad diseases."

The double decker was driven to South Wales by William Joseph Tuningley from Rotherhithe, who in his obituary published in 1965, was stated to have delivered the bus to the Aberavon and District Motor Company and decided to settle in the area. Tuningley lived in Taibach and later drove the bus on services to Aberavon Beach, Cwmavon (Red Lion) and Taibach; the company had cut 18 inches off the top deck so that it could fit under Water Street bridge!

A 26 seat Commer Cars charabanc 'garden seater' was also owned by Aberavon & District — or more specifically, by Oliver Felton. It was used on miners' services from Aberavon to Cribbwr Fawr Colliery and Cwmavon. On Saturdays a special service brought shoppers from Kenfig Hill to W.J. Williams cloth hall in Water Street. These were the first occasions when motor buses were used in the Port Talbot area. Conductors employed in those days included Trevor Saunders, Ivan Smith and Alec and Ivan Grant.

Two incidents involving Aberavon & District vehicles are recorded with a third which might be attributable. The first, in October 1908 involved a child falling beneath a bus at Taibach; fortunately he survived. The second, in April of the following year, was a collision between a bus coming from Kenfig

Hill and a horse-drawn vehicle. The bus was towed to the yard of the Talbot Arms Hotel, Taibach and was described as being only a few months old. The third incident, in Taibach involved the death of a cyclist. The charabanc company was named as the 'Aberavon Motor Bus Company' whose manager was Alfred Haswell.

In 1910 an 'express' charabanc of unknown make was purchased by David Jones and driven by William Tuningley and Trevor Saunders. This, however, might be the previously mentioned Commer changing hands. The Aberavon & District activity seems to have ceased after 1911 with the formation of the Express Motor Co., indicating a possible break up of the company. Some of the vehicles and personalities involved with the Aberavon company appeared with other operators at this time. Captain Oliver Felton, an ardent early motorist whose home was at Aberavon but who prior to the war had been an assistant agent to Emily Talbot, served in France with the 15th Battalion Welsh Regiment and was decorated with the British War and Victory medals. He later retired to Port Talbot and died in 1957 aged 79.

In 1913 there was a brief report in Commercial Motor magazine that:
'The Aberavon Corporation announces its preparedness to assist enterprise with a yearly subsidy in regard to establishment of a motor bus service.'

Nothing else was reported, but world events were soon to take precedence. The outbreak of the First World War in 1914 brought with it a massive increase in the demand for steel to support the war effort. Capacity at Port Talbot was increased considerably with the construction of a new plant at Margam where production included heavy products for shipbuilding. The Ministry of Munitions required as much steel as the country could produce and Port Talbot turned out shell grade steel to produce the ammunition required at the front. The pre-war market-led steel production had been overtaken by the state-driven demand for the war. This, between the wars would lead to over capacity but for the time being Port Talbot had become a profitable, modern steelworks with excellent transport links, turning out up to 364,000 tons a year consisting of a wide variety of products.

For the embryonic bus industry, the war brought a halt to new developments. Many of the motor buses in evidence were commandeered for military service. Their crews were also called up to serve the country in its time of need and petrol was rationed. Use of motor buses for non-essential travel was forbidden.

There is anecdotal evidence that just one petrol engined charabanc was available for use at Port Talbot, old horse-drawn wagonettes had to be dusted off for use. Any expansion was generally out of the question, except of course where it made a contribution to the war effort such as with services to steelworks.

After the war, developments were frustrated by a shortage of new vehicles and the 'Spanish Flu' pandemic, but soon the 1920s dawned, bringing rapid changes, many new operators and with them cut-throat competition. An eventful time lay ahead.

One of the first motor vehicles built to carry 60 people was a D-type four ton Caledon boasting 40hp. The Express Motor Co. of Aberavon was one of the early customers of Glasgow builders Scottish Commercial Cars Ltd.

'The post war years brought an exciting and adventurous time for some, but one of danger for many others'

After the First World War, those who had survived the horrors of the conflict had to seek new jobs when they returned home. Often the work this entailed focussed around skills they had learned in the armed forces, such as mechanical engineering or driving.

The thoughts of many turned to setting up a transport company, either for goods or passengers, sometimes both. This is frequently cited as the reason for the rapid growth of the bus industry at that time, but there were also many from civilian life who became involved along with other factors.

Motor vehicles had become more reliable during wartime and although the manufacture of new ones had yet to increase, there was an ample availability of low priced former War Department lorries. Using a little ingenuity, these could be converted to buses or charabancs. Parliamentary records from the time reveal that one year on from the Armistice, Major D. Davies asked the Secretary of State for War in the House of Commons how many lorries were in the possession of the War Department.

Registered as BX 2764 this 1922 Daimler was owned by Richard Barry, centre, and mainly used on the Aberavon Market to Aberavon Beach service.

Trials and tragedy of the troubled twenties

This Guy BA vehicle in Station Road, Port Talbot, TX 3720 appears to have been on the Goytre service operated by Morgan's Motors which was acquired by Thomas Bros. in 1934.

This is TG 4862, a 1933 20-seat Guy ONDF which was supplied new by dealer Oscar Chess to Richard Hodges of Cwmavon. The bus was sold to Thomas Bros in 1941.

The first vehicle owned by Morgan's Motors was a Ford T registered as L 9515 and seen in this postcard view of Aberavon promenade. The bus service started in 1928.

The Secretary of State, a certain Winston Churchill, replied that at the time of the Armistice there had been 51,950, but that 33,201 had by that time been sold. There was a post war shortage of newly built vehicles and importing them from wartime adversaries was out of the question.

It was an exciting and adventurous time for some, but downright dangerous for others as would-be operators were prepared to use almost anything to start their business. These primitive vehicles had no electric starters of course and often no windscreens. Brake operation could be intermittent. Comfort for passengers and crews was scant with solid tyres, poor lighting and harsh springing. Luxury meant a charabanc with a folding canvas roof. Contemporary reports suggest that on such vehicles, a sudden downpour would soak the passengers before the roof could be deployed, such was the complexity of the task. Moreover, the roads were often in a bad condition with potholes and ruts and were dusty on hot days. The 'emissions' from horse powered transport must have added even more misery to the experience.

Nevertheless many operators were born, many following the same most lucrative routes and the 1920s became a period of intense and relatively uncontrolled competition. In Port Talbot for example, there were at one time 20-25 different operators in the town, some of them owning only one or two buses. The privilege of carrying passengers was at times, quite literally, fought for. Certain operators could hardly be complimented for the quality of service which they offered. Vehicles were run into the ground and maintenance was a challenge in this competitive environment. Under these circumstances many smaller enterprises were short lived as owners gave up or sold out to those in a better position to offer longevity. Others hung on to become successful and respected businesses.

At this time, licensing of vehicles and drivers fell under the control of the local authorities' Hackney Carriage Committees and the local police force who could object to services which caused traffic problems.

In each authority bus drivers were required to wear a badge to show that they were entitled to drive in a particular area. On long routes legislation demanded that a driver carried three or four badges for each town or area within his journey, making sure that he was displaying the correct one as he passed through.

At Port Talbot the busy route from Aberavon to Cwmavon and Pontrhydyfen became hotly contested with up to 14 different operators at one time. Each had the objective of outwitting its competitors and numerous underhand practices were engaged. Buses would run late or early to steal competitors' passengers and sometimes turn back short of the terminus to gain advantage on the return trip. A system of regulatory time clocks was added at key stops but had very little effect. If an operator didn't clock in on or just before their allocated time they were fined for poaching passengers. The way around it was to punch the

A 1927 Star B with 20-seat Willowbrook bodywork, TX 3614, was new to Davies Bros. and ran until 1932 when it was scrapped.

This Commer RC vehicle, registered as BO 3079 was regularly used by Richard Barry on the Bethany Square to Margam route.

cards to certify an arrival or departure time but then wait until a competitor appeared behind them. The less reputable proprietors considered insurance to be an optional extra!

Meanwhile, the development of bus services in Port Talbot became quite tangled with joint ownership, key personalities owning shares in more than one operator, businesses registered at multiple addresses and vehicles (and drivers!) changing hands, being loaned between companies or kept at one another's garages. It became difficult to identify which operator owned any particular bus and some competing operators' families were connected by marriage. As if that wasn't complicated enough, on the Afan Valley route, several owners shared the same surname: Thomas. The buses' paint colours often reflected the previous owner's preference or depended upon the availability of paint. All of this meant that the authorities found difficulty identifying who owned what, where and when.

Benjamin Thomas (no known relation to the Thomas brothers) had started his bus business in 1919 with a capital of £30 and possessed four vehicles — a newspaper report shows him in Bankruptcy Court during November 1935, although by that time he had sold his bus company and become an iron, steel and coal merchant. Latterly, Benjamin Thomas used Bean, Bedford, Guy and Crossley vehicles.

Howell Hopkin Davies and Richard Selway Davies had set up Davies Bros. Ltd. to operate the service between Aberavon Beach and Margam. They had premises in Grugos Terrace which was later renamed Forge Road, and were the local funeral directors and taxi operator. Bus operation seems to have begun in 1923. In the early 1930s they also had horse drawn and motor hearses stabled in Sandfields Road, at premises also used for garaging vehicles. On 7th March 1934 they formed subsidiary company Thomas & James Ltd. which took over Benjamin Thomas who operated on the same route at 6 and 18 minutes past each hour, with the aforementioned Davies Bros. buses departing at 24, 30 and 36 minutes past. Davies Bros. bought Owen E. James's operation at the same time; Benjamin Thomas and Owen E. James were named as directors of Thomas & James Ltd. In 1935 they took over the Lewis & David foundry near Michna Street, Aberavon, as additional garage space. The company operated a mix of vehicles either purchased new or secondhand from other operators. In the 1930s this included a 26 seat Maudslay coach from the London General Omnibus Co. which ran at Port Talbot still with its 'General' fleet name; predictably, the bus became known locally as 'The General'.

In October 1935, under the Davies Bros. name, the pair were summoned by the South Wales Traffic Commissioners for using a motor vehicle as an express carriage vehicle, rather than for contract work and fined £2 each. It has not been possible to identify the vehicle concerned from the mixed fleet owned by Davies at the time.

Another newcomer was Richard Hodges who had first moved to Aberavon from Penygraig in 1914 and joined the police force. He subsequently joined the Army, only to be invalided out. In 1923 he had started running a bus on the Pontrhydyfen to

Aberavon route, by this time alongside 10 other operators. He sold out to Thomas Bros. in 1941 and stayed on as an engineer.

A well-known local entrepreneur, Richard 'Dick' Barry set up another operation after demobilisation from naval service. He ran a Commer Cub (BO 3079) on a service from Bethany Square to Margam and a chain driven Daimler (BX 2764) between the Market and Aberavon Beach. It would appear that by around 1927 he had lost interest in the enterprise and his description changed from being an omnibus proprietor to general merchant. His nefarious activities included trading in rabbit skins, a dodgy magneto and a copper boiler of dubious provenance.
At one point he owned a racehorse though there is no record of him having made any money from this equine enterprise.

Most of the other smaller firms had at least one bus on the Cwmavon and Pontrhydyfen route, all competing and using the already mentioned sharp practices to gain advantage over one another. In subsequent years there were takeovers, mergers and bankruptcies. Attempting to decipher exactly what went on between each of these operators is difficult but court cases reported in the local press provide more than just a hint of what was happening. Fortunately, the Port Talbot Guardian had begun publishing in 1925 and its columns suggest that if a fortnight went past without a case being brought in front of the council or courts, things were going well! Speeding and overcrowding were two of the most common offences, particularly when a competitor was on the road nearby, or at the end of the working day. The situation was exacerbated by the late 1920s with pneumatic tyres being used. Buses were in theory at least then allowed to travel at 20mph.
Those still on solid tyres were limited to 12mph!

On 21st October 1927, a writer in the Port Talbot Guardian observed:

"The buses between Pontrhydyfen and Aberavon seem to conform to the timetables, although sometimes there is a remarkable contrast in rates of motion.

"The other day I had occasion to go by bus in order to catch a connection at Port Talbot. But, to my utter disgust, we were moving forward at a very slow pace. Of course, as the result of a careful driver manipulating the wheel, I found myself so much in arrears as far as time was concerned at Port Talbot that I missed the connection and had to wait half an hour for the next.

"It was a coincidence that I found myself in the same bus returning to Pontrhydyfen late that evening and imagine my surprise when our wary driver of the morning completed the distance in record time. What a remarkable contrast! Why proceed so carefully in open daylight and at such a tremendous pace in darkness? The reason is not too far to seek. My readers will undoubtedly guess it."

Although the lucrative route to Cwmavon had no shortage of operators, still more wanted to get involved and the applications kept coming in. Amid the chaos, some councillors began to think that, if the council ran the services, there would be a more organised approach. The Port Talbot Guardian, 8th June 1928 reported that on an application being made for the granting of more licences on the Cwmavon road, Councillor H. J. Thomas pointed out that the public did not call for more buses as the running of the present services had been greatly improved and most of the present buses belonged to men running them by means of making instalment payments. The matter was referred to the Hackney Carriage Committee.

Councillor J. A. Brown referring to the motor bus question pointed out that the council made the greatest mistake in their lives when they did not run motor buses

Smartly dressed Thomas Bros. staff on parade outside the Jersey Beach Hotel during the 1930s. The 1930 Dennis Dart, left, VX 8830 had a 20 seat front entrance body built by Thurgood. It was purchased in 1933 and broken up in 1940. It is believed that it was heavy on petrol.

themselves, and thus acquire complete control over the services.

Clearly, tensions were running high among operators and sometimes physical violence ensued. The court reporters were being kept busy as is evidenced by a report in the Port Talbot Guardian, dated 29th June 1928:

'D. Richards, a motor bus driver, was summoned for an assault on John Arlon, a rival driver, on June 15th. On the day in question a dispute arose between the drivers when at Market Square, and later in the day, when meeting each other with their buses at the Hospital Road corner of Victoria Road, they again had words regarding the position of their vehicles. Richards got out of his bus and, entering the other one, struck Arlon in the face with his open hand. The defendant was fined £1.'

Trouble between the conductors of rival operators led to another recorded assault in April 1929. It was alleged on this occasion that an unnamed competitor had blocked a Davies Bros. bus in at Bethany Square. The Davies Bros. conductor pointed out to the competitor that he wasn't running to the correct time and received a violent blow to the chin with two fists, cutting his lip. The competing conductor shouted "I'll break every bone in your body."

The council's patience was wearing thin. Trade magazine, Motor Transport reported in August 1929 that they had decided to act: 'Port Talbot Borough Council has decided to notify bus proprietors operating between the town and Aberavon beach that their licences will not be renewed at the end of the year. The council has also decided to invite the South Wales Transport Co., Ltd. to extend its services in the Maesteg district to Aberavon beach, six buses being thus employed.'

If the bus owners expected any leniency from the police, then the following extract from the Port Talbot Guardian in November 1929 under the headline 'The Flying Bus', shows that they really weren't helping their own cause: 'A hurried dash from Margam back to Cwmavon in the early hours of the morning resulted in the appearance at Port Talbot Police Court on Thursday of Mostyn Evans, a bus driver of Danycoed Road, Cwmavon, on two charges of reckless driving and failing to stop. Mr. Trevor Parker appeared for Evans and pleaded not guilty. P.C. Hughes said that at 1.45am on October 25th he was on duty in High Street, Cwmavon, when the defendant's bus came towards him at a speed which he estimated to be between 45 and 50 miles an hour. P.C. Hughes: "The bus was swaying from one side of the road to the other and the witness signalled him to stop, but he took no notice. The witness and P.C. Bush who was with him, flashed their lamps, and shouted, but they had to jump against the wall of a house for safety, and even then the bus only missed them by inches. When the witness "aw Evans later, he said: 'I admit I was shifting. She was all out…I didn't see you until I was right on top of you.'"

Mr. Trevor Parker asked: "Do you suggest that he drove straight at you? — That he was out to deliberately murder you?"

The driver, on oath, denied that he was driving very fast. He had been driving in the borough for four years. He did not see the constables on the morning in question, and he did not tell P.C. Hughes that he was shifting. Superintendent Rees Davies asked: 'Where had you been that night?"

The defendant replied: "At Margam." Superintendent Rees Davies then asked: "What were you doing there – courting?" The defendant replied: "No. I had been listening to the wireless."

The crest of the Great Western Railway.

The Mayor, Councillor John Jones Edwards following a retirement, said that after hesitation they had decided to deal with the defendant on this occasion in the form of a fine. They regarded it as a very serious offence, and any future breach would be met by the suspension of his licence. On this occasion he would be fined £1 for the dangerous driving and £1 for failing to stop. Perhaps if breathalysers had been available at the time, the outcome might have been quite different.

A flavour of these lawless times can be found in Sir Harry Secombe's 1981 novel, 'Welsh Fargo', set around a bus-owning family in a valley community near Swansea. Although the book is a work of fiction, Sir Harry had at least one relative who worked for South Wales Transport, and there is a real possibility that elements of the story are nearer the truth than one might imagine. Either way, it makes a good read!

Pioneer rail replacement bus services

The Great Western Railway was the pioneer of railway-operated bus services in Britain, beginning in Cornwall in 1903 and soon extending services to cover most of its network. Services were usually introduced as feeders to link surrounding towns and villages which were remote from the railway with their nearest station. Others were run to test the market and judge the passenger potential before a new section of track was built.

On 11th April 1927, the GWR commenced a Cymmer Afan to Glyncorrwg bus service. This was not a feeder to the railway as was the original aim of railway motor bus services, but a cost cutting exercise as simultaneously the railway service between those two points was reduced.

It was an early example of a rail replacement bus service! To house the vehicle for the service, the GWR built a shed at Glyncorrwg, on their own land between the Post Office and the railway line to North Rhondda Colliery and South Pit.

This was a one-bus operation, using an older vehicle which had been displaced from elsewhere on the network. On the occasions when the bus broke down, a train had to be reinstated. Eventually, a newer bus appeared on the route. In April 1928 the Port Talbot Guardian reported: 'We are glad to see that a new motor has taken the place of the one formerly plying on the Glyncorrwg - Cymmer Road. It is still a GWR bus but more modern than the old one; balloon tyres have taken the place of the solid rubber tyres and the seating and lighting are much improved. This is a step in the right direction and we hope soon to see more of these modern buses on the Cymmer Road.' Perhaps that last statement was aimed at certain other operators.

A more serious case, involving a fatality, came before the courts in December 1929. At the root of the investigation was insufficient front and rear lights on a bus.

Joseph Mason of Cwmavon had started running on the Pontrhydyfen route in July 1921 as Joseph Mason & Son. They ran a small fleet of around half a dozen buses at any one time. Eventually in 1944 the firm would merge with Rhyd Lewis and W. Jones to form Lewis & Jones which lasted until taken over by Thomas Bros. in 1952.

On the night in question, John Davies, a former full back with Aberavon Rugby Club and a bus conductor with Davies Bros., had died in hospital following a collision between two buses; he had left a widow and two children. Witness Edgar John, a railwayman, stated that he was passing the New Theatre, Water Street, at about 5.30pm and noticed two buses there. One had stopped and the other was approaching from the rear, when suddenly he heard the crash of breaking glass. He had told the police that one of the buses had pulled out from behind the other and that the first bus had no lights.

A second witness, steelworker Darrell Cole, said he was returning home from work at Margam in the leading (Joseph Mason & Sons.) bus going to Cwmavon. He noticed that Davies' bus was right behind them and when, near the Labour Exchange it made an attempt to pass. He had covered about half the length of the bus, when he seemed to realise that he couldn't pass through and attempted to get back. In doing so he struck the corner of the bus in which Cole was travelling. Davies, the deceased, who was the conductor of the overtaking bus owned by Davies Bros., was standing on the step of

Legislation permitting the reorganisation of railway motor bus arrangements led to the formation of the partly GWR owned Western Welsh Omnibus Co., Ltd. in April 1929. The original suggestion had been to call the company Great Western Welsh, but this wasn't proceeded with. It does however explain why a company whose core activity was around South East Wales had Western in its title.

Western Welsh took over GWR bus services in South and West Wales after 31st July 1929. Shortly before this, on 19th July, the GWR in association with Rhondda Tramways and South Wales Transport had introduced a service running from Port Talbot to Cymmer and then over to Treorchy. As a footnote to this, in 1933 Mitchell Brothers, of Bodwenog, Glyncorrwg applied for a licence to provide a new service between Glyncorrwg and Cymmer. The application was turned down.

A rare photograph of a GWR bus on the Cymmer to Glyncorrwg route. This is believed to be YV 1116, a Maudslay ML3 vehicle of 1928 vintage, driven by George Gardiner.

the bus and seemed to be caught.

The witness added, in reply to the Coroner, that the bus in which he was riding stopped and he jumped out to find Davies lying on the steps.

The driver of the Mason's bus, John Mason, the owner's son, in which the witness was riding, said that he had slowed down near the Labour Exchange to pick up a passenger and had resumed his journey. He also admitted that the bus had no rear light but only a red disc on the glass. On examination he admitted that if the lights in his bus were poor, then the red disc wouldn't have been noticeable. The faster he went, the brighter the lights and when stopped the lights were poor.

The driver of the Davies Bros. bus, Daniel Egan, said he was driving a 20 seater Dodge on the night of the accident. (Believed to have been NY 5572, first registered in May 1924 and purchased secondhand from Davies, Pencader - no relation - in 1927). He was approaching the New Theatre at 12-14mph when he felt a crash. He got out and pointed out to a constable who was nearby that the bus into which he had crashed had no rear light. It was a dull, wet night.

Asked if he had a windscreen wiper, Egan replied "No – none of the buses have them. Mason's bus didn't put its lights on until after the accident and then they were dim."

John Mason, the driver, then corrected a previous statement and stated that the bus was actually owned by a man named John Williams. The Coroner then suggested that he had now thrown some doubt on the value of the evidence he had given. Mason's response was that there are three brothers-in-law who are partners in the concern. His statement is of concern as it confirms that buses were changing hands within families to the extent that who owned what had become hazy. After more discussion it transpired that Davies had been leaning out of the bus to identify a 'dark object' ahead when the accident occurred, hitting his head. The jury returned a verdict of accidental death. As a postscript to this sad event, NY 5572 is recorded as having been converted to a lorry at an unknown date; could it be that this accident sealed its fate?

Another of Joseph Mason's vehicles was involved in a fatality in 1935 on Stormy Down, Pyle. On 6th August a coach returning to Cwmavon with a party after a day out overturned, spilling passengers onto the road and sadly one person died. At the inquiry it was stated that the driver was just 17 with only two years experience of driving cars. A verdict of accidental death was returned with the rider that drivers of 'charabancs' should be more carefully selected and tested before being allowed on the road.

Other early bus operators in Port Talbot at this time included E.H. Jenkins & Son (1921), Theophilus Thomas (1921), Stanley Haydn Webb (1922), Leonard Jones (c.1923), William John Clement (1923), David Rhys Williams (1923), William D.T. Stephens (1924), Rees and Mary Ann Morgan (Morgan's Motors) (1928), Rhyd Lewis (1928).

Additional to these of course were a number of

Seen around 1926 are, from left, Thomas Bros. driver Harland Richards with Alec Morgan and Idris Williams, drivers for David Jones & Son, Pantdu.

Very little is known about the Glyncorrwg Motor Co., Ltd which traded as 'The Enterprise', initially using this Commercial Cars vehicle. The service linking trains at Cymmer with Glyncorrwg seems to have begun in 1914 but no trace of it has been found beyond March 1918 when the railway passenger service between the two points began. A Daimler, registered as L 1144 was purchased in 1915. However, it seems that Mitchell of Glyncorrwg operated a service from at least 1919, so possibly GMC was taken over by them.

larger operators which ran longer distance services passing through the area, although a committee of Port Talbot Borough Council had decided against the extension of bus services in the area by Bridgend firms who would stop in the district. The decision was reversed in 1929 which permitted additional services to be established.

From the earliest days of the bus industry operators had formed associations, the functions of which were to protect their members against competition, to regulate the times of the services and to handle legal matters affecting the wellbeing of the bus owners. At Port Talbot, the Port Talbot Motor Proprietors Association (PTMPA) had been formed by 1922, representing a total of 14 vehicles on the Cwmavon to Port Talbot and Taibach to Aberavon Beach routes.

In an effort to exercise some self-control, and fend off criticism from the courts, the local operators who ran services on the Aberavon to Cwmavon and Pontrhydyfen route, eventually came together in 1930 to form the Avon Valley Bus Owners Association (AVBOA). It is not known whether this was a new organisation or a revamp of the PTMPA; either way, nothing is heard of the latter by this date. Part of the remit was that any operator which wanted to sell out would in the first instance offer their business to another association member. Effectively this was a cartel which might prevent a newcomer or one of the large operators gaining a foothold. It is likely also that this was a way to try and find favour with Port Talbot Borough Council, but there can be no doubt that the operators would have been well aware that those in Government were also keeping a keen eye on questionable goings-on in the bus industry. If they failed to get their collective act together, legislation might threaten their livelihoods.

The disorganised operations in the Afan Valley were not unique to Port Talbot; neither were they unique to South Wales. Around Britain, irresponsible operators were at work in virtually every town and city.

Corrupt politicians would support the local operators in exchange for favours even though the larger firms could offer a better service. Companies such as South Wales Transport were seen as outsiders, filtering money away to line the pockets of rich shareholders in London, even though they were good employers with a committed local workforce.

This was an attitude which sometimes still prevails; what is often forgotten is that the shareholders are often pension providers and that the profit is being reinvested in new vehicles and technologies. In the 1920s, something needed to give and Parliament was about to act, but would legislation solve the problem?

The charabanc dream that

Writing in the SWT staff magazine, Ein Newyddion in July 1949, long serving driver D. T. Evans described his early career working on charabancs:

"Operating a service with an open charabanc was a nightmare. There was nearly always a full load and fares were collected while the conductor stood on the running board as the vehicle was in motion at about 20mph. Imagine a bus fitted with solid tyres running over a bad road and the conductor working his way along the outside, tickets in one hand and taking money with the other, hanging on by the elbow and hoping that all doors were fastened securely.

Many accidents did in fact happen through doors being left unlocked. The wheel arch was the greatest difficulty. There was no foothold and the span was such that it couldn't be passed by a short-legged man.

"Some of the charabancs were built on high lorry chassis so that most passengers were quite unable to climb in or out. Short ladders were provided which had to be placed against the door of the compartment so that the brave travellers could enter or alight. The ladder was carried underneath the rear of the vehicle and as the conductor was obliged to handle it continually, his condition at the end of the day, especially on a wet day, is not too difficult to imagine.

"Charabancs were fitted with what the manufacturers humorously called 'one man hoods'. It was a frequent sight to see a conductor, driver and four male passengers struggling to erect the hood in a sudden heavy rain shower. The reason for this was that the bamboo struts had to be placed in slots cut in the top of the body, and if the movements of the man at each side were not made at exactly the same moment, the result was painful both for the occupants of the bus and the men outside.

"Owing to the amount of dust created by the solid tyres on the untarred roads, conductors were issued with dusters for the purpose of keeping the seats clean. At the end of a run in dry weather the conductor looked more like a flour miller than a busman.

"In those days the Road Traffic Act was not in force to limit the hours of duty and road staff rarely completed their day's work until eight in the evening and often carried on till midnight in

A heavil laden early Thomas Bros charabanc proudly displaying the TB monogram on the front door pauses for a photographer on Pentyla Hill, Aberavon.

often became a nightmare!

Charabancs were often the subject of comedy postcards linked to an area, such as this one marketed for visitors to the sands at Aberavon.

the summer months. As a rule, no arrangements were made for meals and in most instances operating staff had very little leisure indeed. The Road Traffic Act, 1930 laid down very definite instructions about the hours of work and meals, which did much to make the busman's life a little easier.

"Uniforms were not issued by the companies and the clothing problem was a serious one. Some conducting fashions were really funny, but the usual outfit consisted of breeches and leggings with a jaunty seaman's cap worn over the ear.

"As well as primitive bodywork, the engines of the early buses left much to be desired. Spares always carried were a length of string, a roll of wire and a can of water. These were of great importance: a journey without any one of them might have meant waiting on the road until the fitters could reach the stranded vehicle, as it was hardly ever possible to operate for a whole day without some trouble being experienced. Often, conductors were forced to lie along the wing, flooding the carburettor to enable the driver to return to depot – an unpleasant task on a wet winter's night.

"There was no such thing as 'resting' in those days. If delegated for a special duty, perhaps during holiday periods and not required immediately on reporting, conductors and drivers had to fill in their waiting time by cleaning buses, office windows, helping the greasers and even painting the vehicles so that when the weekly pay packet was received there was a genuine feeling that every penny of it had been well earned.

In those early days every conductor and even driver was a salesman — selling rides to the public."

'Competition for survival brought bus battles which were fierce, just to steal passengers from rival firms'

Resting at Maesteg Road, Cymmer, Davies C33F bodied JTG 63 was a 1949 Crossley SD42 that was one of 10 buses acquired with the business of David Jones & Son, Pantdu in 1957 when it was rebodied as a Burlingham FC37F before being scrapped in 1965.

The year 1930 was a significant one in the history of the bus industry. Across Britain, cut-throat competition was leading to what could only be termed as piracy. Uneconomical fares were being charged and there was a great deal of wastage in buses and manpower just to pinch a small number of passengers from a competitor.

Relief seemed to have arrived when order came out of this chaos with the passing of the 1930 Road Traffic Act. This led to the setting up of a quasi-judicial body known as the Traffic Commissioners which with the power vested in it, was intended to bring about stability of fares, adherence to timetables and root out the corruption which was holding back the development of bus services.

The granting of licences to operate services which had previously been under the jurisdiction of numerous local councils could now only be obtained through the new authority which was responsible for licensing the vehicles, services and road staff.

Rivalry that brought piracy to valley roads

Garage staff in front of CTG176, a Bedford WTB, with Duple body, new to Thomas Bros. in 1937. Bedford OWB, FNY 192, new to Afan Transport in 1943, also had Duple bodywork. Both had been sold to Smith's of Cymmer when this photo was taken.

Before takeover by Thomas Bros. David Jones & Son of Pantdu operated this Maudslay Marathon III, HTX 626 with Burlingham bodywork.

In advance of the 1930 Act becoming law in April 1931, operators were required to have submitted applications to licence those services which were already in operation. In the case of the Port Talbot to Pontrhydyfen corridor, there were no fewer than 13 identical applications. Moreover, when summer services were required a further 13 applications arrived and again when any fare changes were needed.

The owner-drivers had been particularly vulnerable when it came to running their affairs to an acceptable standard. Having to deal with maintenance, cleaning, legal issues and paperwork after a long day's driving was bound to have created problems. Some proprietors seem to have paid too little attention to maintenance, fixing buses only when they broke down. This often meant a break in the service. At one point vehicle inspectors described the standard of some of them as being mechanically deplorable.

Many of the illegal practices were noticed by the more reputable operators who ran longer distance services through Port Talbot, and were no doubt eager to report any shortcomings in what they saw as the actions of competitors on some sections of a route.

By the 1930s the longer distance routes included: SWT (Swansea to Margam via Morriston or Llansamlet); Llynfi Motors (Aberavon Beach to Maesteg via Bryn, jointly with SWT); Western Welsh (Port Talbot to Kenfig Hill, Aberdare or Merthyr to Porthcawl, Carmarthen to Newport, Port Talbot to Cymmer Afan); N & C Luxury Coaches (Swansea and Neath to Cardiff), Willmore (Neath to Port Talbot) and Associated Motorways (Swansea to Cheltenham). The company of Rhyd Lewis, based at Gadlys Depot, Cwmavon ran a single vehicle on the competitive Aberavon to Cymmer and Pontrhydyfen route from the autumn of 1928. At first it used a 20 seat Dennis G, registered as WN 1353. The firm amalgamated with William Jones and Joseph Mason in 1944 to form Lewis & Jones Ltd.

Licence leaders

The bus owners involved when fare or summer route changes were needed:
- Rhyd Lewis
- Thomas Gwyn Thomas
- Theophilus Thomas
- William Clement
- Richard Hodges
- William Jones
- David Jones & Son
- Joseph Mason
- Elizabeth Ann Stephens
- Benjamin Thomas
- John Williams
- Elizabeth Ann Jenkins

Benjamin Edward Howe, prosecuter for the Road Traffic Commissioner and West Glamorgan Coroner.

David Jones & Son
Avon Hill House, Pantdu,
PORT TALBOT.

36, 34, 33 & 32 Seater Luxury Coaches for Hire.　　Terms Moderate.

A newspaper report on 30th May 1930 revealed that Henry R. Lewis and Daniel Davies, driver and conductor with Rhyd Lewis had been summoned for overcrowding on their bus. Police Sergeant Williams told the court that he had seen Lewis driving a Cwmavon bus into Aberavon which was seriously overcrowded, with passengers standing down the centre aisle and on the footboard. There were a total of 36 adults and three children.

Lewis had told the court: "I stopped the bus for five minutes in Cwmavon to get them out, but they refused."

Davies the conductor added: "They rushed me and I could not hold them."

It was a 20 seater bus and he had been carrying nearly double that capacity. For the defence, Mr. Vivian Deer admitted the breach of the regulations but submitted that there were only 28 adults and not 36 aboard. He called Lewis who said he was the owner and driver of the bus. He said that he had left Pontrhydyfen with only two passengers, but when he got to Cwmavon there was a rush. He stated that when Police Sergeant Williams started to count his passengers they had mostly left the bus and he was counting people who had left the one behind him. He admitted, however, that he had more than 20 passengers aboard. He also admitted, in cross-examination that he had been convicted previously.

Donald Thomas, of Pontrhydyfen, a passenger in the bus, said that he failed to get into the preceding bus because, like all other buses on a Saturday night, it was overloaded: "There was a bus discharging passengers just behind this bus when it arrived in Aberavon and when the sergeant started to count the passengers, many of them had left the bus."

In his opinion there were about eight passengers standing. The bench imposed a significant fine of £5 on Lewis, saying they were determined to put a stop to overcrowding. They dismissed the summons against Davies, the conductor.

Operating a late evening bus on a Saturday then — as now — wouldn't have been the easiest of jobs. No doubt the singing coming from inside the vehicle would have been audible long before the bus appeared and keeping rowdy passengers under control would have been a real challenge. However, the law was there to be obeyed.

The speed limit for buses running on pneumatic tyres was raised to 30mph in 1931. However, those still running on solid tyres remained restricted to a maximum legal speed of 20mph.

It is clear from a report on 18th July 1930 that the offer of a reliable service from SWT was adding to the frustration felt by the council who wanted their bus service properly run by a Port Talbot operator.

A special meeting of the Port Talbot Hackney Carriage Committee was held under the chairmanship of Councillor Herbert Griffiths, to investigate complaints lodged against local bus services. Supporting the Chairman were Alderman K.S. Wehrle, with Councillors Billy Vaughan, E.U. David, Jas. O'Brien. Tom Williams, E.J. Hare, and Joe Brown, with the

Town Clerk and Police Inspector James. An application was read at the outset from SWT offering to run a non-stop service between Aberavon and Pontrhydyfen, making the journey there and back in three-quarters of an hour. Cllr. Billy Vaughan, referring to the continued irregularities on the Cwmavon route, said that it appeared to him that they had been more concerned in the past with pleasing the bus owners than giving the public an efficient service.

Cllr. E.U. David proposed that the committee should threaten the Cwmavon bus owners before doing anything drastic, so that unless they toe the line they must expect trouble. The Town Clerk pointed out that they had been threatened time and again but had taken no notice. Cllr. Brown said that there was a very definite cry on the part of the public for a proper service on the Cwmavon route and thought the council ought to put on one at least which ran to time.

The chairman added that no one had complained more bitterly against the irregularities of this service than he had, but he was loath to put them off the road. If an SWT bus ran, it was bound to mean that some of them would find it impossible to carry on.

Cllr. Tom Williams said that the bus owners had laughed at the council all along. He then seconded the proposal to threaten them.

Ald. Wehrle wanted to give them another chance and tabled an amendment that they should be told that they will have to run a proper service. "Let us get them here before us and tell them straight," he suggested.

Cllr. David added that they had been told on countless occasions, while Ald. Wehrle wanted this to be the last chance. Cllr. Tom Williams felt that the next day they would be running just the same as ever. Ald. Wehrle wanted it known that if that happened, he would be the very first to move that they be put off the road altogether. The amendment was lost. From further comments which were minuted, the council still favoured the small operators with all the implications over larger, more reliable ones such as SWT.

At a subsequent full council, Ald. W. R. Thomas in moving the reference back of the Committee's recommendation that two licences be granted to SWT on the Cwmavon route, said they had to bear in mind that the Cwmavon bus owners were ratepayers of the Borough (and voters too!) who lived locally, some of whom had invested the whole of their life savings in the purchase of a bus. In his opinion the problem should be solved by the police, who had power to suspend any offenders on that route. He understood that since the meeting of the Hackney Carriage Committee the bus owners had made special efforts to run a service and had agreed to form themselves into the Avon Valley Bus Owners' Association (AVBOA). Under the circumstances he thought they might be given another chance.

Ald. Joe Davies, in seconding the reference back, said he agreed that the Cwmavon bus route was the most uncivilised in the country. There were 12 separate owners with the result that they could not organise a

The first edition of the Highway Code issued in 1931 comprised just 18 pages of information.

Purchased from SWT in 1956, GCY 435 was one of four AEC Regal III with Windover C33F bodies. The vehicle alongside, JTX 676, was a 1950 AEC Regal III with Burlingham FC33F Sunsaloon bodywork. The coach had been rebodied from C33F following a fire which destroyed its original body on its first trip in August 1949.

proper timetable. A new element had arisen however, as the owners had formed themselves into an association and he thought they should be given a chance to show just what they could do.

Councillor Tom Williams stated: "The police never had any control over that route," to which Ald. W.R. Thomas replied that they should.

Alderman Dummer added a point of order stating: "There were no licenses on the Cwmavon route. The conduct of operators was so bad last year that they had all been placed on probation."

Councillor Tom Williams suggested that: "The police endeavour to get some sort of order on the routes. The question is whether we are here to see to the interests of the bus owners or the public. If you don't carry this resolution tonight, you are going to make yourselves a laughing stock. Every recommendation that has issued from the Hackney Carriage Committee during the past five years has been referred back by this council. It is scandalous."

Councillor J. Noonan said he was prepared to give the bus owners another chance and Cllr. E.U. David was of a similar opinion.

Meanwhile Cllr. Geo Harris told the meeting: "As long as I have been on this council we have been giving these bus people another chance. It is high time now that forbearance ceased to be a virtue."

Ald. Dummer was also in favour of giving them another chance, adding that the Hackney Carriage Committee has had more trouble with the Cwmavon bus owners than all the other services in the district. It was eventually agreed, by a majority vote, to refer the matter back.

Among the passenger transport entrepreneurs at that time were the two previously mentioned brothers, Thomas Gwyn and Evan Stanley Thomas trading as a partnership called just that — Thomas Bros. Their first vehicles were charabancs converted from War Department lorries. E.S. Thomas died at Port Talbot Hospital on 9th August 1925; his estate was valued at £63 14s. 7d., around £4,000 today.

Almost six years later in 1931 a limited company, Thomas Bros. Ltd, was formed. It operated two services. One was from Aberavon Beach via Taibach to Goytre and the other from Aberavon Beach to Margam.

By 1932, Thomas Bros. was operating its share of the Beach to Margam and Goytre routes with a fleet comprising of Daimler/ADC, Halley, Bedford WLB, and Bean vehicles. Later in that decade, a Dennis, Leylands (Lion, Cub and Cheetah), an Albion, a Thornycroft and another Bedford would join the fleet. All were secondhand and remained painted in the livery of their previous owners until a repaint was due.

In 1933 Thomas Gwyn Thomas and John David Evans who was from West Wales, formed Thomas Bros. (Port Talbot) Ltd. to take over the previous operation. The new company was incorporated on 27th March, with J.D. Evans as Secretary/General Manager. Mr. Evans was a wise businessman and despite limited resources, soon got the company off the ground. The financial records held at the Richard Burton Archive in Swansea University show that book keeping was meticulous, with all transactions neatly listed. The records show that on 1st July 1938, the fleet was valued at £2,054.

The shareholders at this time were mainly existing bus proprietors from Port Talbot: John David Evans (50 shares), Thomas Gwyn Thomas (20), John Mason (50), William Jones (50), John Williams (50), John Jones (50), David Arthur Jenkins (31), David Stephens (21), Richard Hodges (17), and David Rhys Williams (11).

Thomas Bros. (Port Talbot) Ltd. had an office at 129 Station Road and a garage in Sandfields Road, just a short distance from the rear of the Thomas home. This is often referred to as 'Sandfields Garage' but is better referred to as Sandfields Road, to avoid confusion with the new garage constructed in 1958 at Acacia Avenue, on the Sandfields estate.

Sadly, in September 1934, driver Isaac Evans was killed after a bus which he was cleaning and greasing as part of his duties, had caught fire in the garage. Mr. Evans was working underneath the bus when the incident occurred. Thomas Gwyn Thomas left to set up his own company in 1934, later joining forces with H.T. Havard to form Thomas & Havard. This arrangement dissolved in 1937 and Thomas again continued alone, picking up the works contract licences in his own name until takeover by Owen Elias James.

Mr. Thomas seems to have been the bane of the local police and magistrates. In June 1934 he was in court to answer a charge of running an unlicensed car, using it uninsured, fraudulently using a road fund licence and fraudulently using index marks.

On May 14th, a constable had seen Thomas driving a car registered as NY 8082. A few days later he had spotted a Morris Cowley van with the same registration plate being driven by someone else. The constable had spoken to the van driver who stated that the vehicle was owned by Thomas Bros. of Alfred Street. On visiting the Thomas home the police found the original car in a garage, carrying the same registration; the correct number for the car should have been TX 5374. In his defence, Thomas said that he had exchanged the van and car bodies and the registration plate had gone with it.
He was fined a total of £18 for the offences and it was noted that he had some previous convictions. It was around this time that Thomas separated from the Thomas Bros. concern. Was there some connection, perhaps? After all, he had misused a company vehicle. In July of the following year, Thomas, 'a well-known bus owner' was back in court, charged with using a car without insurance. It was reported that there were 14 previous

Former Davies Bros. Seddon MkIV 31-seater JTX 650 was extremely unpopular with both staff and passengers and was eventually disposed of in 1957.

convictions for motoring offences and it was felt that he should be deprived of his licence. However, in the light of his business needs this was not acted upon. The PC reported that Thomas was unable to produce his insurance when asked to and had later turned up with a cover note issued two days after he had been stopped. He was fined £5.

In time, Thomas Bros. would come to dominate local bus services at Port Talbot. There were many small concerns, often inter-related, which have been identified as operating at this time. Those which were partnerships sometimes had vehicles registered to individual partners or even other family members in the company, which further adds to the complexity. Several of them were also shareholders in Thomas Bros. (Port Talbot) Ltd.

By now it seems that the company was considering the introduction of diesel engined vehicles to the fleet and in March 1936 was on a steep learning curve! One of their drivers, Walter Sellars was charged at Port Talbot Borough Police Court on with 'emitting avoidable smoke' which had entered a shop. Thomas Bros. was charged with permitting the offence.

Police Sergeant Usher said that on February 18th he had seen a bus driven by the defendant emitting a dense cloud of thick black smoke. He stopped the bus and spoke to the driver who agreed that the smoke was rather thick and suggested that the mixture was at fault. "It was a new type of engine and we don't know much about it, explained the defendant in court."

The police superintendent observed "Perhaps the public thought there was a war on and you were giving out gas signals!" The trouble had been put right by the next day.

David Jones & Son operated this secondhand AEC Regal III, EM 4687 and had it rebodied in the 1950s with a new Burlingham Seagull-style coach body. Having sold their stage service plus two Daimler buses to Thomas Bros in 1952, their remaining vehicles followed for disposal in 1965.

Thomas Bros. was fined with costs. The vehicle in question was VR 770, a secondhand Halley 32 seater which had been fitted with a Dorman 4HW diesel engine by J.& P. Bevan of Swansea. After this experience, Thomas Bros. bought no more diesel engined vehicles until after the war.

Despite all its best efforts the company was not immune from accusations of various misdemeanors. In April 1937 the company and a conductor were summoned for permitting overloading. The conductor, Ronald Hancorn, aged 22, also answered a charge of not wearing his badge on duty.

Officer Weaver had stopped a bus in Taibach to speak to Hancorn, when five passengers got off and four others boarded. The bus was a 26 seater with 32 passengers on board. When the officer pointed out that Hancorn wasn't wearing a badge and would be reported, he said that he had left it at home, adding: "Give me a chance, I won't do it again."

In the company's defence, it was pointed out that the service only ran every hour and as it was a wet evening, not taking the passengers would have caused hardship. Thomas Bros. were fined £3 and Hancorn was fined £2 for overloading and £1 for not wearing his badge.

To page 38

Transport legislation which

The licensing system which existed in the early days of passenger transport was established under the Town Police Clauses Acts of 1847 and 1889.

Such legislation was originally concerned with the regulation of horse-drawn hackney carriages and the Act of 1889 extended these provisions to deal with the additional problems presented by omnibuses which were, up to this time, legally defined as hackney carriages.

Some authorities failed to exercise their powers at all and others granted licences to anyone without considering facilities which already existed.

In areas such as the Afan Valley, competition went virtually unchecked and the safety of passengers and staff was threatened.

As is frequently the case, warnings to businesses that they need to become organised and operate in an effective way would be, if compliance was resisted, followed by legislation forced upon them. The era of unbridled competition was brought to an end by the passing of the Road Traffic Act of 1930. This gave birth to the Traffic Commissioners who with the power vested in them brought about stability of fares and adherence to timetables.

It established a system of Traffic Courts and licensing. Although opposed by many operators at the time, the elimination of wasteful competition and the removal of 'pirates' was welcomed by the established operators who realised the wisdom of the Act's provisions.

Before any service could be operated, four separate licences were required:

■ **The Certificate of Fitness which related to the state of the vehicle (from the Ministry of Transport), subject to its owner being a 'fit person'.**

■ **Licences for Public Service Vehicle drivers and conductors.**

■ **A public service licence was required for each vehicle.**

■ **A road service licence was required for each operation of the vehicle for which passengers were carried at separate fares.**

These licences were divided into categories of stage carriage (i.e. local bus, express

The first edition of what is now known as 'N&P'; the Traffic Commissioner publishes a notice of all public service vehicle operator licence applications and route changes in this fortnightly publication.

changed the bus industry

Minister of Transport from 1929 to 1931, Labour MP Herbert Morrison who was responsible for the passing of the 1930 Road Traffic Act which brought a national licensing system for routes, vehicles, drivers and conductors. Wikimedia Commons

The hallowed halls of Westminster and the Houses of Parliament where decisions on the future of public transport were taken in 1930.

carriage with a minimum fare of 1s, tours and excursions.) Apart from putting the industry on a firm basis one effect of the Act was to reduce the number of operators on the road. The requirements of the Minister of Transport in matters such as licences and the submission of statistical information were deterrents to the small operator out for a quick return from a small outlay. In the period from March 1931 to March 1932 no fewer than 181 operators went out of business or were acquired by other operators. Of these, 167 owned fewer than 20 vehicles.

This trend continued progressively until by March 1937 there was a total of 4,777 operators against 6,486 in March 1931, an overall reduction of 1,609 or an average of 268 per year. The 1930 Act was the first piece of modern legislation applied to the industry and (with the 1934 Act which followed) marked the recognition of the coming of age of road passenger transport.

It was a situation which was to prevail for the next six decades. In the 1980s the Thatcher Government published a white paper on the bus industry which resulted in the implementation of the Transport Act 1985 on 26 October 1986 – dubbed Deregulation Day. This deregulated bus services in England, Scotland and Wales abolishing road service licensing and allowing for the introduction of competition on local bus services for the first time since the 1930s. To operate a service all an operator was required to do was provide appropriate notice to the Traffic Commissioner of their intention to commence, cease or alter operation on a route.

Exactly as had been the case before the 1930 Act, on well used routes, intense competition often resulted in a bus war which required the intervention of the authorities to stamp out unscrupulous or unsafe practices.

From page 35

A further prosecution followed in November 1937 when a 32-seater bus, returning from a jazz band competition at Maesteg was found to have 51 passengers on board. It was stated in court that one of the several buses being used that night had broken down and its passengers were transferred to join those on another bus. A fine of £1 was imposed.

Unsurprisingly, all the discussions and threats of previous years, and the fact that the Road Traffic Act 1930 was now the law of the land, seemed to be having very little effect at Port Talbot. The South Wales Traffic Commissioners said that difficulty had been experienced in obtaining evidence on which the penalty of the loss of a licence might be imposed. Now however, they had succeeded in obtaining a plain clothes inspector who would travel around the area to detect irregularities.

On 12th May 1930, the Port Talbot Guardian once more reported on cases of overloaded buses following increased vigilance by the police. The identity of the operator isn't revealed, but this led to the appearance of Ivor Morgan, aged 24 and Lewis Davies, aged 18, of Aberavon, driver and conductor respectively, of a bus which PC Page had stopped in Talbot Road at 6.30pm on Saturday, 27th April. PC Page said that there were 29 adults and two children in the bus which was only licensed to carry a maximum of 20. The overloading of nine adults and two children was pointed out to the defendants, who made no reply. A fine of £1 each was imposed.

Theophilus J. Thomas had started his business in 1921 and was another operator on the Pontrhydyfen route. In 1931 he also started running a service to Tonmawr. His small fleet included a W. & G. Du Cros, a Bean, a Commer Centaur, the inevitable Bedford WLB and two ex-SWT Dennis vehicles. Theophilus, aged 48, was in front of the court on 12th May with Oliver Ainesbury, aged 19, a bus conductor of Cwmavon, charged with overloading. On Saturday, 22nd April 1933, PC W. Jones had found a bus to be overloaded; all the seats being occupied, the passengers were standing in a heap in the front of the bus and down the gangway. When asked how many were standing, the conductor said that he had 11 and a boy. The driver made things worse by shouting that there were 18 standing. Constable Jones said that the total carried with the exception of a child in arms and a full-sized greyhound dog, was 30 passengers. He drew the driver and conductor's attention to the seating capacity of the bus, which was 18, and told them they would be reported. Constable Jones added that at this point a slight faint had overcome the driver who was unable to stand. He was taken home in the bus. Once again, a fine of £1 each was imposed.

A Glamorganshire police constable c.1930 - kept busy by the bus owners.

Without wishing to conjure up any gender stereotypes, anyone who expects that a bus company run by a woman would be more law abiding would be severely mistaken. Mary Anne Morgan had taken over the business of Morgan's Motors from her husband in 1930. Services were operated from Goytre to Bethany Square, Port Talbot extending to Aberavon Beach during the summer months. A restriction on the licence prevented the picking up of passengers on inbound journeys beyond Gallipoli Street and conversely, between Bethany Square and Gallipoli Street unless the passengers wished to travel beyond that point. The company's head office was a fish and chip shop run by Mrs. Morgan. The fleet included two forward control Guys and two Thorneycrofts all of which were secondhand and apparently in very poor shape.

In April, driver Frank Jones of Cwmavon was called to answer a charge of driving a public service vehicle without having efficient brakes. With him was summoned Mrs. Morgan, aged 55, of Taibach for allowing the use of a bus in such a state.

Jones pleaded guilty and PC Page, referring to a previous accident involving a motorcyclist — who just happened to be Driver Jones! — with the same vehicle, said that according to the marks on the road, the bus had taken 51 feet to pull up at 15 miles per hour. When travelling on a flat road at 20 mph and the handbrake was applied, the bus took 18 feet to pull up.

The chairman, Sir William Jenkins said that the justices took a very serious view of inefficient brakes on public service vehicles, because they were a real danger to the public. As it was Jones' first offence he would be fined £1 and Mrs. Morgan, the owner, would be fined the same amount.

Exactly a year later, Mrs. Morgan was in court again. On 27th April 1934, the Port Talbot Guardian reported that a bus conductor who had applied for a badge under the Road Traffic Act and then acted without one, appeared at the Port Talbot County Police Court. He was David R. Llewellyn, aged 23 and unemployed. Mary Anne Morgan was summoned for employing Llewellyn while he was not a licensed conductor.

Mr. Benjamin Edward Howe prosecuted for the Road Traffic Commissioner and said that on April 1st the defendant was stopped while driving a bus in Taibach. Had any accident happened whilst defendant was driving, the passengers would have been unprotected.

Inspector D.T.A. Williams, traffic examiner for the South Wales Area Traffic Commissioners, produced the defendant's application for a badge, dated January 6th and said since that date no communication whatever had been received by the department. Llewellyn was ordered to pay £1 and Mrs. Morgan £2.

For those who like some irony in their politics, the eminent Port Talbot solicitor and coroner, Mr. B. Edward Howe, was the father of Sir Geoffrey Howe (1926-2015). He of course was in Margaret Thatcher's Government at the time of the Transport Act 1985 which abolished road service licensing and allowed for the reintroduction of competition on local bus services.
History can sometimes be very strange.

Later in April 1934, Mrs. Morgan again appeared in court. The carrying of 53 persons on a 20-seater bus led to John T. Thomas and Mrs. Morgan being summoned for carrying passengers in excess of the number licensed. Mr. B. Edward Howe again prosecuted for the Traffic Commissioners. Inspector D. T. A. Williams, road traffic examiner, said that on March 26th he saw the bus on the route from Port Talbot to Goytre. Thomas was driving, and he was stopped while the passengers were counted. There were 52 passengers and one spare conductor. Of the 52 persons. 30 were children. The steps and gangway were completely blocked. Previous convictions were proved against Thomas, who was fined £1 and Mrs. Morgan as the owner of the vehicle, £2.

Mrs. Morgan was in trouble again during the following month. A batch of offences in respect of uninsured buses was heard by Port Talbot County magistrates, the defendants being Frank Jones, aged 31, of Cwmavon (who had earlier been fined in the faulty brake case), Glyndwr Thomas, aged 30, and Frederick Williams, aged 24, both of Taibach for offences alleged to have taken place on

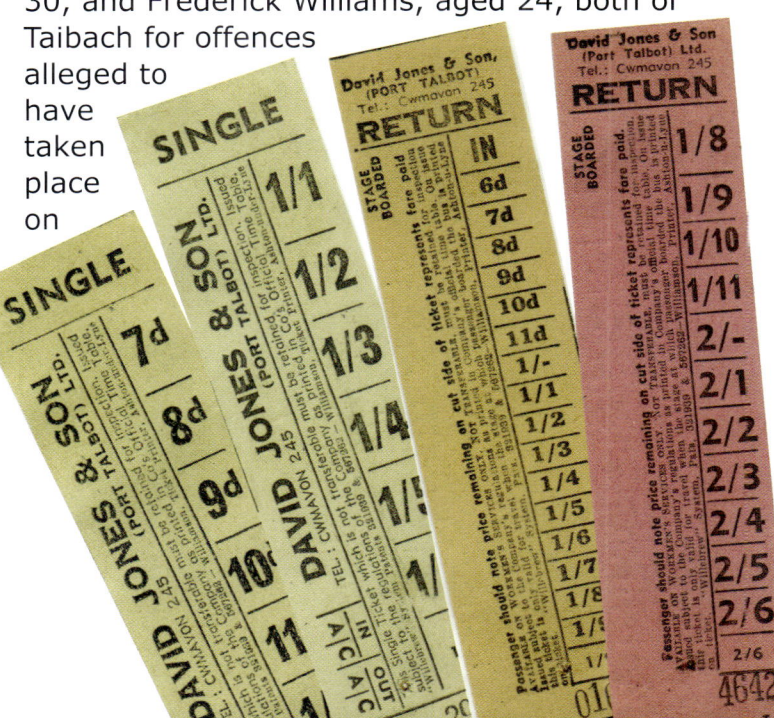

March 25th. The latter defendant was also summoned in respect of an offence alleged to have taken place on March 18th; the employer of all the defendants, Mary Ann Morgan was summoned for permitting the alleged offences. Mr. Dan Perkins defended and pleaded guilty.

PC Albert Page said he saw Thomas driving a Public Service Vehicle in Goytre Road on March 25th; whilst Williams drove another one. The buses were full of people on their way to Goytre Cemetery, preparing for Palm Sunday.

Page said he interviewed Mrs. Morgan later and told her he had found that the vehicles owned by her were not covered by insurance at the time he saw them in service. She said she thought they were all insured and it was simply a mistake.

PC Page said that he saw Williams driving a public service vehicle in Dyffryn Road, Port Talbot. There were seven passengers aboard at the time and Williams replied when asked about his policy of insurance: "Mrs. Morgan keeps them. I have not got one."

Mr. Perkins said that Mrs. Morgan had taken out a covering note for 15 days and was under the impression that the insurance was being continued until after Palm Sunday.

Frank Jones was fined £1, Glyndwr Thomas £1, Frederick Williams, for two offences, £1 and £2 Mrs. Morgan was fined £2 for each offence and for the last offence, the repeated one, £4, making a total of £10.
The drivers' licences would not be affected.

It is clear that financially, Mrs. Morgan's business was failing. In June 1934 she appeared before magistrates because of non-payment of Health and Unemployment contributions affecting six employees, a total of £31. Mrs. Morgan admitted the arrears but said she was unable to pay.

Perhaps illness was at the root of Mrs. Morgan's offences, to the extent that she found it difficult to keep on top of things or perhaps the stress of running the company eventually got to her for in August 1934, the

Port Talbot Guardian reported on her well attended funeral at the Chapel of Ease, commenting that the locality had been robbed of a highly respected personality. The bus business was acquired by Thomas Bros. and with it a 24-seat Thornycroft A6, registered DT 1299 which had been new to an operator in Doncaster. All of Morgans' vehicles were found to be in very poor condition and Thomas Bros. maintained the services initially using Bean vehicles, then a Bedford, a Halley and later a former Devon General Leyland LT2, DV 8504. This bus had found its way to O.E. James and was rebodied by Jeffreys of Swansea; it was later destroyed by fire and Thomas Bros. had purchased the wreck for £60 and again rebodied it with a Burlingham body during the war. Morgans continued as a private hire

penalties that punished them!

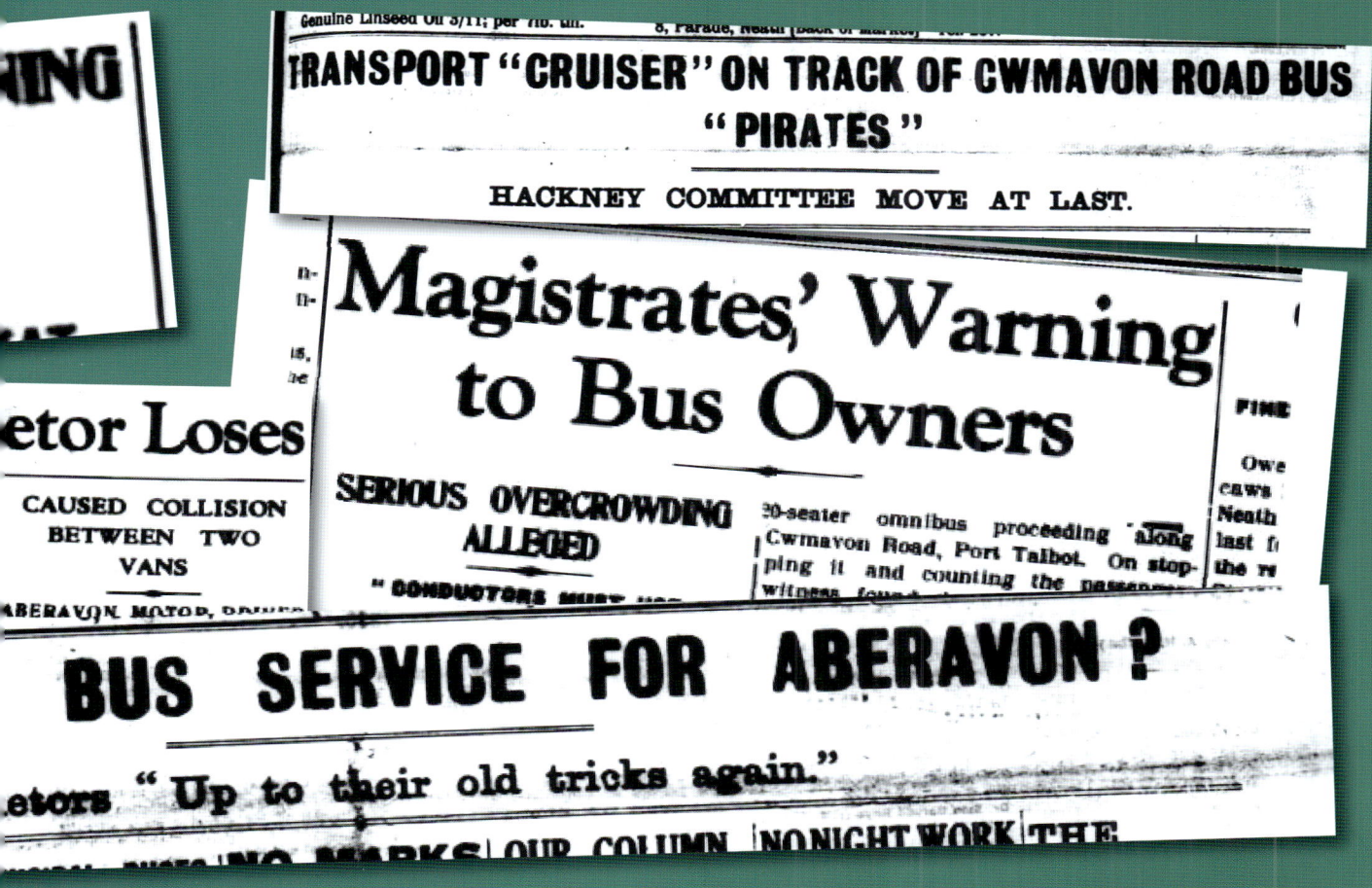

operator using the name Red Triangle Services with a Bedford WTB; the activity ceased in 1938.

After five years trying to unravel the problems caused by the bus operators in Port Talbot, the patience of the Traffic Commissioner, Mr. A.T. James, KC, was wearing thin and a stern warning was issued to them in November 1935.

The Office of the Traffic Commissioner had superseded Port Talbot Council as the licencing authority under the 1930 Act. Now, in desperation the TC was turning back to the council for assistance:

"We have been having difficulty with these services for the past five years," said the Commissioner, "and we should like the Town Council to help us. We have sent inspectors to the district, but as soon as they arrive the scouts are out and as long as they remain in the district things improve.

"Personally, I am not going to put up with it any longer. What I want to know is whether the Town Council is prepared to issue notices of objection to the renewal of these licences.

"We have been having representations from the council with regard to the way in which these services are run and we are piling up a nice little case against the bus owners. I want them to know that the time will come when they will be off the road.

"We have had no end of trouble but have exercised tolerance because we wanted to pursue the policy of keeping the small man on the road. They have been given a chance. The licences will only be granted until

41

February and, by that time, unless drastic alterations are made in the way these services are run, they will be off the road altogether."

> THOMAS Evan Stanley of 1 Alfred-street Aberavon Port Talbot Glamorganshire died 9 August 1925 at the General Hospital Port Talbot Administration London 8 September to Evan Thomas omnibus proprietor. Effects £63 14s. 7d.

The newspaper announcement of the death of Evan Thomas.

On behalf of Messrs. Thomas Bros., Mr. Oliver S. Thomas applied for a half hourly service between Goytre and Aberavon Beach. He added that the service was unremunerative at present because there were two buses on the road. One of the buses was redundant, and if there was no improvement the company would be compelled to withdraw one of the buses.

The Commissioner replied: "It is no use to hold that as a threat over our heads as we have the power to run an unremunerative service as well as a remunerative one." After hearing evidence the application was granted.

Overcrowding of buses was a continuing problem. In February 1936, three cases were brought before Port Talbot Borough Police Court. David Thomas Stephens had started running buses —again on the Afan Valley route — from September 1924.
The company seems to have been a joint enterprise with his wife, Elizabeth Ann Stephens who was named in court as the operator. By the time of the court case the couple were running a Commer Centaur and a Bedford WTB. The conductor on this occasion was David John Stephens, presumably the son of the owners.
The police had pulled up a bus and found that there were 28 adults and three children inside. The gangways were blocked making the bus dangerous to travel in and when spoken to the conductor had admitted wrong doing. Elizabeth Stephens told the court that she was aware of the incident and had nothing to add. A fine of £1, which seems to have been the going rate for overcrowding, was imposed. The bus was stated as being a 20 seater, so could well have been the Waveney bodied Commer Centaur TG 7107.

A large enterprise eventually grew from David Jones & Son of Pantdu. Established in 1924, they had first appeared on the Cwmavon route with NY 5297, a 20 seat Vulcan charabanc and NY 6046, a 14 seat Chevrolet B. A mixed fleet of a Bedford, Commer, Guy, AECs, Leylands and Dennises were used prior to the Second World War. In October 1937, Rees Jones retired and the business remained under the same name but was owned by John Jones.

Brothers John Jones and Rees Jones were identified in court as the vehicle owners and proprietors with David Jones, the conductor. After apologising to the court, all three were fined the customary £1. Once again, the police had stopped a 20 seat vehicle and found 30 passengers on board. At that time, the Joneses owned a Duple B20F bodied Bedford WLB registered WN 4254 and we can safely assume that it was this vehicle which was involved.

Fines of £1 each were also imposed on Joseph Mason, aged 63, and John Mason, aged 34, who owned Joseph Mason & Son of Cwmavon. The conductor was John Stephens, aged 27, who may or may not have had a connection with the previously mentioned family of the same name. A police officer said that when he signalled the driver to stop, two passengers alighted from the emergency exit and three from the front exit and walked away. Once again, mention of a 20 seater — carrying 32 passengers — points towards a Dodge D, registered TX 7752 which the Masons owned at that time.

In imposing the fines the Mayor, Alderman E. L. Hare, JP said that the magistrates considered the offences to be serious in the Port Talbot area and unless heed was taken of their warning, grave steps would follow. The conductors on the buses should use their discretion and refuse to take more than the proper number of passengers.

The decade concluded with more cases of operators overloading, employing under age conductors, working with unsafe operating practices, attempting tax and insurance fraud and not surprisingly, speeding.

During the hearing of one case it was entered as a plea for the bus driver charged that, as no speedometer was fitted to his vehicle, it was largely a matter of guesswork to judge speed. Sir William Jenkins, M.P., the presiding magistrate, said he would like the matter brought to the attention of the bus company, with the suggestion that speedometers should be fitted to public service vehicles. Police Superintendent Doolan commented that he had already made that suggestion, but unless the bus was a stage carriage vehicle, there was no obligation on the part of bus companies to fit speedometers. The industry still had much to learn, but soon another major global conflict would supersede other concerns.

Although there were new legal restrictions, new minor operators continued to emerge in the 1930s. John Williams of Cwmavon appeared on the Afan Valley route in 1934, using vehicles acquired secondhand from nearby operators Mason and D. Jones. P. Waters of Blodwen Street seems to have started up in 1933 but was taken over by Thomas Bros. in 1936. Evan Williams, of Tymaen Street, Cwmavon, ran a workmen's service between Cwmavon and Bryn Colliery; in 1933, Walters & Sons, of Abbey Road also applied for short period licences to operate to Bryn Colliery. Frederick John Clement Adams of Salem Road, Cwmavon ran a workmen's service between Talbot Square and Duffryn Colliery; these were later taken over by Owen E. James.

The new licence applications all played safe by renewing those services already in being at Port Talbot, any need for services extending outside the area — save for a handful of applications to run to Cefn Coed Colliery — having been taken up by the larger operators. One exceptional case, however, is that in 1934 Thomas and James applied to run between Aberavon Beach and Maudlam but the application was refused.

The issue of the level crossing in Station Road again came to the fore in November 1936, when council members discussed some possible solutions for eliminating congestion. The GWR had planned to remove the crossing before the First World War by constructing a joint station in the town for itself, the Port Talbot Railway and the Rhondda & Swansea Bay Railway. An Act of Parliament in 1913 had permitted the work to commence, but the project was shelved on the outbreak of war and never progressed. Among the ideas put forward this time were rerouting the railway, building a viaduct over the road and diverting the road. All seemed to fall into the 'too difficult' category and, as we know, nothing was done for the next 30 years, when the long awaited A48 (M) Port Talbot by-pass opened.

Leyland Cheetah demonstrator ATD 600 was used in Leyland's advertising. It was purchased by Thomas Bros. in 1937, but requisitioned for Second World War service in 1940.

> 'Depression and unemployment were rife, but the flipside was that for most people with a job, living standards rose.'

As the years passed bringing the advent of the next decade it is clear that significant changes in the steel industry and the wider political landscape influenced enormously, not only the bus industry but also the economy of Port Talbot at the same time.

The inter-war years had brought big changes in steelmaking. By the late 1920s, Britain had lost much of its share in world shipbuilding. European countries had expanded their steel production, aiming for self sufficiency. Similarly, Canada, Japan, India, Australia and South Africa were no longer importing as much steel as they had done hitherto.

In the UK, the older, less efficient plants were being closed. In South Wales, this meant steelmaking ended at Cyfarthfa (1921), Blaenavon (1922), Tredegar (1924) and Ebbw Vale (1929). It was a depressed time; Port Talbot's modern plant also suffered and meant that Baldwins, who continued to invest during the 1920s, would find themselves in a difficult position. This led to restructuring, involving a merger of subsidiaries and fringe businesses; a part-merger with Guest, Keen and Nettlefolds to form Guest Keen, Baldwins

Afan Transport JX 2038 was one of four AEC Regents acquired from Halifax Corporation in 1948 to assist with increasing traffic to Port Talbot's developing new steelworks.

Dark clouds broke to reveal a silver lining

If your journey is REALLY necessary and you can choose your times.. travel between 10 & 4
ISSUED BY THE MINISTRY OF WAR TRANSPORT AND THE MINISTRY OF LABOUR AND NATIONAL SERVICE

Davies Bros staff in front of one of the company's Bedfords. The boxes held Bell Punch tickets. *Gillian Davies*

Bedford OB JTG 954, was new to Afan Transport and had Mulliner service bus bodywork. It entered service in October 1949. *Alan B. Cross*

became possible in 1930. The Baldwin element referred to the family iron and steel making business of eminent Conservative politician Stanley Baldwin MP who became Prime Minister three times, in 1923-1924, 1924-1929 and 1935-1937. The second period included the chaotic nine-day general strike of 1926, sparked by events in the coal industry; not for the last time would a Conservative Government find itself at loggerheads with the miners.

In the 1920s and early 1930s, the UK economy had entered a depression. By the start of 1933 unemployment in Britain was 22.8 per cent. However, fortunes began to revive and in 1938 it stood at 10 per cent. New industries such as car and aircraft manufacturing alongside electronics began to prosper in the Midlands and the South of England where unemployment was relatively low. In the mid and late 1930s there were semi-permanently depressed areas in the North of England, Scotland and South Wales.

On the roads, the first electric traffic lights were installed in London in 1925. The 20mph speed limit, dating from 1903 was abolished in 1930, but the 30mph limit in built-up areas and the driving test was introduced in 1934.

Depression and unemployment were one side of the story, but the flipside was that for most people with a job, living standards rose significantly. Poverty had by no means disappeared in Britain by the 1930s but it was much less than in previous decades. There were some terrible inequalities; the wealthy had access to Art Deco furnishings and new homes and fashions, radio and the early labour-saving devices for the home which we all now take for granted. The problems of depression and high unemployment were only really solved by the Second World War, which started industry booming again.

After the 1930 merger there followed a revival in the Port Talbot steel industry's fortunes with GKB's resources being concentrated at Port Talbot. This meant the end of iron and steelmaking at Dowlais and the closure of the plate mill at Cardiff East Moors. This was great news for the Port Talbot economy and for the bus operators who ferried staff to and from Margam.

By 1937 the demand for Port Talbot's heavy steel products had outstripped supply; previous rationalisation meant that the industry might not be able to meet an upsurge in demand. Further investment was needed to increase capacity and further modernise the plant. This was boom time at Port Talbot. By 1938 demand from rearmament was so high that Port Talbot-Margam had become largely immune to other market changes; by July it was running at 97 per cent capacity and had become highly profitable. The wartime Government through the Ministry of Supply took control of the steel industry from 1st September 1939 and by far the majority of production was being used for the war; only seven per cent was used for civilian purposes.

There was no large scale air raid on Port Talbot during the war and certainly nothing on the scale of the Swansea bombings. Overall, the lack of attention from the Luftwaffe is surprising, considering the strategic importance of the docks and steelworks. Workers at Port Talbot had the task of reprocessing 'blitz scrap', the iron and steel recovered from Britain's bombed cities. Ironically, the bombing had provided Britain

NEW COMPANY

THOMAS BROS. (PORT TALBOT), LTD. A private company, registered on March 27. Capital, £600 in £1 shares. Objects: To acquire the business of omnibus proprietors carried on at 2, Talbot-street, Port Talbot, by Thomas G. Thomas and John D. Evans. The subscribers (each with one share) are:—John D. Evans, 5, London-terrace, Cwmavon, Port Talbot, and Thomas G. Thomas, 1, Alfred-street, Port Talbot. John D. Evans shall be first director. Qualification: One share. Remuneration: As fixed by the company. Solicitor: T. Parker, Port Talbot.

A legal notice published in 1933.

with a steady supply of the raw material required to manufacture more armaments, but at a terrible human cost.

Up until 1939, Thomas Bros. still owned only around 10 vehicles which ran between Aberavon and Goytre, Aberavon Beach and Margam plus of course the busy, highly competitive route from Aberavon to Pontrhydyfen and Tonmawr.

With war declared the need to conserve meant that petrol was the first commodity to be rationed; supplies were being interrupted by U-Boat activity. The low octane fuel that was available created reliability problems because it shortened the life of engine valves. The Ministry of War Transport (MoWT) was formed in 1941 and its Road Transport Division viewed bus competition as wasteful. It was made an offence (until 1946) to buy new buses without a permit, available from the Traffic Commissioner under the Defence of the Realm Regulations. The licensing procedure was reinstated in 1945. Operationally, it was a difficult time for bus businesses as vehicles, often the newer, more reliable ones – were commandeered for a variety of uses, including ambulances. Many of the young fitters were called up or sent to work in munitions factories. For those travellers who had to try and get on with their lives, there were requests that they should complete their return journey by 4.00pm, leaving peak services for workers. At Port Talbot, the MoWT and the South Wales Traffic Commissioner intervened to rationalise wasteful competition to save fuel and tyres and improve efficiency. Some would say that the war had at long last given the authorities an opportunity to force the hand of delinquent operators and bring a level of stability to the Afan Valley.

A measure of the economies forced by the MoWT can be judged by looking at service levels on the Port Talbot to Pontrhydyfen route; prior to 1943 there was a requirement of 12 vehicles provided by 10 operators. The service frequency was every 20 minutes (Monday to Friday), every 10 minutes (Saturday) and every 30 minutes (Sunday).

Full operator details were:

- **Mrs. E A Jenkins (aged 39) psv driver, no employees.**
- **David Jones & Son (aged 49) psv driver, nine single deck vehicles (of which two on stage and seven on workmen's services), 10 drivers.**
- **William Jones (aged 61) no psv licence, one single deck vehicle, one driver (aged 39) no other services.**
- **Joseph Mason & Son (aged 43) psv licence, one single deck vehicle. Only service.**
- **Mrs. E A Stephens (aged 41) psv licence, one single deck vehicle. Only service.**
- **Thomas Bros Ltd – I D Evans (aged 43) – Secretary. No psv, ten single deck vehicles (two on stage), nine drivers. Also operated other stage and workmen's services.**
- **Theophilus Thomas (aged 59) psv licence, one single deck vehicle. Only service.**
- **John Williams (aged 51) psv licence, one single deck vehicle. Only service.**
- **Rhyd Lewis (aged 49) psv licence, one single deck vehicle. Only service.**
- **W J Clement (aged 46) psv licence, one single deck vehicle. Only service.**

After MoWT intervention, the vehicle requirement had been reduced to just 4 on Monday to Friday, 3 on Saturday and 2 on Sunday. Under MoWT direction also, the Avon Valley Bus Owners Association — whose members still operated under their respective different names, seen above — was reorganised into the Afan Transport Co. Ltd. in September 1943. This was intended to be an arms-length subsidiary of Thomas Bros. which would acquire the assets of the AVBOA members and run their contracts and local bus services. In the event, it caused a huge administrative problem after the war when accountants sought to separate Afan

To page 50

When Bedfords ruled the road

1 The attractive cover of a Bedford OB sales and marketing brochure produced in 1947.

2 An official photo of HNY 566 by commercial vehicle suppliers Jeffreys of Swansea.

3 This 1946 Duple bodied Bedford OB, FTG 628, was supplied new to Davies Bros. *Alan B. Cross*

4 This narrow bend in High Street was a notorious bottleneck. Here a number of buses attempt to squeeze through, including those of N&C and Western Welsh. Of particular interest is a rear view of the seldom photographed LEH 132, a Bedford OB belonging to W. L. Jones and purchased secondhand from Poole of Alsager's Bank.

5 Wartime, no-frills Duple-bodied Bedford OWB, FNY 672 in 1950. The bus shelter on the left had been converted from an air raid shelter. *Alan B. Cross*

6 Wartime utility Bedford OWB, FNY 348, was a purchased by William Jones and had passed to Lewis and Jones in 1944 as part of the MoWT directive. *Alan B. Cross*

7 Bought new by Thomas Bros. HNY 566 was a 1948 Bedford OB with bodywork by Jeffreys of Swansea.

From page 47

Transport costs and revenue from those of Thomas Bros. With hindsight this was probably to be expected bearing in mind the interchangeability of vehicles and staff between Thomas Bros. and Afan Transport.

After prolonged negotiation, AVBOA members were reduced to just three under MoWT direction in 1944 as follows:

- **Thomas Bros. acquired W.J. Clement, Theophilus Thomas, J. Williams & E.A. Stephens.**
- **David Jones & Son acquired E.A. Jenkins.**
- **Rhyd Lewis & W. Jones created a partnership and acquired J. Mason & Son.**

To discourage non-essential travel, the minimum 'penny fare' had been increased to twopence at the same time, something which displeased the local council who were determined to have the one penny fare reinstated.

As was the case elsewhere, women were employed as conductors during the war years, but even then it became difficult to ensure that shifts were covered. In April 1944, Thomas Bros. were fined £2 for using an unlicenced conductress on a works service between Cwmavon and Port Talbot. This came to light after a passenger fell from the vehicle and the driver failed to report the accident. A conductor's licence in those days cost 5s (25p).

By now, with a dramatic reduction in the number of separate companies in the area, there was a much simpler structure and the South Wales Traffic Commissioner must have found his nights more restful – assuming that the Luftwaffe weren't around, of course.

Bus enthusiasts who visited the area in July 1944 and whose note-taking must have aroused suspicions during wartime, witnessed the situation in the middle of the reorganisation. Their diaries indicate that the poor souls found the transitional situation quite confusing. There was still a variety of liveries though by that time some fleet names and legal lettering had changed since a previous visit in May. It was clear that a pooling arrangement of vehicles was in place with buses now licenced to the enlarged operators but still, of course, in their previous owners' colours; paint was a scarce resource at the time. It is apparent that the visitors expected to see everything neatly ordered. Life in the bus industry isn't always like that; as in all businesses, after a merger there would be a long interim period before resources were fully consolidated. It didn't help either that one of the observers was using Garcke's Motor Transport Year Book and Directory of 1936 as a reference; the

Driver Ron's fight to save blazing bus

On Sunday 23rd January 1949, Ron Davies, a driver with Davies Bros. returned to Port Talbot in the small hours with a bus he had been driving on a weekend trip. Having dropped off the last of his passengers, Davies made his way to the company's depot in Isaac's Place where about 20 other vehicles were garaged.

As he approached the depot, he found Edward Hill who was a near neighbour raising the alarm that a fire had broken out in one of the buses. Together, Davies and Hill attempted to fight the fire which was in the centre of one of the vehicles, using the extinguisher from the bus. Their efforts had little effect and together they decided to tow the bus outside; it then became wedged in the doorway, threatening the structure of the garage and the other buses within the building.

The Port Talbot Fire Brigade arrived while they were struggling and assisted them to

River Afan had passed beneath several bridges in the intervening eight years. Unfamiliarity with Welsh place names such as Tonmawr and Goytre (one of them was looking for a non-existent place called 'Coytre') added to the confusion.

Up until the war, the various Port Talbot operators had used as diverse a selection of vehicles as could be imagined. In the early days the names Vulcan, Bean, Dodge, Dennis, Guy, Ford and, as one might expect, Leyland and AEC could be found. More exotic imports had included an Oldsmobile and a Lancia. All were single deck vehicles with a capacity of between 20 and 30 seats. As has already been mentioned, former First World War WD lorry chassis were fitted with charabanc - also sometimes called 'torpedo' - bodies. This variety was all good fun for enthusiasts but it presented a nightmare for the operators who needed to source spares from numerous manufacturers and it would have been difficult to set up any price advantages based on bulk purchases.

By 1940 the UK automotive industry had turned production over to manufacturing items deemed essential for the war effort, ranging from tin hats and jerry cans to weapons, tanks and aircraft. In the UK no private cars, commercial vehicles or parts were made for personal use during the Second World War with fuel strictly rationed and non-essential car owners' vehicles decommissioned. Nevertheless, what was needed in Port Talbot was a new, reliable, economical bus suited to the needs of local conditions so that essential services could continue throughout the conflict.

Some of the rationalised companies were permitted to acquire quantities of lightweight wartime utility Bedford OWB vehicles which arrived between 1942 and 1945 and allowed some ageing pre-war buses to be taken out of service. Basically, the new Bedfords were similar to the pre-war Bedford OB but were to a Ministry of Supply specification with components made from valuable metals like aluminium — needed of course for aircraft — replaced with those made from cast iron. The OWB was fitted with an austere, no frills bodywork featuring 32 wooden slatted seats without upholstery; initially, some of the wood used in these buses had been imported for use in furniture manufacturing. The bodies were designed and built by Duple Coachbuilders and similar bodies to Duple drawings were also built by Charles H. Roe in Leeds, Mulliner in Birmingham and Scottish Motor Traction in Edinburgh. The total OWB production which finished in 1945 was 3,398. After the war Thomas Bros., in common with

move the bus outside where it was allowed to burn itself out. Fortunately, the service bus had been one of the last in that night and was near the door. It might otherwise have been in the centre of the other buses in the garage and impossible to move.

Apart from the burned out bus itself, just two others suffered minor scorch damage. The bus destroyed was 1944-built Bedford OWB FNY 873, one of the wartime utility vehicles. It was later sent away for rebodying and reappeared before

Rebodied and revived, FNY 873.
Alan B. Cross

the end of the year with a new postwar OB-style body. The bus survived in the later Thomas Bros. fleet until 1954 after which it was sold to an operator in Neath.

many other operators, fitted more comfortable upholstered seats, at which point the capacity was reduced to 30, to reflect the extra space needed for safety and the cushioned seats. As was so often the case throughout industry, utility items produced quickly and cheaply with a short expected lifespan were found to perform reliably for many years after the conflict.

The longevity of such vehicles was extended by continued rationing after the war. In the early post-war period, government policy was to ensure that manufactured goods should be exported rather than sold at home as the country sought to make good the huge financial losses incurred during the conflict. Statistics given by the Ministry of Supply showed that 3,137 double deck bus chassis and 1,897 bodies were produced in 1946. Of these, 574 chassis and 152 bodies were exported. In 1948 the government limited the number of buses which could be supplied to the home market to 6,000. Considering the hundreds of bus companies operating throughout the country, this was a very small number indeed and efforts had to be made to conserve existing fleets.

The constant requirement for steel had meant that during the war years Thomas Bros. had continued to operate with success. Largely because of the steelworks, revenue from services and contracts increased rapidly and the business expanded.

The steelworks operated at or near full capacity which was reflected in growing profits and a major contribution to Britain's war effort during the war. To keep ahead of projected post-war demand, a new modern strip mill, the Abbey Works, was planned. This integrated steelworks would be a massive undertaking and, in a direct parallel to what had been going on in the local bus industry, several steel manufacturers in south Wales pooled their resources to form the Steel Company of Wales, a public company. The planning application for Abbey Works was made on 6th June 1945. Building work by the main contractor, George Wimpey, started in 1947. 500 acres of land were leased for the steelworks from the Margam Estate with an additional 1,200 acres to the seaward side of the works. The massive project required raising the whole site by 10 feet and this involved adding over five million tons of material.

During May 1945 the Ministry of Town and Country Planning reported that it anticipated difficulty in recruiting sufficient numbers of skilled builders. An estimated 2,500 builders would be needed during 1947-48, later rising to 5,400. In time, the construction workforce peaked at 7,700. Many were housed at the former RAF base at nearby Stormy Down; yet again, an excellent opportunity for the local bus operators!

One further legacy of the war years was the presence of foreign prisoners of war who were available for work; in 1947 there were still about 250,000 PoWs in Britain and the Secretary of State for War

A joint timetable issued by three operators of the Aberavon to Tonmawr route which was issued on 1st June 1948.

ABERAVON-TONMAWR TIME TABLE

WEEK DAYS.

	a.m.	p.m.	p.m.	p.m.	p.m.	p.m.
ABERAVON Dept.	10.30	1.00	3.30	5.00	8.30	
WAUN	10.40	1.10	3.40	5.10	8.40	
PONTRHYDYFEN	10.45	1.15	3.45	5.15	8.45	
EFAIL FACH	10.50	1.20	3.50	5.20	8.50	
TONMAWR	10.55	1.25	3.55	5.25	8.55	
	Operated by D. Jones & Son	Afan Transport Co., Ltd.	Lewis & Jones Ltd.	Afan Transport Co., Ltd.	Lewis & Jones, Ltd. Alternative fortnights with D. Jones & Son	

	a.m.	p.m.	p.m.	p.m.	p.m.
TONMAWR Dept.	11.05	1.35	4.05	5.35	9.00
EFAIL FACH	11.10	1.40	4.10	5.40	9.05
PONTRHYDYFEN	11.15	1.45	4.15	5.45	9.10
WAUN	11.20	1.50	4.20	5.50	9.15
ABERAVON	11.30	2.00	4.30	6.00	9.25

SUNDAY.

	p.m				p.m	p.m
ABERAVON Dept.	1.15		TONMAWR Dept.		1.50	4.50
WAUN	1.25	4.15	EFAIL FACH		1.55	4.55
PONTRHYDYFEN	1.30	4.25	PONTRHYDYFEN		2.00	5.00
EFAIL FACH	1.35	4.30	WAUN		2.05	5.05
TONMAWR	1.40	4.35	ABERAVON		2.15	5.15
		4.40				

Sunday Service Operated by Afan Transport Co., Ltd.

1st June, 1948.

D. W. Jones (Printers) Ltd., Port Talbot.

This 1933 Leyland TD3 with English Electric bodywork, was HG 2935, new to Burnley, Colne & Nelson Joint Omnibus Committee. *Alan B. Cross*

One of the first buses to be transferred in by the British Electric Traction group following their takeover of Thomas Bros. in 1951, FWL 647 was a 1938 Park Royal bodied AEC Regent which came from City of Oxford Motor Services. *Alan B. Cross*

made a policy statement which was of interest to bus operators:

"It has been decided that German prisoners of war in this country, other than those classified as ardent Nazis, whose output of work is satisfactory shall be allowed to draw part of their pay in sterling and to use shops, cinemas, restaurants and public transport within five miles of their Camp, but not to use licensed premises. These arrangements will come into force about the middle of July. They are intended as incentives to good work and will be subject to review in the light of experience."

Six former Burnley Colne and Nelson Joint Omnibus Committee — Bus companies don't have names like that any more! — high bridge double deck Leyland Titan TD3s were obtained between 1947 and 1949: HG 2298/2301/2303/2935/2961/2962) followed by a further one (HG 2303) the following year. These were operated very successfully thanks to the efforts of the engineering staff. From Halifax Corporation came AEC Regents JX 1912/3, 2038 and 2305. More double deckers appeared in 1950 in the form of a pair of former Bolton Corporation Leyland Titan TD7s. The price of a secondhand double decker in those days was between £250 and £400, depending on condition.

Low bridges at Port Talbot meant that the double deckers, which also ran on the Cwmavon services couldn't access the depot; they were kept on land at the Waun, Cwmavon belonging to haulage contractor Mostyn Evans where there was a basic inspection pit and a small shed. Works services and contracts were operated under the Afan Transport wing which was intended to keep such work separate from Thomas Bros. so that revenue could be apportioned to the respective owners.

By having a 'works' fleet, the companies ensured – as far as was possible – that passengers dressed in their finery didn't have to use the same buses as workers whose clothes would have been past their best at the end of a long shift.

Standing outside the Plaza Cinema en route for Goytre. HG 4476 was a 1936 Leyland LT7c/English Electric B38R which had been new to Burnley, Colne & Nelson as their No. 143. Purchased in 1948 it was withdrawn in October 1951. *Alan B. Cross*

A similar situation existed between Davies Bros. and its subsidiary, Thomas & James.

In postwar Britain, the first general election since 1935 took place in July 1945. This was after Labour leader Clement Attlee had refused Churchill's proposal to continue with the Wartime Government until the end of the conflict with the Japanese. The Labour Party ran a 'Face the Future' campaign which appealed to voters who feared that the Conservatives might bring a return to the stagnation of the 1930s. Labour won a majority with 394 seats to the Conservatives' 210 and quickly set about introducing legislation which would prepare the way for nationalisation of Britain's principal industries; cable and wireless, railways, civil aviation, coal, gas, iron and steel, the Bank of England and road transport. Over one fifth of the British economy went into public hands. Political dogma aside, some of these industries had fared particularly badly during the war and nationalisation was sold as the best way to pump new money into them.

In 1946, the postwar Labour Government published a Transport Bill which, when law, would set up a British Transport Commission (BTC) to nationalise and integrate all inland transport networks in Great Britain. Northern Ireland was dealt with separately, but along the same principles. In time, the Transport Act 1947 was passed and the BTC came into existence on 1st January 1948 at which point British Railways (later British Rail) was born. The railways, through legislation which had been passed in the 1920s, owned about 50 per cent of shares in the BET, Tilling and Scottish Motor Traction (SMT) groups which were provincial Britain's largest bus owners. So by default a substantial part of the bus industry also became part-nationalised at this time. Notably in South Wales, the South Wales Transport Company was exempt from this, having no railway shareholding.

With the incentive of a generous payment, Tilling, which in state ownership would become the Transport Holding Company

With a 33 seat Burlingham coach body HNY 415 was a 1948 Leyland PS1. Then the height of luxury, it was fitted with a radio at the seemingly high cost of £72 15s 6d.

This 1937 AEC Regal had a Cravens 32-seat body. DWE 606 had been new to Sheffield Corporation and is seen here in service with Thomas & James at the original Talbot Square bus terminus for valley routes.
Alan B. Cross

(THC) and SMT both later sold out in full to the BTC. Moreover, the Government had a plan to set up regional transport boards which would buy out the group companies, the municipalities and independent bus operators in the respective areas, which included South Wales. Similar proposals would re-emerge in the late 1960s under Barbara Castle, leading to the formation of the Passenger Transport Executives serving the UK's biggest conurbations.

In the 1940s, BET, whose South Wales interests then included Western Welsh, Rhondda Transport and South Wales Transport obstinately refused to sell out to the Government and in due course shareholders were told that the income they received from profits was greater than that they would have received on the interest for the purchase price. Result!

One of the worst winters ever known hit the UK in early 1947 in Port Talbot as with the rest of the country bus services were suspended because of heavy snowfalls and thick ice. Workers were often unable to reach their homes and forced to spend the night at their place of employment.

Meanwhile, an unfortunate incident took place in September 1948. Two Thomas Bros. coaches had arrived at Tintern on a day trip from Port Talbot. Also there, on a half day tour from Gloucester, was a Bristol Tramways vehicle carrying day-trippers which had stopped at Tintern for tea and was heading back via Monmouth. Near the Wye Valley Hotel, the leading Thomas Bros. vehicle met that from Gloucester head on. The force of the collision ripped seats from their mountings and approximately 20 people were taken to hospital.

Meanwhile, wartime rationalisation had meant that by 1948 the number of local bus operators in Port Talbot had been whittled down to just the following: Thomas Bros (Port Talbot) Ltd./Afan Transport which was operating the frequent (every 7-8 minutes) service from the Beach to Margam along with Thomas & James and Davies Bros. and the hourly service from the Beach to Goytre; David Jones & Son and Lewis & Jones operating the infamous Pontrhydyfen route.

This list of course excludes any non-service operators who existed purely for private hire and those which offered longer distance services; principally The South Wales Transport Co., Ltd., Western Welsh Omnibus Co. Ltd., Neath & Cardiff Luxury Coaches Ltd., Rhondda Transport Co., Ltd. and Llynfi Motors.

The Government's nationalisation of electricity generation and supply under the Electricity Act 1947 had taken away BET's slice of that industry but left the group with a healthy financial base, so it could afford some 'retail therapy' to soften the pain of its loss. It went in search of businesses to replace the earning potential of the electricity interests, including Rediffusion and Eddison Plant and invested in transport operations in Africa, Canada and Jamaica. There was also an expansion of BET's interests in 'textile maintenance'; laundry services in plain language!

'Demand for skilled labour boosted wages and provided money in the pay packet to buy cars and televisions.'

In 1950, like the rest of Britain, Port Talbot was still dealing with the scars of the Second World War. Petrol, sweets and sugar were all still rationed and manufacturing was focused on orders for export, rather than the home market in an effort to pay off the country's £21bn wartime debt.

The following year, this battle of a different kind was powered up by the 1951 Festival of Britain. This was effectively a huge shop window for the country's industry and importantly a hopeful tool to boost its wounded finances.

By the middle of the decade, there was a more positive outlook. The demand for skilled labour brought higher wages. The Coronation of Queen Elizabeth II in 1953 also boosted the mood of the nation.

More good news for consumers was the availability of television sets and the rebirth of car production for the home market with a selection of affordable small cars becoming available. Unfortunately, both these developments would eventually lead to a decline in bus usage. By 1958 of the 14,000 homes in the Borough of Port Talbot, 8,000 of them already boasted a TV.

Built in 1931, AEC Regal TG 5167 operated by Jones, Pantdu passes the well patronised Emlyn Davies electrical store where many bought their first records and home appliances, early 1950.

Austerity to affluence via the positive route

The back end of the bus heading down a busy Station Road, Port Talbot in 1951 belongs to former Birmingham City Transport EOG 275, a 1939 Leyland TD6c/MCCW H28/24R which Thomas Bros. and Afan Transport operated on works services between 1951 and 1952. The AEC coach alongside was N&C's FNY 556 and hides a Thomas Bros. Bedford OB.

Bill James in front of DOD 466, one of the AEC Regals Thomas Bros. obtained from Devon General in 1952.

DAVID JONES AND SON
(PORT TALBOT) LTD.
PANTDU GARAGE, PORT TALBOT

IF YOU WANT THE
BEST COACHES FOR THE PRESENT SEASON
BOOK EARLY!

We can offer 41, 37, 33 and 29-Seater
LUXURY COACHES FOR YOUR PARTY

★ LOOK OUT FOR FUTURE ANNOUNCEMENTS OF ADVERTISED TOURS

The General Election of 1950 had returned Labour to power but with a majority of just five seats. A second election in 1951 returned a Conservative Government under Winston Churchill and it seemed that for the most part, the threat of full nationalisation of the bus industry had retreated.

The two decades when Thomas Bros. (Port Talbot) Ltd. became a company worthy of the town of Port Talbot brought with them some interesting developments.

This 1951 Albion Victor had been new to Gough of Pembroke Dock and came with the takeover of David Jones in 1965, but was never used by Thomas Bros.

1950
Another Acquisition

With the state ownership threat receding, BET went on the lookout for companies which could be purchased at low cost, but which had potential for substantial growth. Acquisition of these would also be of strategic importance, to prevent the THC making incursions into strong BET territory. In South West Wales, three operators in particular stood out. Two of them were J. James of Ammanford and Neath & Cardiff Luxury Coaches. The third was Thomas Bros. of Port Talbot. There can be no doubt these companies were chosen after consultation with the larger BET subsidiaries, possibly because they were becoming a thorn in their side and because there was potential for growth and profitability. A further reality is that by absorbing these smaller operators, BET was preventing the THC group from making further inroads into South Wales. They already had a strong base in east Wales with Red & White and around Swansea and Neath with United Welsh.

On 6th November 1950 a representative of SWT visited D.W. Jones & Son of Pantdu for discussions about a possible sale. His report was submitted to the SWT General Manager and then to the BET board. The Joneses, as might be expected, were after the best possible price and made a point of telling SWT that they were expecting a visit from the British Transport Commission on the 8th!

Mr. Jones was reportedly 'anxious to dispose of the whole of this business'. Financial commitments included three vehicles on hire purchase, but he had recently been successful in a fare increase application. It was also noted that Mr. Jones held one ninth of the shares in Afan Transport and one sixth of the shares in Thomas Bros. (Port Talbot) Ltd.

The report reveals that at the time the Jones fleet totalled 18 vehicles made up of five coaches, 12 saloons and one double decker. The coaches were on Tillings, AEC, Crossley, Dennis and Maudslay chassis

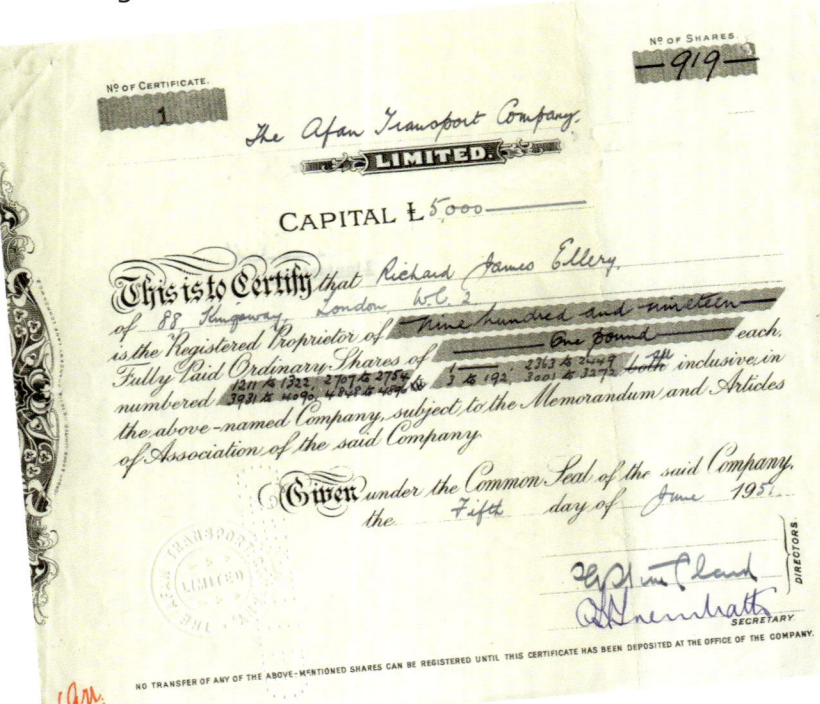

A share certificate for the Afan Transport Co., Ltd. issued on 5th June 1951.

Two of the former 1936 Birmingham City Transport Daimler COG5s with MCCW 34 seat bodywork alongside the Jersey Beach Hotel on Aberavon seafront. Both had spent the war years converted to work as ambulances in their home city.

and were in good condition. The saloons were four AEC Regals and eight Bedfords. The double decker was a Leyland and all seemed to have been earning their keep.

Two buses were needed for the services between Pontrhydyfen and Tonmawr and Port Talbot which were shared with Lewis & Jones and Afan Transport. The requirement for stage carriage works services between Pontrhydyfen and the Abbey Works was much larger. Five vehicles were required before 5.00am; nine vehicles by 7.30am; three were required from Cwmavon at 1.20pm and 9.20pm, four for the return at 4.00pm and three at 5.00pm.

Other contracts were to the Carbide Works, NCB Garth and Newlands Collieries and there was a 'Railway Contract' from Pontrhydyfen to Margam and from Blaengwynfi to the Abbey Works for the day shifts. Schools contracts were operated from the Afan Valley to the Eastern Schools at Taibach and the County Grammar School in Port Talbot.

As a consequence of the visit by SWT, the local bus services of David Jones & Son were acquired under the Afan Transport name in February 1952. The company was originally set up by David and Martha Jones who lived in Pantdu and was by then run by son John. The firm had previously taken over B. Thomas of Port Talbot (1934) and Jenkins, Pantdu (1943). The livery was green and cream. After takeover, John Jones continued with his contracts until he finally sold out to Thomas Bros. in 1965. John Jones also bought Thomas Brothers lorries (no direct connection with the Thomas Bros. bus company), which eventually became Pantdu Haulage. In conjunction with Nelson's of Taibach they also ran a fleet of long distance lorries called Blue Line Transport. Later, they took on an Austin/Morris agency and they were an agent for National Benzole; the car business was eventually taken over by the Fletcher family of Swansea. With the Jones business came their two ex-Birmingham Daimler COG5 single deckers, AOP 52 and BOL 35 which immediately passed to dealers.

1951
All change!

Early in 1951, Thomas Bros. had a 'Birmingham moment' when it purchased a Leyland Titan TD6 and three Daimler COG5s (two single deck, one double deck) which Birmingham City Transport had passed to the well-known dealer, Bird of Stratford-upon-Avon. Neighbouring operator Davies Bros. also bought two COG5 single deckers from the same source, at the same time. There must have been occasions when all six of these dark blue and cream vehicles rolled up at the steelworks for the same shift change, making quite a sight!

In March 1951 it was announced that the share capitals of Thomas Brothers (Port Talbot). Ltd., and the Afan Transport Co., Ltd. had been acquired by BET. In a familiar scenario the former directors of the two companies duly retired and were replaced by representatives of BET. That June, BET took over fully and in due course combined Thomas Bros. with its Afan Transport subsidiary and Davies Bros. with its Thomas

To page 62

Routes that tested the best

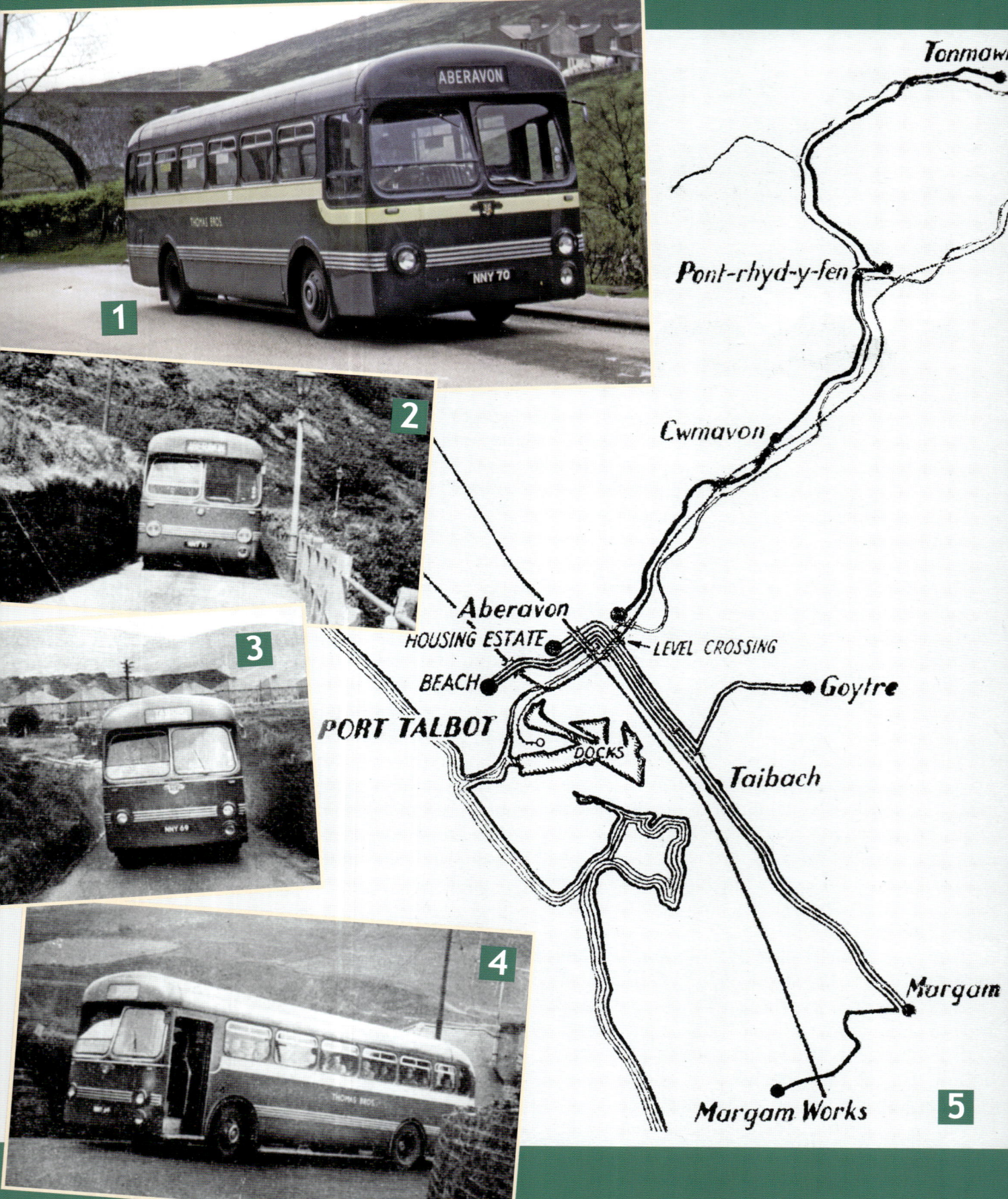

One of Thomas Bros. early Hermes-bodied Leyland Tiger Cubs crosses the River Afan in late 1959, long before the town centre redevelopment of the 1970s. The first floor bay window on the pine end of the white building on the left, was that of the company's office in High Street above a chemist's store, until the new premises at Acacia Avenue, Sandfields, opened.

Two buses at Danybont, Pontrhydyfen, possibly waiting for passengers before heading back down the valley. In the background is the impressive nine arch viaduct built in 1898 by the Port Talbot Railway Company. It was built from brick rather than stone as it was cheaper. The bridge linked collieries at nearby Tonmawr to Port Talbot docks. Actor Richard Burton's birthplace is visible, bottom left.

Valley views

1. Saunders Roe bodied Leyland Tiger Cub NNY 70 waits at Pontrhydyfen before its return run down the Afan Valley to Aberavon in May 1967.
Roy Marshall, copyright The Bus Archive.

2. Illustrating why this stretch of road was known as 'The Narrows' with a 10 minute headway NNY 71 returns to Port Talbot from Pontrhydyfen.

3. Heading up the single lane road to Tabor meant squeezing between stone walls and high hedges for NNY 69 on this day in the early 1950s.

4. The hairpin bend on the Brynbryddan and Tabor route was used by up to 17 journeys each day calling for some skillful driving.

5. An outline map giving an indication of how in the company's early days Thomas Bros, linked coast and country, communities and workplaces.

THOMAS BROS. (PORT TALBOT) LTD.

4, HIGH STREET
ABERAVON
PORT TALBOT

DIRECTORS:
W. T. JAMES, O.B.E. (CHAIRMAN)
P. G. STONE CLARK
T. R. WILLIAMS, M.A.LL.B.

TELEPHONE: PORT TALBOT 181
OMNIBUS PROPRIETORS
SANDFIELDS GARAGE
ABERAVON

..............195........

From page 59

& James subsidiary. For the new-look company of Thomas Bros. (Port Talbot) Ltd., the next 20 years would see modernisation and expansion as it was assimilated into the BET Group. Not until the post-National Bus deregulated era of the 1980s would issues of underhand competition re-emerge.

Coincidentally, in the same month as the takeover by BET, the new hot strip mill at Abbey Works commenced its commercial output. It was officially opened on July 17th by Chancellor of the Exchequer Hugh Gaitskell, deputising for King George VI whose failing health was giving considerable cause for concern at that time.

Meanwhile, the Steel Company of Wales was placing advertisements in local newspapers to recruit workers:

"The Steel Company of Wales Limited has a large number of vacancies for Production and Maintenance Workers of many grades, including General Labour, for their Abbey Works. All these jobs offer excellent prospects of early promotion for young and energetic workers. Houses are being made available for workers whose homes are not in the Port Talbot area, and in the meantime accommodation is available in the Steel Company's hostel near Porthcawl, at very low rates, with free transport to and from work."

The hostel was the former RAF base at Stormy Down where some huts were used as billets for workers. In 1948 the gymnasium there was converted to a cinema by the steel company. It was open to the general public and remained so until it closed in 1953.

A huge boom in demand for sheet steel for consumer goods and cars meant that eventually the Abbey Works would become Europe's largest steel producer and the largest single employer in Wales with a workforce of over 18,000. With so many well paid jobs in the area, Thomas Bros. suffered from an ongoing shortage of drivers. Recruits were brought in from West Wales and the council considered that the bus service was of such importance that it was willing to allocate housing to bus company staff. With the first service due out of the depot shortly after 5.00am and the last back around 11.45pm, staff transport was supplied.

BET inherited around 50 vehicles with the takeover. A large number of these were the previously mentioned lightweight Bedford OB and OWB models. The rest were a mixed bag of Daimlers, Dennises and some ageing AECs and Leylands, including the double deckers which had been slogging away on works services. There was a Seddon, described as being totally unsuitable for service which was disliked by drivers, maintenance staff and, possibly passengers. A start was immediately made in repainting the fleet into a new livery of royal blue and electric blue.

The new management team at Port Talbot had BET's reputation to protect and their personal ones to build, so they were probably quite risk averse when it came to taking over vehicles from operators who may, or may not, have been diligent in their record keeping. The company quickly put into action a plan to replace as much of the fleet as practicable with more durable and reliable vehicles whose maintenance history was known, even if some of them were of similar age or even older than those which were being condemned.

The replacements were sourced from within the BET Group, so had known histories. AEC Regent double deckers and AEC Regal saloons were brought in from City of Oxford Motor Services. The Regents were allocated to the Afan Transport fleet for use on services to Cwmavon. A sole Leyland Titan TD5 came from SWT for use on a contract service to the National Oil Refinery (later BP) at Llandarcy. A further eight SWT AEC Regents of 1937 vintage, originally purchased for tramway replacement at Swansea were also available to Thomas Bros. had the need arisen. SWT had undertaken an AEC Rehabilitation Scheme for pre-war vehicles but was by now replacing them with newer buses, so there was an availability of recently reconditioned vehicles. All of this meant that a start could be made on standardisation of the fleet and no doubt sorting out the large variety of spare parts which were held. The first engineering stocktake must have been a revelation to those involved.

the 1,000th had been opened in September 1951 by Hugh Dalton, Minister for Local Government. Construction would continue for the next 25 years. In 1952, British Oxygen erected a works at Longlands Lane, Margam, to serve the steelworks.
For Thomas Bros., having a giant steel plant and associated industries on one side of town and workers living on the other, was the perfect scenario for profitability.

The fleet of little wartime Bedfords had served the company well, but they had severe limitations. By 1952 they were exhibiting the signs of having had a hard life and as lightweight buses it was clear that they would be unable to cope with the challenges which lay ahead. To replace them, the company bought fifteen 35-seat AEC Regal saloons with Harrington and Weymann bodywork which were surplus to the requirements of Devon General, another BET subsidiary.

These were overhauled and repainted by Devon General at Torquay before being dispatched to South Wales. After the first 10 had been in service for just a fortnight in 1952, a letter was sent to Devon General expressing the company's delight with the buses and asking whether any more were available! They were given a notional value of £100 each, plus tyres and the overhaul costs to which 10 per cent was added to keep the accountants in Devon on side.

One of the Harrington-bodied AEC Regals from Devon General in 1952, DDV 443 outside the Sandfields Road depot while a sister bus receives attention.

1952
5,968,553 not out

Clearly, with such a large steelworks, there was a need for housing for the workers and their families. In 1951-52, hundreds of homes were built at Sandfields including many prefabs;

They're all coming back for *more* Tiger Cubs

This lively Tiger Cub is lapping the M.I.R.A. test ground at over 67 miles an hour. (Illustration by courtesy of "The Commercial Motor").

Right from the start, the Tiger Cub 44-seater bus has been an unqualified triumph. Performance and economy have exceeded operators' most sanguine expectations, and a steady volume of repeat orders is flowing in. Despite the low kerbside weight of well under 6 tons, its brilliantly designed chassis is packed with economy features from stem to stern.

The high efficiency 90 h.p. underfloor diesel is wonderfully low on fuel, consumption figures ranging between 13-16 m.p.g., varying with routes. The Tiger Cub 44-seater coach is similar in layout to the bus, but a 108 h.p. engine is fitted, permitting a 9½ ton gross maximum weight. Write for leaflet No. 716 for specifications of both vehicles.

Leyland TIGER CUB BUSES & COACHES

LEYLAND MOTORS LTD. Head Office & Works: LEYLAND · LANCS · ENGLAND
London Office & Export Division: HANOVER HOUSE · HANOVER SQUARE · LONDON, W.1.

Passengers for stops to Abergwynfi board Leyland PSUC1/1 TTG 6 at Bethany Square on a sunny summer's day in July 1969 while stablemate TTG 5 noses behind prior to a journey to the closer village of Tonmawr in the Pelenna valley. Fred Bowden meanwhile simply spread news of his bookmaking business on the bus!
Roy Marshall, copyright The Bus Archive.

It is known that 10 of the Bedfords were eventually sold on to a dealer for around £200 each and later passed to a variety of small operators around Britain. The Thomas Bros. management were no doubt more than satisfied with the deal.

In 1952 Lewis and Jones also came into the Thomas Bros. fold. This was, in turn, a 1944 amalgamation of William Jones of Port Talbot, Rhyd Lewis and Joseph Mason of Cwmavon. This brought a bus-seated Bedford SB/Duple Vega coach, KTX 476, with a breathtakingly poor petrol consumption of just 5 mpg. The machine ended up with Hastelow of Malvern who used it on its Malvern to Gloucester service. Hastelow's fuel suppliers must have been rubbing their hands with glee although one suspects that by then it had been given a diesel engine.

At this time, even as renewal of the fleet was in hand, the first financial year (1951-1952) since BET took control, 5,968,553 passengers were carried over 792,006 miles.

1953
Hermes delivers the goods

Four more ex-Devon General Regals arrived in April 1953 at a cost of £1,250 per bus. Again, all were overhauled at Torquay before being forwarded to Port Talbot.

These secondhand vehicles were only ever intended as a stop-gap. What Thomas Bros. and the long suffering residents of Port Talbot really needed was new buses.

First though, an AEC Regal IV coach arrived in March. MTG 172 was the first new item of rolling stock since BET takeover even though it had been ordered prior to BET ownership. It was also the first underfloor engined vehicle in the fleet and carried the short lived Mark 2 version of the Burlingham Seagull centre entrance body with the untidy double trim around the side panels.

It was finished in a two-tone blue livery and carried the name Port Talbot Monarch. Coach names with a local theme became a notable feature of the Thomas Bros. fleet throughout the 1950s and 60s.

Morale at the company must have been quite high towards the end of 1953 when a batch of nine new Leyland Tiger Cubs arrived, registered NNY 54 to NNY 62. These had the iconic and durable Weymann Hermes all-metal lightweight 44-seat bodies which were ordered in very large numbers across the UK, notably by sister BET company Western Welsh who at one time had 180. They were the first new buses to be delivered in the new 'Thomas Bros. Blue' livery.

The bodywork was of excellent build quality, and for ease of maintenance included detachable single piece skirt panels for access to the engine. Thomas Bros. played an important role in the design of the Weymann bodies with 2ft 11in doorways, a lower than normal step height and a ramped floor. The batch would remain a feature of the South Wales scene for many years. Once they had done their 12 or so years

After heading along Church Street buses passed beneath the low bridge carrying the main Paddington to Swansea railway line with limited clearance, necessitating slow running. The route was from Sandfields to Aberavon Market, to the left of this view.

work with Thomas Bros., most were sold to other local operators for further service.

In the event, NNY 58 lasted longer than any of its sisters as for several years it was fitted with a removable rear panel and a towing bracket, doubling up as the depot towing vehicle. The new vehicles meant that the double deckers could be withdrawn and all had gone by the end of the year.

A long-running thorn in the side of all road users in Port Talbot was the former Rhondda & Swansea Bay Railway level crossing on the A48 at Station Road, in pre-bypass days this was the main route between Cardiff and West Wales. The congestion would extend into Water Street which was the main route from the beach. Traffic on the bottleneck at Water Street would remain static until Station Road and High Street had cleared. It was estimated that an extra 10 minutes could be added to journey times and this could accumulate through the day; the level crossing was closed between 90 and 100 times per day, an aggregate of four hours. A report from the National Road Transport Federation rightly described the situation as a 'traffic handicap of the first magnitude'.

1954
Investors in people

This year saw Thomas Bros. apply for the four (Afan Valley) licences of the Afan Transport Co., Ltd. after which it was wound up and combined with Thomas Bros. In May a further nine Leyland Tiger Cubs with 44 seat bus bodies arrived (NNY 63 to NNY 71) however no coaches were bought.

The low numbered registrations meant that some people came to know the buses individually. Local resident Sue Masrani said: "I have always been a numbers nerd and remember that NNY 66 was my favourite Thomas Bros. bus. I used to watch for the Velindre bus in the hope it was NNY 66."

The new additions had bodywork built by Saunders-Roe of Anglesey, a handsome new single deck body for underfloor engined chassis was introduced in 1952 known as the SARO body which sold well on Leyland Tiger Cub chassis to BET group companies. Following an overall drop in demand for bus bodies in the mid 1950s the last Saunders Roe bus bodies were built in 1956 and the factory was sold in 1959.

The innovative construction method produced an attractive, distinctive and modern design. Moreover, increasing costs meant that lightweight bodies such as those built by SARO were preferable while at the same time mainstream manufacturers were experiencing production difficulties. SWT was also trialling several lightweight 44-seat buses for its hilly routes at the time, including demonstrators from Guy and Leyland. These were:

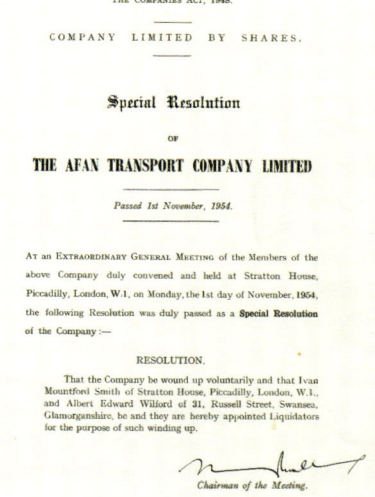

- ■ **A Leyland Cub (sic) with 5.76 litre engine, Eaton 2 speed axle, UW 5-14-3. This is likely to have been Saunders-Roe bodied PTE 592.**
- ■ **A Guy Arab with Gardner 6HLW, UW 6-3-3. This is believed to have been another Saunders-Roe vehicle, Guy Arab LUF LJW 336, now preserved at Aldridge Transport Museum.**

One of the routes on which SWT had been trialling the demonstration vehicles was that on service 20 between Aberavon and Maesteg where the hills provided an excellent testing ground. Presumably, Thomas Bros. management had been invited to view them as well. They would certainly have been aware of the trials. The nine new buses were delivered to Port Talbot in workshop grey and painted by Thomas Bros. staff. There were by now 18 new buses in town which would definitely have been appreciated by passengers. The extra internal capacity was much needed on services in the growing Sandfields Estate.

By February there was progress in construction work on the Central Road and Central Bus Park area of the Abbey Works. This was expected to take three to four months. The revised bus park at the works duly came into use from 28th June 1954, but just a few years later, in 1960 a totally new and redesigned layout was opened.

Newly delivered Saunders-Roe bodied Leyland Tiger Cub NNY 71 alongside Beulah Chapel in Groes Village. Also known as the Round Chapel and dating from 1838, it was moved in 1976 to make way for construction of the M4.

The limitations of single aperture destination displays are evident in this view of NNY 64 which has subsidiary information propped in the windscreen. Several of the SARO vehicles lost much of their brightwork after several years in the rough and tumble of working life at industrial Port Talbot.

The first batch of nine Leyland Tiger Cubs arrived in late 1953. One, NNY 55 is seen below.

In July, it was announced that General Manager J.H. Gilbert would be leaving to join A. Timpson & Sons, Ltd. in London to succeed W.A. Timpson when he retired. He was succeeded in October, by Peter Hornblow. A former BET trainee, Peter had previously been with SWT as Swansea area traffic superintendent. This move highlights BET's focus on, and commitment to, developing management skills. Having impressed the board with his work at Swansea, he was then given his 'own' company to manage.

BET's training scheme, though ground breaking in its time, was by today's standards, a catalogue of discriminatory practices. Applications were open to men (this was specified!) between the ages of 21 and 25, though men — this was re-emphasised — outside those ages would be considered, based on character, past record and general suitability. In other words, you needed to be a decent sort of chap. This was a legacy perhaps of the military origins of senior management; to this day many bus companies call their supervisors 'officers' rather than managers and road staff are often referred to as the troops.

The programme was designed to fit recruits to managerial posts in the local bus companies, spending up to three years with one of the selected 'training' operators. After this they would be attached to one or more operating companies to gain further experience. All being well, they would then move on to a first appointment proper, often with one of the smaller companies, as a first full managerial post.

A perfect example in the context of this story is that of Owain G. Davies who, having

Buses between Sandfields estate and the town centre had to use Church Street which had two-way traffic and roadside paking, so that mounting the pavement was inevitable.

John David Evans   J.H.Gilbert   Peter A. Hornblow   Anthony Beetham   D. N. Flower

Faces of the five at the top

General Manager	Previous Company	Next Company
John David Evans 1931-1952	Thomas Bros (Port Talbot)	Retired
J.H. Gilbert 1952-1954	Western Welsh	A. Timpson & Sons, London.
Peter A. Hornblow 1954-1962	South Wales Transport Co	Salisbury United Omnibus Co. Rhodesia (Zimbabwe)
Anthony Beetham 1962-1968	Southdown Motor Services	City of Oxford Motor Services.
D.N. Flower 1969-1969	N&C Luxury Coaches	Aldershot & District Traction Co.

joined his father's business at Port Talbot a couple of years before BET takeover, went on to receive further training with Western Welsh and then became Assistant Traffic Manager of Rhondda Transport. This explains why BET kept some smaller operations such as Thomas Bros. and N&C Luxury Coaches separate as 'training companies', rather than combining them with SWT or Western Welsh, which would have seemed a more logical and cost effective step. In a small company, a trainee manager had the opportunity to prove whether or not he (again, it was invariably 'he') was worth his salt. If he wasn't, then there was an element of damage limitation at play.

1955
More of the same

A new face joined the team during the year. Perhaps with a nod towards what the future might bring. Mr. Donald P. Drew took up the role of joint accountant for Thomas Bros. and SWT. He was appointed company secretary of both the following year. Five more brand new vehicles arrived in March 1955. By now the pattern of the annual intake had emerged; usually a handful of Leyland Tiger Cub 44-seat buses and one or two AEC coaches. The Tiger Cubs, registered PTX 197 to PTX 199 and PTX 202, had Weymann bodywork, similar to those delivered in 1953. The engines were horizontally mounted Leyland O.350, driving through an Albion 5-speed crash gearbox to the well liked single-speed Eaton/Leyland spiral-bevel rear axle. PTX 203 was an AEC Reliance, the successor to the Regal IV, with a Burlingham 41-seat centre entrance body, which took the name Pride of Port Talbot. This was a Seagull Mk.3, with the design errors of the poorly received Mk.2 now a thing of the past. The chassis was designated **MU3RA**, meaning: **M**edium-weight, **U**nderfloor engine, **3**-pedal, **R**ight-hand control with **A**ir brakes. It was powered by AEC's 7.7-litre AH470 engine.

Several older coach-type vehicles were redesignated as 'dual purpose' at this time. For the layman this means that they could

Weymann bodied PTX 198, one of the 1955 intake of four Leyland Tiger Cubs at South Wales Transport's Ravenhill, Swansea, works undergoing maintenance after the 1969 fleet merger.

be used on both coach work — tours and contracts — as well as local bus operations.

On October 31st, the A48 Briton Ferry Bridge opened. Construction had started back in 1949 and at the time it was the largest civil engineering project in the UK after the Second World War. This did little to ease congestion in Port Talbot, but it would become a useful tool in the marketing of Aberavon Beach in future years. At the beach itself, a one and a quarter mile sea wall was built primarily for sea defences to protect the increasing number of homes, mainly for steelworkers which had been built on the dunes at Sandfields.

> A coach fitted with a radio was a talking point for passengers in 1948. This was Leyland Tiger HNY 415 seen in an advertisement that year.

They all ask for the "RADIO" COACH

Leyland Coach recently equipped by us with "RADIOMOBILE," for THOMAS BROS. LTD., PORT TALBOT.

Why not use the slack season to equip your Coach, Commercial Vehicle, or Car with RADIO.

Consult the RADIOMOBILE Accredited Dealers:

MOORWELL MOTORS LTD.
2, WESTGATE STREET, CARDIFF. Tel. 8335

1956
A taxing time

In February, Thomas Bros. along with the other major South Wales operators applied to the Traffic Commissioner for a fare increase. Costs had increased by £14,542 and extra revenue of £7,600 was required. The fare increase was granted on the basis that it should only apply to routes where Thomas Bros. competed with other operators, but not on services which they operated alone. BET's modernisation plan was proceeding well. TTG 3 to TTG 6 arrived in late July, again, these were Leyland Tiger Cubs with 44 seat

Three former SWT AEC Regal IIIs with Windover coach bodies at Acacia Avenue.

There was no shortage of passengers when this image of 1956 Leyland Tiger Cub TTG 3 was captured as it prepared to depart Bethany Square, Port Talbot for Sandfields Estate.

Weymann Hermes bodies. By now, the type had become the standard workhorse of the fleet, giving reliable service and helping to create a new modern and trustworthy image for the Thomas Bros. brand. These enabled the withdrawal of some of the former Devon General Regals. Another AEC Reliance with a Burlingham Seagull Mk. 3 body, TTG 2 was named Port Talbot Princess. A good quality coach fleet was gradually being constructed in line with the BET group's aspirations.

For works contracts, three secondhand vehicles also appeared in 1956. The first was GCY 432, a 1950 AEC Regal III with a Windover Huntingdon coach body, displaced from the SWT fleet by the delivery of its new state of the art Weymann Fanfare Reliances. The price paid was £750. Three more SWT Regal III coaches would arrive at Port Talbot in due course, again mainly for use as works vehicles, continuing the need to keep the worker and local resident markets apart. Similarly, as a further temporary measure until more Tiger Cubs could be delivered, two former Western Welsh Leyland Tigers were obtained for works services. These were BBO 893 and BUH 55.

In April 1956, Princess Margaret visited the Abbey Works and, later, Aberavon Beach where she opened the new road across the seafront to be named Princess Margaret Way. This was more significant than a simple road-opening ceremony. It marked a milestone in the development of the beach as a summer destination which would later include the Afan Lido and Miami Beach funfair.

A meeting to discuss the possible provision of a central bus station at Port Talbot was convened by Glamorgan County Council in May. The bus station would form part of the town centre redevelopment which was precipitated by the by-pass plan. Representatives from N&C, SWT and WW were present, together with Mr. Hornblow from Thomas Bros. Surprisingly, there was disagreement from the operators about the need for a bus station in the form suggested; those operating 'through' services preferred not to have those services using it, while Mr. Hornblow said that if services from Margam to Sandfields Estate and the beach used it, there would be serious congestion.

Conductress Sarah Thomas in front of VTX 7 at the Acacia Avenue depot. *Steph Evans*

Thomas Bros. would also require a booking office and waiting room. It was resolved that the local authority would seek to accommodate 'through' services in a layby adjacent to the proposed bus station thereby undermining the need for a bus station! While operational issues may well have been a factor in opposing the plan, the council was looking to the bus operators using the bus station to contribute financially by way of rent. This in turn might involve increasing fares. It was not a good time to be asking bus companies to increase their running costs.

By this time, the ugly expressions 'cost management' and 'economies' were spreading through the bus industry and would continue to dominate matters up to the present day. Generally, fares in the BET Group had remained static since 1939 and it could be argued that bus services were being undersold, but it no doubt contributed to the 'bus boom' of the early post-war years. Across Britain, BET's buses had carried 1,480,760,927 passengers in 1938 and that this had risen to 2,327,723,893 in 1955. On its own, this would have been great news for the group, but other factors were at play.

In 1945, the tax on bus fuel was 9d. (4p) per gallon. The incoming Labour Government doubled this tax and a year later increased it by a further 4½d. (2p). In 1952 the Conservatives raised it by 7½d to 2s 6d. (13p). Other costs were also rising such as wages, new vehicles and spares. With the abolition of petrol rationing in 1950, the use of private cars doubled between then and 1958. A running complaint about the Traffic Commissioners was the length of time it took to approve — or not — fare increase applications. In some cases months might pass before a decision was reached, putting operators in a difficult financial position.

More bad news was to follow. Late in 1956 the Suez crisis erupted and the Suez Canal was closed from October 1956 until March 1957. This restricted Britain's oil supply and put the national finances into a dire situation. Chancellor Harold MacMillan temporarily raised fuel duty by 1s. (5p) per gallon and permitted bus operators to 'make a temporary and limited increase in fares' without the need for obtaining further authority. The Bill allowed companies operating more than 50 buses to increase fares only to the extent that the new charges would give them an extra one twelfth, or a 1d. in the shilling, on their gross receipts.

1957
Life continues

A further ex-SWT AEC Regal III coach of 1950 vintage arrived in April 1957; GCY 435, again with a Windover body at a cost of £775. Although it was only seven years old, this coach had again been ousted by SWT's new Weymann Fanfare bodied AEC Reliances. It is likely that Thomas Bros. had a good deal with this low mileage vehicle; SWT were justifiably proud of their growing Continental Tours programme — for which Thomas Bros. was an agent, thereby earning commission — and its coaches were well maintained. Only the latest vehicles would do, to impress regular customers and SWT had to be seen to offer an up to date fleet to its clientele. Image was everything!

The interior of one of the 1957-built Tiger Cubs. The roof was painted 'sky blue grey' to hide nicotine stains and the seat backs were covered in Formica for ease of cleaning.

Having rounded the junction of the A48 into Water Street, drivers had to follow a badly cambered road that allowed just eight inches of space when two 8ft. wide buses passed one another. Here TTG 5, heading towards the junction, waits behind a cyclist as PTX 199 heads towards Aberavon Beach.

On 25th April, construction work at last got under way on the new depot and head office at Acacia Avenue, Sandfields.

In May, following removal of the Suez tax, fares were reduced but Thomas Bros. warned that a more permanent increase would soon be required as operating costs were still rising.

June saw the arrival of VTX 7 and VTX 8, another two Weymann 44-seat Tiger Cubs. By now the numerical part of the registrations were following a sequence, which would be used to identify individual vehicless. A detail difference on this pair was the addition of a destination display above the entrance door. These, it was felt, would reduce time being wasted by people running round to read the front display. These blinds were used when the buses were new but painted over by the mid-1960s.

A management report of May 1957 looked forward to vehicle deliveries expected until 1959. It stated that deliveries beyond that would depend on future housing development and the position arising from the Port Talbot redevelopment scheme to eliminate the level crossing bottleneck in Station Road.

Consideration needed to be given to the condition of the last four Devon General AEC Regals, HTT 480, 500/1 and JTT 708 which were due for examination that July. Clearly, they were in fair condition because they were still in service at the end of the year, along with four of the company's ageing works fleet.

1958
More Acquisitions

The year's secondhand intake included a further two ex-SWT AEC Regal III/Windover 'Huntingdon' coaches, GCY 436 and GCY 438 to be used on works services. These were

To page 76

A view of 1958-built XNY 9 clearly showing the destination box fitted above the passenger door, which was painted over in later years.

The electrifying financial

Most people will be familiar with at least one of the current bus owning groups in the UK, with names such as Arriva, Stagecoach, First or Go Ahead.

BET began in a small way with the formation of the British Electric Traction (Pioneer) Company, founded in November 1895 to arrange finance for any organisation wanting to use electrically powered tramways.
The idea for setting-up such a company came from Mr. Emile Garcke who had been born in Germany in 1856.

The better known British Electric Traction Co., Ltd. (BET) was formed in October 1896 and during the next few years subsidiary operating companies were formed in towns in the British Isles. In many cases horse buses and later, motor buses were operated as feeders to the tramways. The first BET subsidiary to be formed specifically to run motor buses was the Birmingham and Midland Motor Omnibus Co., Ltd., registered in 1904. Better known as Midland Red, it grew to become the largest operator in the entire BET Group.

Negotiations were held with local authorities and in South Wales the BET network included Merthyr Tydfil Electric Tramways, Swansea Improvements and Tramways and the Swansea and Mumbles Railway.

Separately, in 1914 Thomas Tilling Ltd., which grew out of one of the early London horse bus proprietors found itself limited to just 150 buses in London and sought to expand elsewhere.

Tillings took the view that to work with the BET was the way forward. This resulted in close co-operation between the two groups. By 1920 BET began to diversify. One of the first acquisitions was Stoll Picture Productions, a film production company. Another was Advance Laundries and Laundry Services Limited. BET sold its shareholdings in a number of companies including the British Automobile Traction Company, the London and Suburban Traction Company, and the Shropshire, Worcestershire and Staffordshire Power Company, and in

One of the Mumbles Railway's 13 106-seat trams seen at Mumbles Pier terminus. Operated by South Wales Transport, BET bus operations in South Wales eventually also included Rhondda Transport, Western Welsh, N&C Luxury Coaches and of course Thomas Bros.

idea that was BET

1930 purchased shares in several gas companies and acquired the National Electric Construction Company.

BET's bus fleet grew rapidly. By 1944 the company owned 8,500 buses which operated throughout the country. In 1947 the country's power station and electricity distribution network was nationalised and BET lost the once important electricity generation and distribution part of the business. The company continued to diversify with a number of businesses from construction and plant hire, leisure and entertainment, printing and publishing, textile maintenance and waste management, to a trust company in South Africa. One of its acquisitions was a significant portion of Broadcast Relay Service Limited, otherwise known as Rediffusion. In 1967 BET acquired a controlling interest in the company, and in 1983 acquired the remaining equity.

After the Second World War the Labour Party announced its intention to nationalise the road transport industry, forming the British Transport Commission in 1948.
In September of that year, Tilling Motor Services sold out to the BTC for £25 million.

In 1954 BET acquired 22 percent of the shares in Initial Services, the hygiene and towel company. When commercial television started in the UK in 1955, BET and Associated Newspapers funded the formation of Associated-Rediffusion which began broadcasting in London.

The company's last tram, which ran on the Swansea and Mumbles Railway, made its final journey on 5th January, 1960.

In 1962 the Transport Holding Company took over the nationalised transport industry which still faced severe problems. As well as declining passenger numbers, there was a need to shed unremunerative services, constant rounds of fare increases and a loss of platform staff to more rewarding jobs.
In 1967 BET sold its bus business to the THC.

In an attempt to solve some of the bus industry's problems, the 1968 Transport Act formed the National Bus Company, which came into existence on the 1st January 1969, amalgamating the interests of The Tilling Group with the recently acquired BET Group.

In 1968 BET acquired Boulton and Paul Limited, Grayston Limited, J. D. White Limited, Biffa Limited, Re-Chem International Limited, and became involved in the search for oil in the North Sea. In the same year it completely took over Initial Services Limited, and in 1996 was itself taken over by Rentokil, which then became Rentokil Initial.

In just over 100 years BET had risen from small beginnings to become a vast industrial organisation, controlling many businesses, in many different fields.

The company changed beyond recognition from its early days when it operated trams, to diverse activities including leisure industries, film and TV, waste management, and oil exploration. It was one of the country's great business success stories.

> **CESSATION OF SERVICE. SALE OF BUSES & COACHES.**
> A number of A.E.C. Buses and Coaches for Sale including 1957 Reliance 45 Str. Bus. No reasonable offer refused. Inspection and test at Pantdu Garage, Port Talbot. Telephone Cwmavon 245

From page 59 followed by two AEC Regal III buses, FWN 633 from the SWT fleet and GNY 764 from Rhondda Transport, both for works services. FWN 633 was one of five buses which SWT had bought in 1949 with 34 seat bodywork by Longwell Green Coachworks of Bristol, an unusual choice for SWT at that time. GNY 764 had been bought by Rhondda in 1948, coincidentally also with a Longwell Green body; before passing to Thomas Bros. it was overhauled at Porth, the work including refinements such as sliding window vents. At the end of its working life in the UK in 1960, the latter bus was exported to Malta where, having been rebodied, it still exists.

Summer service changes included a Sandfields to Velindre service replacing the Beach to Velindre service up to 2.30pm.

A further pair of Weymann bodied Leyland Tiger Cubs arrived in August. These were XNY 9 and XNY 10, again with the unusual destination indicator located above the entrance door. In a separate development from the Thomas Bros. story but related to it, a series of advertisements which appeared in the press in August offering vehicles for sale. Further advertisements mentioned that Tilling (Stevens) and Bedford vehicles were also available. This marked the downsizing of the David Jones & Son fleet following a dispute between them and the Steel Company of Wales. Until July the SCoW had been subsidising the fares of up to 1,000 workers at the plant for several years; this was additional to the on-bus fares paid by the workers. SCoW was now ending the subsidy and Jones needed to raise their fares by 40 per cent or withdraw the service. No satisfactory resolution was found and the buses were eventually taken off.

The AEC Reliance mentioned was Park Royal bodied PCY 546 which Jones had bought new in 1957 and which probably wouldn't have looked out of place in the Thomas Bros. fleet. Meanwhile, Jones continued with other private hire work, including a contract for Tonmawr Rugby Club, until it sold out to Thomas Bros. in 1965. The one year old Reliance was soon snapped up and went on to take its place in the fleets of operators in Pontllanffraith, Gloucester and Telford.

1959
Costa del Aberavon

The 'a-couple-of-buses-and-a-coach' pattern of deliveries continued in 1959 with the arrival in July of 12 CNY and 13 CNY, Leyland Tiger Cub 45 seaters. These had been bodied by Park Royal to the latest BET styling which would become the group standard for the next few years. Almost identical styling would be produced by several manufacturers to the same BET group specification.
The fleet now stood at 48, comprising 32 Leylands, 14 AECs, one T.S.M. and one Dennis Lancet J3. The coach for the year was 11 CNY, Port Talbot Crusader, an AEC Reliance, again with Burlingham Seagull body. This was a Mark 7 version of the body, which

Former Rhondda Transport 1948 AEC Regal III with Longwell Green B34R body, GNY 764, later found its way to Malta, where it was heavily rebuilt.

Burlingham

Three Burlingham Seagull-bodied AEC Reliances formed the front line coach fleet in the late 1950s, each reflecting the evolution of the design. From left: TTG 2 of 1956, PTX 203 of 1955 and 11 CNY of 1959 are seen in the depot. MTG 172 was a 1953 Regal IV carrying a Mark 2 version of the Seagull design with double side trim, which many considered unsightly. Front entrance 11 CNY was a Mark 7 version of the type with larger side windows. These proved to be the achilles heel of the design, making the structure less rigid than previous models.

Burlingham had redesigned in an effort to keep up with other coach designs. The side mouldings were considered untidy and the market wasn't yet ready for the panoramic windows which in themselves proved to be an Achilles heel; some operators had to strengthen the bodywork. Prior to 1959, BET companies had purchased up to 40 Seagulls each year, but that year there was only one, 11 CNY. One redeeming feature was that the entrance door was at the front. In later life 11 CNY became a mobile uniform store with SWT, being withdrawn after a fire in 1969. With the new Princess Margaret Way opened across Aberavon seafront the borough council had embarked on a programme to turn the area into a first choice resort, or as was anticipated, 'The beach with the £1 million look'. The developments which appeared over the next few years certainly matched the ambition. Already, £400,000 had been spent on the sea wall and promenade. There were going to be shops, a boating pool, sunken gardens and a pavilion. The aim was to attract upwards of 300,000 visitors per year. This was without doubt excellent news for the bus operators.

Was that colour Thomas

Nothing in the bus industry has ever been more contentious than colour, whether it is the ties worn by drivers, publicity material or that of the all-important vehicles themselves.

For bus operators with a large number of services circulating in any particular area, the colour of the fleet can have an impact on the location itself. A street full of buses in a drab livery can present a negative image and the converse is true – all of which will be noted by civic leaders. A tacky, inconsistent or unimaginative colour scheme can detract from the company's perceived value as an operator, while a livery which holds more gravitas can give a feeling of permanence and reliability. In recent times it has been argued that a group standard livery across the nation gives shareholders some idea of exactly where and how their money is being invested.

Up until 1934 the repaints were in fleet livery of grey/green with a grey waistband. The arrival of brand new Duple-bodied

Bedford WLB WN 5834 in 1933 which was finished in a light blue and cream livery focused minds and that became the new standard although over the years it took on a more greenish hue. The acquisition of secondhand Bedford WLB TH 4096 from Davies Bros. Pencader caused a change for the war years when Thomas Bros. adopted the grey waist and bonnet top. When the war was over, the blue and cream livery reappeared. Unlike some of the modern bus-owning groups, BET seems to have maintained a laissez faire attitude to liveries. While many companies took what was called BET Red as a base for their liveries it was by no means applied uniformly. Devon General and East Kent had greater areas of cream than SWT, City of Oxford added duck egg green to its red

The final vehicle to be delivered in traditional Thomas Bros. bus colours, albeit to a revised arrangement was RTG 140F in 1968.

Bros. blue or green?

A comparison of the 'Danube Blue' liveried 117 LNY, with 122 NTX in the usual fleet livery. *Glyn Bowen*.

The colour which would prevail for the next 20 years, although distinctive, left much to be desired. Oil-based coach enamel was the order of the day, with polyurethane and two-pack paints a thing of the future. Like many darker colours it soon deteriorated, helped by the salty, sea air, the pollution from the steelworks, bleaching of the sun, whatever detergents were thrown at it during washing and just plain old wear and tear.

At no point did Thomas Bros. vehicles feature fleet numbers, individual buses being identified by their registration numbers. The fleetnames on the AEC Regals which were obtained from Devon General were applied in that company's house style, using a Gill Sans font in cream and which was then carried through to the rest of the fleet.

AEC Reliance 126 SNY with its high backed, dual purpose seating. The bus carried a unique livery with Danube Blue window surrounds, Thomas Bros. Blue lower body and cream roof.

livery and Midland Red – who championed the spray booth, covering everything – had its own interpretation of what a red bus should look like. In some areas there was no red at all; Southdown used green and East Yorkshire blue, providing just two examples.

When BET took over Thomas Bros. the fleet was painted in Royal Blue and the lighter Electric Blue with cream relief. When the new Saunders Roe Leyland Tiger Cubs appeared, they were delivered in workshop grey primer and painted by the company in a curious deep turquoise and cream livery which became known as Thomas Bros. Blue. One of the possibly apocryphal theories behind this unusual shade is that the turquoise colour was a mix of the existing blue at the time with green from one of the constituent companies. Either way, if blue and green are mixed in equal amounts on an RGB colour chart, the result is quite interesting!

79

NNY 58 was one of the initial batch of Leyland Tiger Cubs purchased by the company in 1953 and is seen at Western Avenue, Sandfields, heading for Margam.

Several attempts were made to brighten up the livery over the years, most notably in 1965. 118 LNY was given a cream frontal 'V', reminiscent of City of Oxford's livery and sister 117 LNY appeared in a lighter 'Danube Blue' colour. 117 was also painted into reverse coach livery in an another attempt to brighten up the fleet; when first repainted, it too featured a 'V' on the front, but it didn't impress and the 'V' was painted out before it left the paint shop. 117 LNY was repainted into traditional fleet livery in less than a year. The livery experiments introduced a bold extended font which was adopted for the fleet post-1965. The coach and open top fleet carried the primrose cream and Danube Blue livery. Coaches and open toppers were finished in a primrose and Danube Blue livery and carried names which had a Port Talbot theme, a useful device when multiple coaches were in use on a single tour or a private hire job. It meant that passengers returning after a stop could identify their coach more easily. Later dual purpose vehicles had additional cream roofs. On repaints, paint was applied using the traditional brush method by resident coach painter, Tom Warmington. Meanwhile, in 1963 dual purpose Reliance 126 SNY broke

Leyland Tiger Cub B44F, TTG 5 awaits delivery from the Weymann factory to Port Talbot in July 1956 at the start of its 17 year career.

Talbot Square, Aberavon, in the 1960s with the New Hall as a backdrop. How many people would have realised that the Thomas Bros. company and Initial Services were part of the same group?

In 1969, dual purpose AEC Reliance TTX 141G was delivered in what was effectively coach livery. It included additional features such as a boot and a chrome front bumper and found use on the tours to Minehead.

new ground when it was delivered in dual purpose livery, but with Danube Blue window surrounds, a livery which later was changed to the standard Thomas Bros. Blue dual purpose colour scheme.

Two tone liveries always seem to work quite well and 126 SNY's original livery, with a little adjustment, wasn't a million miles from one of the UK's best loved colour schemes – that of West Bromwich Corporation. The final vehicle to be delivered new in Thomas Bros. blue bus livery was Tiger Cub RTG 140F in 1968. By this time, nationalisation and the merger of the SWT group of companies was on the cards so in 1969 VTG 142G and VTG 143G were delivered new in SWT bright red, but with Thomas Bros. fleetnames. All later repaints were in SWT red, with Thomas Bros. names until full takeover in 1971 when South Wales fleet names and fleet numbers were applied. The first Thomas Bros. bus to be repainted in the new red but with original fleet name was VTX 7.

AEC Reliance 125 SNY, new in 1963 was on a private hire at Worcester in 1964 when this image was captured.

Displaying an illuminated advertisement panel 118 LNY shows off the experimental V arrangement of the cream band and the new bold extended Thomas Bros. fleetname in 1965. *G.H.Truran.*

In 1969 also, TTX 141G was delivered. This was a dual purpose vehicle but featured coach livery, a boot and was set off by a chrome bumper across the front.

'Decade that brought the Beatles, one small step for man, spies, scandal and the end of the Mumbles train'

The 1960s were an exciting time. The country was becoming more affluent with a higher disposable income to be spent on a wide range of luxury goods. The music of the time, offshore radio stations, TV and fashion all gave the young new freedoms, not all of which were approved of by their parents. And if their parents didn't like it, then so much the better!

It was an eventful decade with the Profumo spy affair of 1963; Harold Wilson became the youngest Prime Minister in 150 years in 1964. British Rail finished running steam locomotives in 1968 along with Armstrong and Aldrin setting foot on the moon in 1969. Closer to home, the Mumbles Railway closed in January 1960. The Aberfan disaster brought tragedy in 1966 with 144 people — mainly schoolchildren — losing their lives.

No-one working at Thomas Bros. could have predicted that by the end of the decade the company would be no more. After all, in its present form it had only been in business since 1951. There was still a programme of modernisation to complete and the increasing popularity of Aberavon Beach

Two Thomas Bros. Leyland Tiger Cub buses pick up passengers for Aberavon Beach and Baglan Estate on a Station Road, Port Talbot busy with both traffic and pedestrians.

New freedoms but state control was looming

Leyland Tiger PTX 202 turns from High Street and the A48 into narrow Water Street, a move which occurred on as many as 22 occasions an hour and involved some overhanging of the pavement.

Heading for its Bethany Square terminus, 15 HTG, a 1960 Leyland Tiger Cub passes Chidzoy's fruit and vegetable store, Station Road on 4th April, 1968.

AEC Reliance OTX137F passes a Park Royal bodied SWT AEC Regent V at Aberavon Beach in September 1970 as it waits to return to Swansea. *Roy Marshall, copyright The Bus Archive.*

The remains of 16 HTG following a fire started by schoolchildren. Alongside, the bus awaiting a repaint after rebuilding and finally, back in service. By this time the vehicle was displaying a number of different details that set it apart from its sisters.

meant that the full potential of passenger numbers had yet to be reached.

1960
An act of Vandalism

A further three Leyland Tiger Cubs appeared in 1960; 14 HTG, 15 HTG and 16 HTG, all to the same standard BET design but this time built by Metro-Cammell.
16 HTG later suffered from vandalism when it was set on fire by children at Glyncorrwg. The front end was rebuilt by United Welsh at their central works at Neath Abbey. After that, it was easily identified by having separate front numeral and destination indicators and a cab window of a type normally fitted to one of the United Welsh Bristol MWs. The vehicle eventually survived long enough to enjoy an extended life as a towing vehicle with SWT at Neath.

An open-top seafront service started in 1960 bringing two 1940 Bristol K5Gs which were acquired from Brighton, Hove and District for the first season.

The Sandfields and Aberavon Beach to Margam services were curtailed to run as far as Tollgate Road, Margam, instead of Groes although some Sunday morning services continued to Margam Post Office as did services on show days. The service between Tollgate Road and Groes School ran on schooldays and to Groes (SCoW Sports Club) in the evenings.

The huge number of bus services coming into the Abbey Works meant that the plant had its own bus station. It has been recorded that at one time there were 32 buses entering and leaving the works on each of its three-shifts covering 24 hours. The original main bus terminus was at the Hot Mill Canteen. Buses ran right into the works and eight continued to carry workers whose jobs were some distance from the main gate.

To improve facilities, Mill Row in Taibach was demolished in 1960 to make way for the Vivian Bus Park. Each of the four islands in the new bus station could accommodate up to seven buses and was equipped with umbrella pattern Blakeley shelters.
There was a cabin for an inspector/regulator at the end of one island. Services then ran via the new bus station instead of via Penrhyn Street as they had done previously. Buses from Sandfields ran via a private road,

avoiding Aberavon and Port Talbot town. For buses which actually went into the works, where in some areas kerbs were higher than normal, a tyre type with reinforced side walls was fitted to the nearside, rear outer position to prevent damage from rubbing along kerbs. These were known as tunnel tyres, as used by London Transport on its Blackwall Tunnel bus services. A new town tour including a run via the steelworks was introduced in May 1960 using single deck buses.

In August, an amended timetable was in operation on the Margam, Tollgate Road to Margam Post Office route. This allowed the withdrawal of the Tollgate Road to Groes, SCoW Sports Club journeys. On the services to Brynbryddan, the terminus was changed from Cefn Coed Road to Brynna Road.

Winter visitors to Acacia Avenue depot included AEC Regal IVs belonging to N&C Luxury coaches. These were put into storage at Port Talbot for the winter because they had inefficient heaters and were prone to skidding on icy roads.

1961
Getting up to date

The construction of a petrochemical works at Baglan Bay was first announced on 31st January when Glamorgan County Council gave outline planning permission to British Hydrocarbon Chemicals and its subsidiary, Forth Chemicals Ltd. As construction progressed over the following years, the construction workforce reached around 1,500. The eventual operational workforce was about 500. Conveniently, the main entrance to the plant was near the Western Avenue terminus of Thomas Bros.

In February, everyone at Port Talbot was awaiting a decision from the Ministry of Transport relating to the Baglan to Sandfields link road, later named Seaway Parade. The project, costing £125,000, took around 18 months to complete and was designed to improve access to Aberavon Beach and the steelworks as well as playing a part in reducing town centre traffic jams.

In an effort to reduce the effect of Port Talbot's other source of congestion, the level crossing at Station Road, a new service was introduced for the summer, from Bethany Square to Goytre on Mondays to Fridays only. Although Bethany Square was a central terminus, buses heading there from Aberavon had been able to use side streets on the inward journey. The new service ran via Abbey Road, Tanygroes Street and Danybryn Road.

Predictably, two more Leyland Tiger Cubs with Park Royal B45F bodies went into service in July; 117 LNY and 118 LNY. The latter had a number of new refinements to the company's specifications that allowed illuminated exterior and interior advertising spaces. It was the first vehicle of its type in Britain to be constructed in this manner. The orthodox method of filament

To page 90

Exterior and interior views of 1961-built Leyland Tiger Cub/Park Royal 118 LNY illustrating the illuminated advertising panels and the improved interior lighting.

The topless belles of 'Bravon

As developments on Aberavon seafront progressed, on high days and holidays there was a requirement for duplicate journeys on services which connected Sandfields Estate to the beach.

General Manager Peter Hornblow decided to play a trump card for Thomas Bros. and prove the company's commitment to the seaside scheme by creating a service which still springs to mind whenever the Thomas Bros. name is mentioned. In 1960 it was revealed that from that summer, an open top bus service would link Port Talbot town centre and Sandfields Estate with the beach. Initially running from Aberavon market, in 1965 the service was extended to Port Talbot General Station. There was however, one major concern relating to the operation of open top vehicles; the behaviour of children on the upper deck, something which still haunts open top bus operators. Fearful of what might happen, in April 1960 General Manager Peter Hornblow wrote to his opposite number at Devon General, T.L.C. Strange, for advice on the matter and whether additional signage would be needed on the vehicles.

In 1960, the Four Winds public house, originally intended to be named the Marine Hotel, opened. At he same time two 1940 Bristol K5Gs were acquired from Brighton, Hove and District for the first season. One of the K5Gs was kept only for the first summer, after which two secondhand AEC Regents entered the fleet. One of these was replaced in 1965 with a further Bristol K5G.

One of the AEC Regents was OD 7497, a 1934 vehicle purchased from Devon General for a mere £100 plus Dunlop tyres and a tank of fuel. It was collected from Devon General's head office in Torquay at midday on 10th March. Thomas Bros. had in fact planned to take two of these buses from Devon General, but one had been cancelled in February after Port

An excited group of children wait to head back to Port Talbot aboard open topper CAP 205.

The open top name game

Name	Reg.	Built	Vehicle make and builder	With TB
The Afan Belle	CAP 205	1940	Bristol K5G/Eastern Coachworks	1960-1970
The Margam Belle	CAP 237	1940	Bristol K5G/Eastern Coachworks	1960 only
The Sandfields Belle	JK 7431	1938	AEC Regent/Northern Counties	1960-1965
The Margam Belle	OD 7497	1934	AEC Regent/Short	1961-1965
The Sandfields Belle	GHT 127	1941	Bristol K5G/Eastern Coachworks	1965-1969

Derby Day at Epsom Racecourse and GHT 127 is a long way from home as it waits outside the Downs Hotel.

Talbot Borough Council revealed that roadworks along the seafront would not be ready for that summer and so reducing the need for a second vehicle.

The other AEC Regent purchased at this time was 1938-built JK 7431, which came from Eastbourne Corporation. After the 1962 season, it was planned to dispose of this bus but as no replacement could be found it was reconditioned during that winter and stayed with the company until 1965.

Initially, the service ran half hourly in the mornings using one bus, with a second taking the frequency to every 15 minutes after lunch and at weekends. As the summer progressed and the nights drew in, the buses would run back to the depot earlier. In 1961, the Bristol, CAP 205, was usually the first bus out, doing the higher mileage.

The open top services were effectively duplicates for the existing routes to the beach and the company was able to dispense with one peak hour relief vehicle on Mondays to Fridays. However, by linking Sandfields with the town, they still had reasonable loadings even when the weather was poor.

The open top buses attracted new traffic of their own. Children persuaded their parents to take them for a ride and they became a hit with the elderly, too. Running these buses through a housing estate certainly turned the heads of children during the school holidays! Revenue, taking into account the low fares, was considered to be quite good at 30.92 pence per mile in 1960.

The open top buses were painted in what was effectively the coach livery of primrose cream and danube blue and given local names along the 'Belle' theme. The names were chosen by means of a staff competition, as Susan White recalled:

"My dad Viv Davies drove for Thomas Bros. for years. I remember he won a competition for naming the Afan Belle."

Out of season, the open top buses were delicensed and stored at the depot. Occasionally additional work would be found for them, including tours to Royal Ascot and the Epsom Derby. An attempt to use one of them on the Port Talbot town tour was

Three 'Belles' parked up in the depot. Left to right: CAP 205, GHT 127 and OD 7497, while another belle, a conductress, puts on a headscarf to protect her hairdo from the wind, before setting off for the seafront aboard OD 7497.

refused on safety grounds as the itinerary included the road through the steelworks. On June 21, 1964 one of the open top vehicles – believed to have been OD 7497 was filmed by TWW — the predecessor to HTV Wales and ITV Wales — for a summer edition of its programme, Land of Song. The bus was renamed Llanelli Belle for the occasion and appeared at various points along the south Wales coast before arriving at Penarth. A further snippet of film exists showing GHT 127 at Oystermouth being used by the BBC for filming of a tourism-related programme.

In January 1970 the company announced that the open top services, by then numbered 7A and 7C, would be withdrawn and would not run during the 1970 season. In a letter to the council, Traffic Manager Brian Horner said:

"As you will be aware, these services operate subject to

An immaculate OD 7497 leads a pair of Thomas Bros. open toppers operating at Epsom Racecourse.

As it begins its return No 2 run to Sandfields Estate and Aberavon Beach 1938 AEC Regent JK 7431 is seen near St. Mary's Church, Aberavon.

suitable weather conditions and in accordance with traffic requirements. The traffic has diminished considerably and now it is completely unremunerative. The routes are largely covered by other existing stage carriage services and another point to be considered in the surrendering of these licences is the fact that there has been an acute staff shortage at Port Talbot for some time."

The letter went on to point out that it was important to maintain regular services rather than a summer season service.

Bristol K5G GHT 127 in full flight along Victoria Road.

FATE OF THE FIVE

On leaving the Thomas Bros. fleet the open toppers suffered mixed fates:

CAP 205: Withdrawn in 1970. Exported to D. Arnold of Cobourg, Ontario in Canada by October 1971. Photos exist of it in very poor condition with Seeboyers, Agricultural Engineers, Havelock in 2012.

CAP 237: Withdrawn in September 1960. Sold to dealer AMCC Ltd. in London E15 and then to Shangri-La Holiday Camp at St. Osyth in Essex in 1961. Believed to have been scrapped after that.

JK 7431: Withdrawn in 1965 and sold to Way's scrapyard in Splott, Cardiff. It was still there 10 years later! It then passed to the West of England Transport Museum, Winkleigh in 1978. By 1985 it had moved on to the Chalk Pits Museum, Amberley, Sussex. It then moved back home to Eastbourne and was stored in a shed at Wenhams. The shed was destroyed in the great storm of 1987 and it is believed that JK 7431 was scrapped after that.

OD 7497: Withdrawn in 1965 and sold to preservationists in Devon and Somerset, then run as a PSV with Nostalgic Transport Ltd., Broadhempton and Quantock Heritage in 2018. Sold in 2020 to a hospitality company in the West of England. Used on a West Somerset Railway replacement bus service between Dunster and Minehead in the summer of 2021.

GHT 127: Passed to Bristol Omnibus in December 1969. Then to Bristol Omnibus Preservation Society in 1979 and back to Bristol Omnibus and later Badgerline. It was repainted for use on Bath City Tours and then taken out of service in 1996. From there it passed to First Bristol/First Somerset and Avon and loaned to Bristol Vintage Bus Group.

Ready for action; the new Vivian Bus Park at Margam shortly after completion in 1960.

From page 85

bulb lighting was replaced by fluorescent tube lighting with the offside interior luggage rack dispensed with. In addition flush fitting fluorescent lighting was installed above the gangway of the vehicle. On the exterior of the body, both sides of the roof above the cantrail were redesigned to provide illuminated Perspex advertisement panels.

At a launch to demonstrate the buses to Port Talbot Borough Council and the Chamber of Trade, Peter Hornblow said: "The final result is a big improvement in the standard of lighting provided over the conventional type of lighting fitted in public service vehicles, and it is felt that this brightly lit and attractive interior will not only be of benefit to passengers travelling in the hours of darkness, but will also encourage more people to travel at these times."

Representing part of the £20,000 capital investment 117 LNY was built more along the lines of vehicles already in service at Port Talbot and special features in this instance included Formica side lining panels, white plastic interior roof and dome sections, recirculating heaters, a safety device to warn the driver whenever the emergency door was open and a continuous strip conductor's signal bell.

Two AEC Reliance coaches were also added to the fleet in 1961. These were 119 LNY and 120 LNY with Harrington Cavalier 41-seat bodies. Representing the most modern design available at that time, the pair were purchased with the increasingly popular Saturday departures for Blackpool in mind. Costing in the region of £5,000 each, the pair included a radio, heaters, demisters, controllable ventilation, special double deflecting windows, double skinned roof, special low back seating to permit improved visibility and Formica side lining panels. They carried AEC's 2MU3RA designation, with five-speed all-synchromesh gearboxes. The coaches were named Port Talbot Cavalier and Maid of Port Talbot. At the other end of the age scale, two more open top AEC Regents joined the fleet in 1961.

In August came news of an increase in fares, effective from the 25th. The revised fares, recently approved by the South Wales Traffic Commissioners, followed wage awards to drivers, conductresses and other grades of staff, as well as increases in other costs. It only applied to areas of the town where fares hadn't been increased for some years. The Afan Valley, Velindre, Goytre and parts of Sandfields Estate were cases in point with many of the fares not having been increased for nearly nine years. Fares over the section of route between Bethany Square and Margam were unaffected on this occasion as passengers had previously faced increases which those in other parts of the town had missed. Nevertheless Thomas Bros. fares were still some of the lowest in the country and since the last general fares increase in February 1953 it had to pay no fewer than 11 separate wage increases.

General Manager Peter Hornblow seems to have been keen to integrate Thomas Bros. into the local community by, for example, becoming involved with the newly opened Sandfields Comprehensive School. In October, he chaired the Annual Road Safety Quiz there. No doubt behaviour in and around buses would have been part of the evening.

Vivian Bus Park was built by the Steel Company of Wales at a cost of £85,000 plus a further £50,000 for the new access road. Bus services came from a broad area and apart from Thomas Bros., operators included SWT, Western Welsh, Rhondda and Llynfi of Maesteg. Buses were required to arrive at the works 20 minutes before each shift to give workers adequate time to transfer to works buses which took them to their workplace. Many buses ran to the terminus near the central time office and there were connections for other parts of the works at Vivian Bus Park. Some of these were extensions of incoming services from elsewhere, while SCoW also ran its own small fleet although some of that activity was eventually transferred to Thomas Bros.

There was considerable overmanning at the Abbey Works at this time. By the end of 1952 the workforce was 9,071, peaking at 18,352 in 1960. Every craftsman had a mate to undertake each job which doubled the number of workers required. Fitters removed the tools from the locomotives claiming that repairs were their job. Job demarcation spread throughout the works; in nearby Port Talbot Steelworks there were just six people in the personnel department. At the Abbey each section had its own personnel department which numbered over 100 staff. Overmanning became more significant in the auxiliary functions than in the main production process. This clearly explains why so many buses were needed to ferry workers to and from the plant.

The Government had helped SCoW to build the Abbey Works and they expected them to absorb the unemployment resulting from the closure of many smaller metal works. Management expansion of the Abbey was subject to approval by Ministers, who needed to be convinced that the additional workforce would be forthcoming. Thus, in a difficult labour market the SCoW was under pressure to hoard workers. By building up manpower in the ancillary functions, there would be sufficient staff to be moved across to production when the need arose. Unfortunately, the process re-introduced some outdated working practices which would cause difficulties in future years. Management was aided and abetted in this practice by the trade unions who probably couldn't believe their luck! It also gave the management opportunity to extol to the workers the benefits of a private industry when nationalisation was being discussed. Later in the 1960s SCoW management took the view that things had gone a little too far. New vacancies began to be filled internally and an enforced retirement age of 65 was introduced, all of which only reduced the numbers employed by about 1,000. Further attempts to redress the balance led to a long period of industrial unrest with many strikes.

1962
Beetham and Beeching

In 1962 Sandfields Estate services were extended to the new roundabout at Western Avenue. On 3rd May the eagerly anticipated new Baglan to Sandfields link road opened. The first Thomas Bros. services made use of it from Sunday 3rd June with a new service from Baglan Estate instead of the existing SWT service, running via Sandfields Estate to the town centre. In summer this service operated via Aberavon Beach so that people in Baglan Estate had a direct link with the seafront. At the same time, the Abbey Works services operated by SWT from Baglan Estate were taken over by Thomas Bros. and run via Sandfields and a private road into the Abbey Works. In addition, Thomas Bros. extended to twice hourly the existing service terminating at Sandfields out to Baglan roundabout to connect with the westbound through services of other operators'.

Further service changes from the same date were a new Sunday service for Tabor and direct buses to Aberavon Beach from Pontrhydyfen and Cwmavon. The Velindre service was extended from the promenade via Dalton Road, Sandy Ridge and Farm Drive to Western Avenue.

By June, Peter Hornblow had found a new challenge within the BET Group and took up a post with the Salisbury United Omnibus Company in Zimbabwe. On leaving he was presented with a plaque by the local authority. There must have been a strong feeling of déjà vu for Mr. Hornblow for in 1954 BET, together with United Transport had set up Rhodesia United Transport to bring together 14 separate operators with the objective of modernising and also co-ordinating their operations. Peter Hornblow's successor at Port Talbot was named as Anthony Beetham, who had previously played a role at Southdown.

A great way of keeping a bus company in the consciousness of the local population and improving staff morale is through Safe Driving Awards. A total of 14 Thomas Bros. drivers received awards in 1962, having covered the estimated 30,000 miles around the town with no blameworthy accidents. At the 7th annual presentation dinner held in Newton the drivers were among 32 who qualified for awards for the year. The Mayor of Port Talbot presented the medals and diplomas on behalf of the company and commented: "The manner in which you do your jobs adds to the welfare and dignity of the town. The awards are evidence that you do your jobs to the best of your ability and probably better than most people could."

Recipients were: C. Lambert, 11 to 14 years' safe driving; W.H. Pike, C. Richards,

Strangely, Tiger Cub PTX 202 was used to illustrate a Leyland sales document for the outwardly similar, but integrally built Olympian in 1964 by which time the vehicle itself was nine years old!

H. Thomas, H. Stephens and R. Williams six to nine years' safe driving. Recipients of diplomas for the completion of four accident-free years were O. Davies, A. Edwards, D.W. Jones, C. Mitchell, J. Patterson, C. Routcliffe, R. Warren, A. Wilson, C. Thomas and G. Evans.

New buses for the year included a further two Leyland Tiger Cubs to BET 45-seat design, this time with bodywork constructed by Walter Alexander Coachbuilders of Falkirk (122 NTX and 123 NTX). These Z-type bodies were fitted with fluorescent tube lighting similar to that which had been included in the 1961 buses. Another AEC Reliance with Harrington Cavalier coachwork was 121 NTX. This received the name Afan Star. The vehicle differed from its sisters, being a 2MU4RA model, with a six-speed constant mesh gearbox. At 31' 8" it was also slightly longer taking advantage of the revised Construction and Use regulations at this time, though retaining the seating capacity of 41 passengers. Thomas Bros. was now catching up with SWT in terms of the quality of its coaching fleet.

Addressing the Port Talbot Committee of the Industrial Life Offices on 'Economic Problems in Bus Operations', Anthony Beetham described the loss of revenue to the large bus companies caused by minibuses, pointing out that they were not strictly legal. They were effectively collecting individual fares by way of a fuel contribution and fell outside the restrictions imposed on ordinary operators.

Another problem which faced bus operators, said Mr. Beetham was the very unfair fuel tax imposed on bus services. "Buses," he said, "use the same fuel as diesel trains on the railway, yet the railways proceed untaxed, while fuel for buses is taxed at the rate of 2s. 9d. per gallon. A reduction of fuel tax is most urgently desired and would be a great help to alleviate economic problems." Mr. Beetham explained to the meeting that bus services over the country had suffered the loss of many passengers. In the past few years mainly due to the steep increase in privately owned cars on the road, with the medium of television proving an attraction at home curbing evening travel.

"To attract passengers," continued Mr. Beetham, "bus companies try to operate economic and efficient services but all over the country, and in Port Talbot, the traffic congestion problem provides a headache."

Paradoxically, the Thomas Bros. garage at Acacia Avenue wasn't on any scheduled bus route. Anyone wishing to visit it on business or who lived nearby either needed to drive a car or walk from – say – the bus stop at Western Avenue. To make life a little easier for everyone, including those who lived near, it was announced in November that buses travelling between Sandfields and the depot would be permitted to carry passengers, alighting at a new stop in Southdown View.

Newly delivered in 1962 and yet to have fleetnames applied, this was 123 NTX, one of a pair of Leyland Tiger Cubs with standard BET-style bodywork supplied by Alexander.

Accordingly, destination blinds were updated to include 'Sandfields Estate and Garage'.

A sad event – though possibly not for those who needed to travel through Port Talbot by road – was the announcement that the Rhondda and Swansea Bay Railway line was to close. The passenger service was to cease at the start of December with goods traffic ceasing in November 1964. The British Railways notice at the time read:

> **BRITISH RAILWAYS Western Region**
>
> **"British Railways will withdraw the passenger train service between Treherbert and Swansea on and from Monday, December 3, and the stations at Aberavon (Seaside), Aberavon Town, Cwmavon, Pontrhydyfen and Duffryn Rhondda Halt closed to passengers. On the same day a revised train service, worked by diesel cars will be introduced between Treherbert, Cymmer Afan and Bridgend. Treherbert will continue to be served by trains from the Cardiff and Pontypridd line, and Briton Ferry, Neath General, Skewen, Llansamlet (North), Landore and Swansea (High Street) by Cardiff to Swansea main line services. Alternative bus services are operated in the area between Cymmer Afan, Port Talbot and Neath by United Welsh Services, South Wales Transport Company, Western Welsh Omnibus Company, Thomas Bros. and Llynfi Motor Services."**

By now, Thomas Bros. had a near monopoly of local bus services within Port Talbot, but there were still opportunities based on rationalisation within the BET group. SWT was a long-term operator of its service 20 between Aberavon Beach and Maesteg, which must have come at a cost since the nearest SWT depot was at Neath and would have required several dead positioning runs. The service was run jointly with Llynfi Motors and so SWT wanted to hand its share of the service over to sister operator Thomas Bros.

Moreover, there was a restriction that service 20 journeys could not pick up after Abbey Road on journeys towards Aberavon, or set down before Abbey Road on the return; this restriction wouldn't apply to Thomas Bros. In November, Llynfi Motors opposed the Thomas Bros. application and put in their own to take over the whole route.

The situation was still unresolved by the following spring, when in April the traffic commissioners turned down both rival applications and advised all three operators to meet to agree the way forward. It seemed unlikely that the two BET companies would agree to the independent Llynfi company taking over the full timetable. A compromise was found whereby Llynfi would run the entire service on a reduced frequency during the winter months running only between Maesteg and Port Talbot. The service became joint SWT/Llynfi in summer when it was extended to Aberavon Beach.

In December, Thomas Bros. joined the Ministry of Transport and Brewers' Society annual Drink-Drive campaign, displaying advertisements proclaiming 'Christmas Driving Needs a Clear Head!' The British Minibus Companies Public Relations Committee had produced posters some carrying the slogan 'Enjoy your Party - Go home by Bus.' Clearly, Thomas Bros. was hoping for increased patronage during the seasonal festivities.

1963
Summer Specials and an Autumn Accident

Revised services were announced for 10th February, including a new direct service from Baglan Estate (Ash Grove) to Margam via the A48 which had been requested by the community. The service replaced the Western Welsh route between Baglan Estate and Bethany Square. This service was to run half hourly on weekdays and hourly after 7pm and on Sundays. The new service was in addition to the route from Baglan via Seaway Parade and Sandfields was being

The 1963 vehicle intake consisted of these three AEC Reliances with Marshall bodywork, 124-126 SNY. 126 SNY originally had a 49-seat dual purpose body; the other two were to 53 seat bus configuration

The interior of 126 SNY when new.

A new holiday service to Butlin's at Minehead was granted permission at a public hearing in Swansea at the end of April.

More locally, summer bus services were announced at the end of May. From the 20th, the Margam to Aberavon Beach service was extended between approximately 11am and 9.30pm daily from its terminus at the Jersey Beach Hotel to run via the Seafront to the Four Winds Hotel. On the same date, journeys on the service from Baglan Estate to Velindre via Sandfields Estate were diverted via Sandy Ridge, Dalton Road, Four Winds, Princess Margaret Way and Victoria Road to provide a service to Aberavon Beach to Velindre and Baglan residents. The half hourly Sandfields Estate to Goytre service continued to run via Dalton Road, Four Winds, Aberavon Beach, Princess Margaret Way and Victoria Road. On summer weekends the Aberavon Beach to Pontrhydyfen service was extended to Efail Fach with a school holiday service on Thursdays also. The Brynbryddan/Tabor service was improved to run on summer Saturdays. Add the open top services to these changes and it can be seen that in summer Aberavon Beach was now

To page 98

revised to run half hourly via Sandy Ridge and Sandown Road, extending to Velindre. This doubled the Velindre frequency.

To meet requests for a service to Sandfields Estate and Aberavon Beach adjacent to the Four Winds Hotel, the services between Goytre and Aberavon Beach and between Goytre and Sandfields Estate were replaced by a new service operating every half-hour between Sandfields Estate and Goytre via Aberavon Beach.

The route was via Western Avenue, Fairway, Vivian Park Drive, Dalton Road, Four Winds Hotel Roundabout, Princess Margaret Way, Victoria Road and then via the existing route to Goytre. Consequently, timings of the Margam to Sandfields Estate and Margam to Aberavon Beach services were adjusted.

Routes around town

The following is a detailed description of the network of routes operated by Thomas Bros. during the Summer of 1969. Route numbers are followed by termini and then the way the two were linked, followed by the frequency of service.

T1 Margam (Tollgate Road) to Sandfields Estate.
Route: Tollgate Road, Margam Road, Commercial Road, Talbot Road, Station Road, Water Street, Victoria Road, Hospital Road, Vivian Park Drive, Fairway, Western Avenue. Weekdays a combined frequency of every 15 minutes, Sundays a combined frequency of every 20 minutes. Renumbering from December 1970: 231.

T1A Margam (Tollgate Road) to Sandfields Estate.
Route: Tollgate Road, Margam Road, Commercial Road, Talbot Road, Station Road, Water Street, Victoria Road, Golden Avenue, Silver Avenue, Parry Road, Purcell Avenue. Weekdays a combined frequency of every 15 minutes, Sundays a combined frequency of every 20 minutes.

T2 Margam (Tollgate Road) to Sandfields Estate.
Route: Tollgate Road, Margam Road, Commercial Road, Talbot Road, Station Road, Water Street, Victoria Road, Sandown Road, Dalton Road, Sandy Ridge, Western Avenue. Weekdays a combined frequency of every 15 minutes, Sundays a combined frequency of every 20 minutes. Renumbering from December 1970: 232.

T3 Goytre to Sandfields Estate Via Aberavon Beach.
Route: Goytre Road, Dyffryn Road, Commercial Road, Talbot Road, Station Road, Water Street, Victoria Road, Princess Margaret Way, Dalton Road, Vivian Park Drive, Fairway, Western Avenue. Weekdays a combined frequency of every 30 minutes, Sundays a combined frequency of every 30 minutes. Renumbering from December 1970: 234/235.

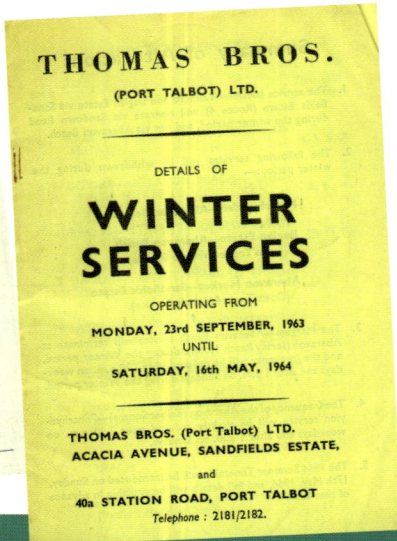

T4 Velindre to Baglan Estate.
Route: Forge Road, Water Street, Victoria Road, Sandown Road, Dalton Road, Sandy Ridge, Western Avenue, Seaway Parade, Willow Way, Albion Road, Greenwood Road, Laurel Avenue, Willow Grove, Church Crescent, Baglan Road, Seaway Parade, Western Avenue, Sandy Ridge, Dalton Road, Sandown Road, Victoria Road, Water Street, Forge Road. Some journeys extended to Abbey Works. Weekdays a combined frequency of every 30 minutes, Sundays every 60 minutes. Renumbering from December 1970: 238/239.

T4B Velindre to Baglan Estate.
Route: As above but via Sandy Ridge, Dalton Road, Princess Margaret Way, Victoria Road and not via Sandown Road. 4B was the summer equivalent of 4A, but via Aberavon Beach.

T5 Port Talbot (General Station) to Baglan Estate.
Direct Service. Route: Station Road, Pentyla, Baglan Road, Church Crescent, Willow Grove, Laurel Avenue, Hawthorne Avenue, Mayberry Road, Albion Road, Old Baglan Road, Willow Way, Baglan Road, Pentyla. Weekdays a combined frequency of every 30 mins, Sundays a combined frequency of every 60 mins. Renumbering from December 1970: 240.

T7A Sandfields Estate (Purcell Avenue) to Market.
Route: Parry Road, Silver Avenue, Golden Avenue, Princess Margaret Way, Victoria Road, Water Street. Weekdays every 30 minutes, Fridays and Saturdays early summer, daily mid summer. Sundays every 30 mins. Summer only open top, 1st June to 15th September.

T7C Sandfields Estate (Fairway) to Market.
Route: Western Avenue, Sandy Ridge, Dalton Road, Princess Margaret Way, Victoria Road, Water Street. Weekdays every 30 minutes, Fridays and Saturdays early summer, daily mid summer. Sundays every 30 minutes. Open top service, 1st June to 15th September.

T8 Port Talbot to Tonmawr
Route: Bethany Square, Pantdu, Cwmavon, The Waun, Pwllyglaw, Pontrhydyfen, Efail Fach, Tonmawr. Weekdays 7 journeys, Sundays 4 journeys. Some journeys extended to Abbey Works. In summer, some extended to Aberavon Beach. One man service.

T9 Sandfields Estate to Brynbryddan and Tabor.
Route: Western Avenue, Aberavon Beach, Talbot Square, Cwmavon (Police Station), Brynna Road, Tabor Chapel, Cwmavon (Tabernacle Terrace), Talbot Square, Sandown Road, Western Avenue. Weekdays every 30 minutes, Sundays service T9A. Renumbering from December 1970: 236/237.

T9A/T9B Sandfields Estate to Tabor and Brynbryddan.
Route: Purcell Avenue, Hospital Road, Talbot Square,

and up the valley

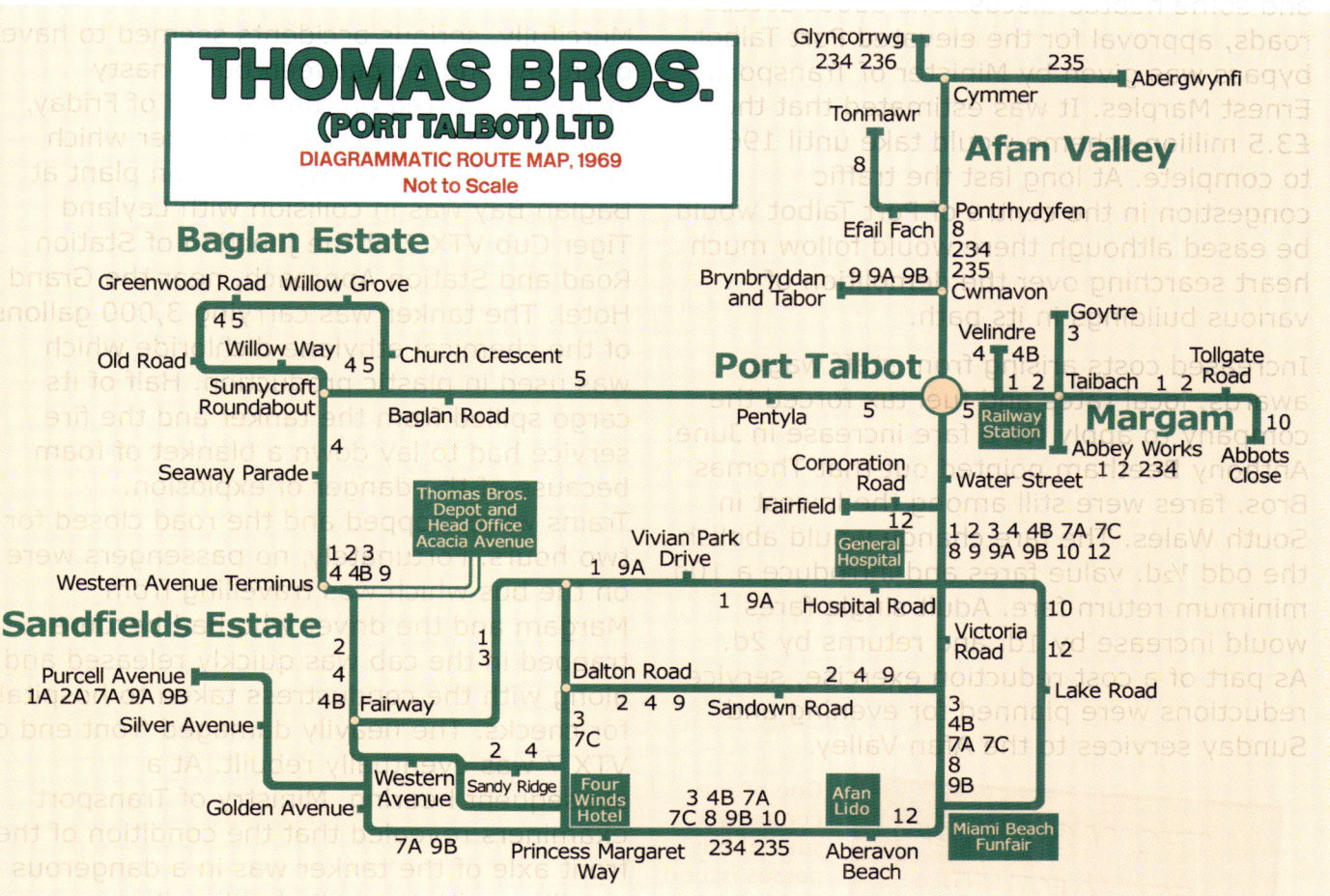

Cwmavon (Tabernacle Terrace), Tabor Chapel, Brynna Road, Cwmavon (Police Station), Talbot Square, Sandown Road, Hospital Road, Purcell Avenue. Weekdays every 30 minutes, Sundays every 30 minutes. Between May and September, one Sunday journey per hour ran via Golden Avenue and Seafront as service 9B.

T10   Margam to Aberavon Beach.
Route: Abbots Close, Tollgate Road, Margam Road, Talbot Road, Station Road, Water Street, Victoria Road, Lake Road, Princess Margaret Way, Afan Lido, Four Winds, Purcell Avenue. Weekdays every 30 minutes (summer), every 60 minutes (winter), Sundays every 60 minutes. On summer Sundays, the service was extended into the evening, running Afan Lido to Abbots Close. Renumbering from December 1970: 233.

T12   Beach, S/fields and P. Talbot Station (Circular).
Route: Lake Road, Victoria Road, Julian Terrace, Corporation Road, Water Street, Station Road, Abbey Road, Tanygroes Street, Danybryn Road, Forge Road, Water Street, Corporation Road, Julian Terrace, Fairfield, Corporation Road, Water Street, Newbridge Road, Lake Road, Victoria Road, Princess Margaret Way. Weekdays every 60 minutes, Sundays every 60 minutes (pm only). Flat fare between any two stops; 6d. Adult, 3d. Child. No return tickets available. One man operated service. Renumbering from Dec 1970: 241.

T234, T235 Port Talbot to Abergwynfi or Glyncorrwg via Cwmavon and Pontrhydyfen.
Route: Bethany Square, Pontrhydyfen, Cymmer. Weekdays 8 journeys to Glyncorrwg, 10 journeys to Abergwynfi with additional connections at Cymmer. Sundays 1 journey to Glyncorrwg, 6 journeys to Abergwynfi with additional connections at Cymmer. Route numbers in the Western Welsh series. Taken over from the Western Welsh company on closure of its Port Talbot depot in 1966. In summer, some journeys extended to/from Aberavon Beach. One man operated service.

T236   Glyncorrwg to Cymmer Afan.
Route: Via Heol-y-Glyn. Weekdays approximately every 30 mins, Sundays approximately every 30 minutes, pm only.

From page 95

very big business, no doubt boosted by the recent construction of the optimistically named Miami Beach Funfair on the Little Warren.

After several months of preparatory work and some heated discussions about access roads, approval for the elevated Port Talbot bypass was given by Minister of Transport, Ernest Marples. It was estimated that the £3.5 million scheme would take until 1966 to complete. At long last the traffic congestion in the centre of Port Talbot would be eased although there would follow much heart searching over the demolition of various buildings in its path.

Increased costs arising from staff wage awards, local rates and fuel tax forced the company to apply for a fare increase in June. Anthony Beetham pointed out that Thomas Bros. fares were still among the lowest in South Wales. The fare change would abolish the odd ½d. value fares and introduce a 10d. minimum return fare. Adult single fares would increase by 1d. and returns by 2d. As part of a cost reduction exercise, service reductions were planned for evening and Sunday services to the Afan Valley.

On 16th October, Sir Keith Joseph, Minister for Welsh Affairs, officially opened the £13 million British Hydrocarbon Chemicals plant at Baglan (later BP Baglan Bay) which had by this time come into production and which was another important employer in the town.

Mercifully, serious accidents seemed to have been few and far between but a nasty incident occurred on the evening of Friday, November 15th. A chemical tanker which had just left the new hydrocarbon plant at Baglan Bay was in collision with Leyland Tiger Cub VTX 7 at the junction of Station Road and Station Approach, near the Grand Hotel. The tanker was carrying 3,000 gallons of the chemical ethylene dichloride which was used in plastic production. Half of its cargo spilled from the tanker and the fire service had to lay down a blanket of foam because of the danger of explosion.

Trains were stopped and the road closed for two hours. Fortunately, no passengers were on the bus which was travelling from Margam and the driver who had become trapped in the cab was quickly released and along with the conductress taken to hospital for checks. The heavily damaged front end of VTX 7 was eventually rebuilt. At a subsequent hearing, Ministry of Transport examiners revealed that the condition of the front axle of the tanker was in a dangerous condition with the bolts holding it on one side of the vehicle completely sheared off. Violent braking might lock the front wheels and send the vehicle across the road.

The tanker driver was charged with dangerous driving or alternatively driving without due care and attention and having dangerous parts on the vehicle. The owners of the vehicle, Tyburn Road Tanks Ltd., of High Wycombe were fined £40.

One of the company's special bus passes issued in 1969.

Among the company's longest routes was from Port Talbot to Glyncorrwg where 14 HTG is seen waiting at the Bridge Street terminus before its return to Port Talbot.

Changes to the Construction and Use Regulations from 1st August 1961 had seen the maximum size of buses extended to 36ft x 8ft 2½ins but while the bus industry quickly latched on to the 36 foot long single decker as a way of converting services to one man operation, there was virtually no interest in double deckers of this length. Indeed, with around 53 passengers able to be seated in the longer single deck buses, many operators chose them to replace older double deckers which had seated around 56. After almost a decade of buying Leyland Tiger Cubs to the old permitted length, one might have expected the Leyland Leopard to be the choice for new buses at Port Talbot.

Instead, in 1963 Thomas Bros. took delivery of three AEC Reliance 36 foot buses, 124 SNY, 125 SNY and 126 SNY. All three were on the 4MU3RA chassis, so had AH470 engines and five-speed synchromesh gearboxes. The last, 126 SNY was delivered as a 49-seat dual purpose vehicle, perhaps with the new Minehead run in mind. It had an experimental two-tone livery; all three had illuminated cantrail advertising panels. In later years 126 would give up its dual purpose status to a newer vehicle.

1964
Election Year

The deterioration in industrial relations at the Abbey Works was an issue which would affect most of Port Talbot throughout the year. In January, Anthony Beetham said that they had already cut their special services to the steelworks by 50 per cent. Staff buses continued to run but with reduced loadings.

In February Port Talbot Borough Council and workers at the Abbey Works welcomed the

A promotional photograph of 1964 Marshall-bodied AEC Reliance 130 WNY, taken at Sunnycroft, Baglan. The 'passengers' were all employees of Thomas Bros. *G. H. Truran*

introduction of a through bus service from Pontrhydyfen and Cwmavon to the works. The service, provided as the result of numerous requests from steelworkers, was operated to coincide with the 3pm and 10pm shifts. Previously, workers had to change buses at Talbot and Bethany Squares.

In part, these were replacements for the services which David Jones & Sons had withdrawn back in 1961. At the same time, improvements were made to the service between Talbot Square and Tabor/Brynbryddan. However, there had been some complaints about services running between Port Talbot and the Sandfields and Baglan Estates.

Four new AEC Reliances arrived during the year. The first, in January carried a 36ft. version of the Harrington Cavalier coach body with 49 seats. it was named Afan Venturer and registered as 127 WNY. Only 11 of the 36 ft version of the Cavalier were built that year and 127 WNY was the only one purchased by a BET Group subsidiary. Again, the coach was acquired with the Blackpool runs in mind and an application had been submitted to re-route those tours via the newly opened section of the M6 near Knutsford.

The three others, which arrived in May, 128 WNY, 129 WNY and 130 WNY were also 4MU3RA models. They had Marshall 53-seat bus bodies to the updated BET design with a peaked rear dome, the cost was recorded as being approximately £5,000 each.

A conductress wiats for her driver at the depot. This is DNY 131C, a Weymann bodied AEC Reliance delivered in 1965 to dual purpose specification.

On 26th April, a bus outstationed at Glyncorrwg was stolen by a local 19 year old youth who collided with a gate post. At the Magistrates Court, the youth was described as someone who 'spent too much time on licensed premises' and fined £27. Fortunately damage to the bus was minimal, being valued at less than £7.

The summer service for 1964 was introduced on 16th May. The Margam to Aberavon Beach service was extended from its winter terminus at the Jersey Beach Hotel to the Four Winds between 11am and 9.30pm daily. Once again, some journeys on the Velindre to Baglan Estate service ran via Aberavon Beach during the summer. The weekend summer service which ran between Efail Fach, Pontrhydyfen, Tabor, Brynbryddan and Aberavon Beach was also reintroduced. A sad occasion during August brought together many familiar names from the history of Thomas Bros. It was the funeral of Joseph Hodges, son of Richard Hodges, one of the original operators on the Cwmavon service who had sold out to Thomas Bros. in 1941. Mourners included many names from the early days of Afan Valley bus services, including the Mason family (of Joseph Mason & Son) who were related by marriage. Staff from N&C Luxury Coaches (where Joseph worked as a driver) and Thomas Bros. attended.

During 1964, with the Rhondda and Swansea Bay railway line no longer in use, the

To remind people of its achievements and possibly as a softening up exercise for future fare changes, the following appeared on a leaflet early in December 1965:

SERVING PORT TALBOT

To meet the changing pattern of public demand we keep our services under constant review. Where new housing developments justify it, new or revised services have been introduced to bring a bus service within easy reach of most people's homes. To quote only a few examples in the last two years: increased services to Tabor and Brynbryddan: a new service to the Purcell Avenue area of Sandfields Estate: a service via Lake Road to cater for Little Warren Estate: a new service to Fairfield for the new housing development in that area.

Later in December, following the usual public bluster about bus fares, the company issued the following notice:

Fares are good value company tells passengers

ARE FARES FAIR?

We think that our bus fares are very reasonable. Although there have been increases in recent years to meet the increased costs we have to pay for materials, wages, Fuel Tax, Rates, etc., the percentage increase in fares is in many cases less than the general rise in the cost of living over the last 25 years. For example, the return fare from Margam to Aberavon Beach 25 years ago was 8d., today it is 1/5d. Although this fare has doubled, the cost of many other goods has gone up four times.

Our Fares are Good Value for Money.

crossing gates on Station Road, were at long last, and to the relief of many, removed.

The Labour Party, under Prime Minister Harold Wilson, won the 1964 general election with a majority of just four seats even after Profumo had brought the entire political system into disrepute. A second election in 1966 saw Wilson increase his majority to 96 and nationalisation was back on the agenda.

Now with a decent fleet of coaches, the company advertised Christmas shopping tours to Pontypridd Market in December. No doubt to appease local traders, the advertisements included a reminder that shopping in Port Talbot was much easier by local bus services.

1965
A Final takeover in the Afan Valley

Another open-topper appeared on the scene in March; GHT 127 came from Brighton, Hove & District and was a 1941 Bristol K5G. Four new Weymann bodied AEC Reliance 4MU3RAs were delivered in June: DNY 131C to DNY 134C. The first was a 49-seat dual purpose vehicle, the other three were 53 seaters to local bus configuration.

On 20th September, the remaining business of David Jones & Son (Port Talbot) Ltd. based at Pantdu was acquired and with it, 10 vehicles.

None of them was taken into the Thomas Bros. fleet and all were quickly disposed of. Included in the mix was 1953 AEC Regal IV/Burlingham MTG 172. This had previously, been owned by Thomas Bros. and it developed something of a charmed life. After Thomas Bros. disposed of it for the second time it went to dealer and breaker, W. North of Sherburn in Elmet, Yorkshire from where it escaped to become a mobile home. At the time of writing it is in store at Barry, Vale of Glamorgan awaiting restoration.

The contract services taken over from David Jones & Son were integrated with other work:

- **Tonmawr and Margam to Newlands Colliery.**
- **Pontrhydyfen and Port Talbot to the Abbey Works**
- **Velindre and Port Talbot to the Abbey Works**
- **Pwllyglaw and Margam to the Carbide Factory**

The Olympic size, Afan Lido Swimming Pool was formally opened by H.M. Queen Elizabeth II on 25th June 1965. Its first manager was Graham Jenkins, brother of actor Richard Burton. The facility included a 50m competition swimming pool and became the centrepiece of developments at Aberavon seafront. A further announcement in 1965 was that a new relief road later named Afan Way, was to be built through Sandfields along the trackbed of the former Rhondda & Swansea Bay Railway.

To page 106

Driver Doug Stephens with AEC Reliance, OTG 529, a Roe Dalesman bodied coach new to Jones, Pantdu in 1954. It passed to Thomas Bros. with the remaining part of the Jones business in 1965, though was never operated by them.

A crusader, highwayman

Coach hire and excursion work had restarted nationally, after the Second World War when fuel rationing regulations began to be relaxed.

As a result the 1950s and early 1960s became busy times for the luxury coach industry, before air travel and package holidays became popular and car ownership grew. Cutbacks in the rail network under controversial Conservative Minister of Transport Ernest Marples and chairman of the British Railways Board, physicist Richard Beeching in the early 1960s generated more traffic for coach operators. The speed limit for buses and coaches on open roads had been increased to 40mph in 1961.

As paid holidays for manual workers reached 96 per cent in 1955, demand for days out by coach grew accordingly. Customers' expectations had been raised by SWT and Western Welsh who ran fleets of top of the range vehicles. Following the BET takeover, the Thomas Bros. coach fleet was slowly renewed, usually by adding one or two new coaches anually. Each was given a name with a local flavour which, apart from being a useful PR exercise, assisted passengers to find the correct coach after a refreshment stop when two or more vehicles was used.

Coaching generally encompasses one of three areas of activity: express services, tours and excursions and private hire. Thomas Bros. activity on express services was limited to providing the occasional duplicate coach for other operators.

A rear view of 119 LNY showing the name 'Port Talbot Cavalier' emblazoned across the boot lid.

and the maid...

Representing the Thomas Bros. coach fleet in the early 1960s are from left: Leyland PS1, HNY415; AEC Regal IV, MTG 172; AEC Reliance, PTX 203; AEC Regal III, JNY 675; Leyland PS1, HNY 377; Dennis Lance, JTG 549; AEC Regal III, JTX 676; Tilling-Stevens, KNY 418 and Dennis Lance, JNY 336.

A full programme of day and half day tours was offered, to destinations such as Tenby, Cardigan, Gower, Abergavenny, New Quay and Symond's Yat. There were also the obligatory mystery tours, often to one of the listed destinations. Passengers on the day tours were handed complimentary copies of daily newspapers. The key holiday destination was Blackpool. In June to September during the 1960s, the weekly Saturday departure offered two options: An eight day tour to Blackpool with or

For their time the Harrington Cavalier bodies were well appointed.

Carefree Holiday Tours

Coaches, comfort and class!

without booked accommodation or transfer via Squires Gate Airport to a British United Airways flight to the Isle of Man, probably on board one of BUA's DC3s. Leaving Port Talbot at 6.00am, passengers could be picked up at any bus stop on route 1 between Acacia Avenue and Bethany Square, or along the A48 between Bethany Square and Baglan. The 1964 fare was a mere 40/- (£2) adult or 26/9d (£1.34) child.

Three and four day variants of the Blackpool tour were run in the autumn, tailored to view the illuminations. The three day tours left on Fridays, the four day version on Mondays. Fares were 35/- (adult) or 23/6d (child). Initially, the mainstay of these services was the Burlingham bodied AEC Reliances which at Blackpool were maintained by Ribble Motor Services.

At a press launch for some new coaches in 1961, Peter Hornblow said: "The tours are becoming very popular and last Saturday for instance, four coaches left Port Talbot for Blackpool. New coaches have been introduced under the company's normal stock replacement programme and will greatly assist in meeting demand. Permission for a new holiday service to Minehead was granted at a public hearing in Swansea at the end of April 1963. This took the form of an eight day holiday tour to the new Butlin's Holiday Camp, along similar lines to the tour operated to Blackpool. Running July to September coaches left Port Talbot on Saturdays at 6.15am. Once again, passengers could request to be picked up along route 1 or between Bethany Square and Pyle on the A48. Adult fare was 55/- (£2.75) or 36/9d (£1.84) for a child.

Some of Thomas Bros. private hire and tours leaflets produced down the years.

A youngster manages a quick game of tennis while AEC Reliances TTG 2 and 126 SNY in its original condition wait to make the long journey home from Blackpool Coach Park.

Just four years separate these two AEC Reliance coaches which show the evolving trends in coach design. 1964-built 12 WNY with 36ft Harrington Cavalier body is seen passing the BOAC terminal in Buckingham Palace Road, London while Duple (Northern) PTG 239F of 1968 is seen when new.

Anthony Beetham explained at the hearing that the company already provided for some of the holiday needs of the people of Port Talbot, but a number of passengers recently had suggested Minehead as an alternative trip to the Blackpool run. Four local residents gave evidence at the hearing supporting the application and each stated that they would use the tour if permission was granted. The only objection seems to have come from Associated Motorways on the grounds that they operated a route to Cheltenham, where passengers could change to a coach which would take them on to Minehead. This was not as bizarre as it may sound; the Severn Bridge had yet to open, so any service to the West Country would need to be routed via Gloucester. The application was granted and the service began within a few weeks and continued into the National Express era under the summer Holiday Express banner. It retained its popularity with a need for duplicate journeys in high season.

If you needed a coach for your organisation to visit a particular destination, the company was only too pleased to help. It published a leaflet entitled 'Luxurious Motor Coach Tours' which listed the most popular destinations along with the route, return mileage, journey time required and price for a 32-seater coach. The latter might appear a little odd, since by revealing their prices, they were playing into the hands of competitors. Or maybe they felt that no-one else could match the quality of what they had to offer.

Prices were all mileage based and created some interesting anomalies. In the pre-motorway era, three routes to Birmingham were offered with prices ranging from £22 14s (£22.70) to £25 10s (£25.50). There was no Severn Bridge of course, so hiring a coach to go from Port Talbot to Bristol (via Gloucester) involved a 248 mile round trip costing £23 12s 6d (£23.63).

Monarchs, Princesses, Crusaders, Cavaliers, they all shared the pride of Thomas Bros.

The following are the names of coaches proudly operated by Thomas Bros. from 1953 until the end of the company's life.

Port Talbot Monarch MTG 172
1953 AEC Regal IV/Burlingham
In service 1953-1965

Pride of Port Talbot PTX 203
1955 AEC Reliance/Burlingham
In service 1955-1966

Port Talbot Princess TTG 2
1956 AEC Reliance/Burlingham
In service 1956-196?

Port Talbot Crusader 11 CNY
1959 AEC Reliance/Burlingham
In service 1959-1969

Port Talbot Cavalier 119 LNY
1961 AEC Reliance/Harrington
In service 1961-1971

Maid of Port Talbot 120 LNY
1961 AEC Reliance/Harrington
In service 1961-1971

Afan Star 121 NTX
1962 AEC Reliance/Harrington
In service 1962-1971

Afan Venturer 127 WNY
1964 AEC Reliance/Harrington
In service 1964-1971

Afan Highwayman HTG 179D
1966 AEC Reliance/Duple
In service 1966-1971

Afan Commander PTG 239F
1968 AEC Reliance/Duple
In service 1969-1971

Afan Crusader* UWN 67H
1970 AEC Reliance/Duple
In service 1970-1971

*This name was allocated, but never carried. Instead UWN 67H was given the name Afan Commander as well as PTG 239F.

From page 101

With the introduction of the winter 1965-1966 timetable on September 19, there were again some alterations to bus services. The Margam to Aberavon Beach service was revised to run half-hourly on weekdays, most journeys being diverted to run via Victoria Road, Lake Road, Newbridge Road and Victoria Road to serve Little Warren Estate, meeting requests from residents and the Borough Council. A new service was introduced running on weekdays only, from Margam and the General Station to Sandfields via Water Street, Corporation Road and Julian Terrace to serve a new housing development. At the same time there were some slight reductions in the frequency of services relating to demand on the Aberavon to Pontrhydyfen routes.

In 1965 it was revealed that the population of Port Talbot had risen from 41,000 in 1952 to 51,322, mainly of course due to the expanded steelworks and BP Baglan Bay. For Port Talbot at least, the 1950s and early 1960s had indeed been a boom time.

1966
It's Hello motorway and Goodbye Western Welsh

In January, General Manager Anthony Beetham continued the policy of moving in circles of influence and keeping Thomas Bros. as a community-based operator when he was installed as President of the Port Talbot Chamber of Trade.

In late summer, fare increases applied for by Western Welsh were opposed by several parties and the application was turned down by the Traffic Commissioner.

In consequence, Western Welsh announced that it would be carrying out its promise to cut some routes and close depots.
The garages at Port Talbot and Kenfig Hill were closed from 25 September.
The company was in "A serious financial position", said the Traffic Manager, Mr. F. H. Pengelly. "The depots are being closed as a necessary economy measure," he added.
Mr. Pengelly blamed uneconomic services,

This German MAN 750, MN-AR 142 coach brought schoolchildren from Port Talbot's former twin city of Heilbronn on an exchange visit in 1964. During the visit it was garaged at the Thomas Bros. depot. Geoff Fulgar, Ronnie James, Dennis Richards, Ron James and Chief Engineer Ernie Lewis are seen alongside it here. *Les Davies*

the Government's credit squeeze and the rejection of the company's recent application for a fare increase for the closures. "We warned that we might have to make some changes when the Traffic Commissioner turned down our application to increase fares. This is the first," he said

The company had retained a depot at Port Talbot since it was formed in 1927. Staff were offered alternative jobs at the company's Bridgend and Neath depots but 44 redundancies were made. Financial issues apart, it actually seems like a logical move. BET had both Western Welsh and Thomas Bros. based in the town, competing on some sections of route. The latter no doubt had lower operating costs and modern facilities at Acacia Avenue. Moreover, the former Cridlands depot in Margam Terrace which housed Western Welsh was earmarked for demolition. The rebuilding of Port Talbot General station in 1961 had released part of the land – along with Margam Terrace - for what became Heilbronn Way. The Margam Terrace depot had remained on the books of WW until 1973 when it was sold to Port Talbot Borough Council for £14,850. As part of the reorganisation within BET Thomas Bros. received the important Western Welsh 'other' Afan Valley routes 234 and 235 which ran from Port Talbot via Abbey Road and Ynysygwas, then via the A4107 to Abergwynfi. There was a connecting service at Cymmer for Glyncorrwg, where a vehicle was outstationed, a legacy of GWR days. There were two outstation drivers and three clippies, with the 'late' crew sweeping out the bus at the end of daily service.

There was no regular vehicle allocated to Glyncorrwg. Changeovers were effected at Cymmer during mid-morning on Mondays to Saturdays. The fresh bus from Port Talbot would have been serviced, cleaned and fuelled prior to leaving Acacia Avenue. The ex-Glyncorrwg bus worked back via Blaengwynfi. The GWR's shed at Glyncorrwg was too small to accommodate 30ft buses, which were stabled overnight outside, as they had done in Western Welsh days. Crews had access to the building for consumables and cleaning equipment.

As from 22nd May 1966 a new experimental timetable was introduced on the Fairfield service (12). This ran between Port Talbot

General Station (Plaza) and Fairfield with some journeys extended to Aberavon Beach (Afan Lido). The route was then via Talcennau Road, Danybryn Road and Forge Road to avoid the congestion on Station Road. This also gave Danybryn Road residents a service to Bethany Square, Aberavon Market, Fairfield and the beach.

On 22nd July the final section of the Port Talbot bypass was opened by the Rt. Hon. Cledwyn Hughes, MP, Secretary of State for Wales. This event was welcomed by almost everyone, not least Thomas Bros as it brought much needed relief from the traffic problems which had dogged the town for many years. It was built by A.E. Farr Ltd. to motorway specification and so designated A48(M), making it the first motorway in Wales. The wisdom of the planners at that time was questioned by many. Hailed as a major engineering achievement it required the demolition of large swathes of the town and the displacement of hundreds of people from their homes and businesses. Over 200 homes, three churches and several schools were demolished with those inhabiting quiet terraced streets finding themselves faced with living directly against the concrete structure and the noise and pollution the new road brought.

On the positive side, the redevelopment solved the annual flooding of the Aberavon area of Port Talbot and increased air quality in Station Road. Some felt that a less brutal solution could have been found; restoration of some of the classic buildings and sensitive landscaping in a town with a river flowing through it might have been preferable. Instead, the heart of the old town was replaced with a shopping mall and multi-storey car park. This, though, was the 1960s and cities such as Birmingham were being applauded for celebrating cars; it seemed everyone wanted to follow them.

For Thomas Bros. the motorway meant that lost mileage on services running through Port Talbot had reduced substantially from 3,100 miles in a month in 1965 to just 980 miles in the same month in 1966.

A new coach, an AEC Reliance 2MU4RA with a Duple (Northern) 41 seat coach body, HTG 179D delivered at the end of February. It had forced air ventilation with individual controls for passengers. Following a competition among staff it was christened Afan Highwayman.

Three Strachans bodied Leyland Panther Cubs (HTG 180-182D) arrived just before the National Eisteddfod was held in Port Talbot during August. Designated PSRC1/1, they were being touted as a rear-engined version of the trusty Tiger Cub. To a completely new design, these had the engine located at the rear of the bus instead of the more usual position amidships. This enabled the floor level to be much lower and passengers needed to mount only one step at the entrance instead of the usual three on a Tiger Cub or Reliance. A feature of the new buses was a compartment near the entrance for folding push chairs and luggage. The new buses were the first of their type to operate in Wales. Unfortunately, the trio were notoriously unreliable, particularly in SWT days as they grew older.

When they were produced in 1966, the concept of rear engined single deckers was still relatively new and its contemporaries such as the AEC Swift, Daimler Roadliner or Albion Viking VK43 also had severe shortcomings. Thomas Bros. had trialled the first built AEC Swift at Port Talbot, FGW 498C with a Willowbrook body, but were clearly less than impressed. Only the Bristol RE succeeded, along with the later Leyland National, but at first that wasn't widely available to non-THC companies. The Panther Cubs were underpowered using Leyland's O.400 engine and tended to overheat. There wasn't space for the larger O.600 unit. Maybe all might have been well if they had been limited to the flat routes through Sandfields but that would have been too restrictive. At any rate, they became limited to use on contracts and extras from comparatively early on in their lives.
The story goes that the engineers at Leyland knew it was underpowered and didn't really have much time for the project but the type

had emerged following a request from a good customer, Manchester Corporation. Only 94 were ever built. Attempts to rectify the problem continued with SWT moving the radiator to the rear and housed in a bulge in the bodywork.

Fitter Dai Morris felt that the bodywork and finish of the Panther Cubs was excellent, despite their obvious mechanical shortcomings: "It was such a shame as these three Panther Cubs were really nice vehicles in every other way. They were bright with fluorescent lighting and wipe clean formica surfaces to give a pleasant travelling environment," he said. At that time Strachans Coachbuilders were keen to expand and to make inroads into the lucrative BET bus market so one is left wondering if favourable terms were offered for purchasing what was still an experimental design when it came to such vehicles. As a postscript, a Leyland Panther radiator was discovered in the engineering stores at SWT's Ravenhill Depot in the late 1980s. By then the Panther Cubs had long gone so it was of little use or value and was donated to preservationists.

Another important development which would help secure the future of the steelworks was the start of construction of the Port Talbot tidal harbour, south-west of the existing dock. It was completed in 1970 and was the first dry-bulk cargo terminal in the UK capable of taking vessels of over 100,000 tonnes.

Unexpectedly, three Leyland Panther Cubs were purchased in 1966; HTG 180-182D. Here, the first is seen at Cedar Gardens, Sunnycroft, Baglan.

Leyland Panther Cub HTG 182D with its peculiar rear bustle to accommodate an additional cooling system.

1967
You can't please them all . . .

Two significant industrial developments occurred at Port Talbot during 1967: the Steel Company of Wales was absorbed into the giant British Steel Corporation in July and BP Chemicals acquired the British Hydrocarbon Plant site at Baglan and its associated businesses. Each of these events helped to secure employment in the area.

Four new vehicles arrived during 1967: MNY 135E was an AEC Reliance 6MU3RA with a Marshall 49-seat dual purpose body, while

109

Trials of AEC's new rear-engined Swift model took place in 1966/7. Here, Marshall-bodied demonstrator LYY 827D is seen at Aberavon Beach in June 1967. *Roy Marshall, copyright The Bus Archive.*

OTX 136F, OTX 137F and OTX 138F were a trio of identical 36ft AEC Reliances with 51-seat Marshall bus bodies that arrived in November. They were all fitted with more powerful AH505 engines and five-speed all-synchromesh gearboxes. With no power steering, they were heavy vehicles to manoeuvre, but were superb buses otherwise. Favourable comments received about the luggage pens fitted to the Panther Cubs resulted in these being fitted to the OTX Reliances. Sadly, these buses brought the end of the road for some of the 1953-4, 44-seat Leyland Tiger Cubs which began to be taken out of service by the end of the year, having achieved some substantial mileages on the streets of Port Talbot.

In July, the company announced revisions to the Port Talbot to Abergwynfi, Glyncorrwg and Cwmavon services. The changes were being brought about because of requests for the services between Glyncorrwg and Cymmer and between Abergwynfi and Cymmer to have improved connections with the United Welsh service to Maesteg. The revised timetable aimed to improve the connections between bus and rail services at Cymmer Afan. There had also been requests for services from Glyncorrwg and Abergwynfi

The first AEC Swift built was Willowbrook-bodied demonstrator FGW 498C, seen here at Seaway Parade.

to be extended through to Aberavon Beach during the summer. A passenger survey had revealed that between Oakwood (Pontrhydyfen) and Port Talbot there might be a benefit from diverting via Cwmavon Road instead of Penycae Road, the latter being served by the Port Talbot to Maesteg route. Services in the area had reached the point where changing needs meant adjustments were needed.

Housebuilding in Brynbryddan and Tabor had precipitated a need to increase the frequency of buses to that area, while patronage on services to Pontrhydyfen and Cwmavon was diminishing. A new road, Heol Jiwbili, meant that it was now possible to cover Brynbryddan, Tabor and parts of Cwmavon on the same service. Moreover, reduction in traffic at Port Talbot since the opening of the bypass meant that a cross-town service between Brynbryddan, Tabor and Aberavon Beach was now feasible.

The proposed new services were:

- **Sandfields Estate via Sandown Road to Brynbryddan and Tabor.** (A basic half-hourly service leaving Sandfields Estate terminus at 00 and 30 minutes past the hour on weekdays.)
- **Purcell Avenue via Hospital Road, Depot Road, Cwmavon Police Station, Heol Jiwbili, Tabor and Brynbryddan.** (An hourly service leaving Purcell Avenue at 14 minutes past the hour during most of the day on weekdays.)
- **Purcell Avenue via Golden Avenue, Aberavon Beach, Depot Road, Cwmavon Police Station. Heol Jiwbili, Tabor and Brynbryddan.** (An hourly service leaving Purcell Avenue at 44 minutes past the hour during most of the day.)

There would be short journeys from Port Talbot to Abergwynfi and Glyncorrwg or to Pontrhydyfen and Tonmawr using one-man operated buses. The terminus in Port Talbot for these services was to be at Bethany Square, thereby avoiding the need for the use of Talbot Square as a terminal point for buses. Certain journeys would be extended to or from Port Talbot General Station.

Almost immediately there were complaints. Mostly, it seems, they were a reaction from the vocal minority. There were those who didn't like any form of change or found the new network confusing.

There were those who didn't like the new cross town service because it didn't stop at Talbot Square. There were those who didn't like one man buses because they had to queue to get on. Nevertheless, most of the changes it seems, had been introduced because of customer requests and new timetables always need time to bed in as drivers get used to new procedures. Interestingly, in a large survey carried out by Port Talbot & District Consumer Group later in 1967, 88 per cent of those questioned said they were happy with bus services.

The Road Safety Act of 1967 introduced the first maximum legal blood alcohol limit in the UK. This was set at a maximum blood alcohol concentration of 80 milligrams of alcohol per 100ml of blood or the equivalent 107 milligrams of alcohol per 100 millilitres of urine. It became an offence to drive, attempt to drive or be in charge of a motor vehicle with a blood alcohol concentration that exceeded the maximum prescribed legal limit. With it came the 1967 Breathalyser Act. Transport Minister Barbara Castle introduced the breathalyser as a way of testing a person's blood alcohol concentration level at the roadside.

It seems incredible now, but at that time, people protested about the introduction of the limit and publicans claimed that bankruptcy would follow. In November, no doubt with Christmas in sight, Thomas Bros. took this as an opportunity to promote its private hire business under the headline, Worried about the new Breathalyser Test?

In December, the death was reported of Howell Hopkin Davies, one of the partners in Davies Bros. Ltd. a company which became part of Thomas Bros. in 1951. Another link with the heady days of the 1930s had been lost. At the end of the year, Thomas Bros. had a fleet of 53 vehicles, 66 drivers — of which 43 had received safe driving awards — and was operating 1,800,000 miles annually.

AEC Reliance OTX 137F passes a Corona pop delivery lorry as it noses through Sandfields Estate on its !A route.

1968
Clouds begin to gather

In Westminster, the Labour Government was in talks to place BET's bus operating interests in public ownership. This was made easier in South Wales because SWT had no railway investors and so its transfer to the THC who already owned United Welsh was straightforward. The Transport Act of 1968 initiated the National Bus Company (NBC) as an entity which would take over the THC group operators together with those of BET from 1st January 1969. In South Wales, it was South Wales Transport which became the lead company in the NBC mergers but it didn't necessarily follow that SWT's policies would dominate the new set up.

The loss of another contract came with the closure of Newlands Colliery at Kenfig Hill in March. The last local colliery and employing 358, it tapped seams of coal which ran out under Swansea Bay. Thomas Bros. had inherited the contract with the acquisition Jones of Pantdu in 1965.

An important piece of legislation was passed in 1968 with the implementation of the New Bus Grant. This offered a 25 per cent grant for new vehicles provided they complied with particular specifications to ensure that they were suitable for local bus work. Luxury coaches designed for touring or private hire work were not eligible for Government grants. However, dual-purpose single-deckers with luxury type seating, used on both express and stage carriage services, did qualify for grants. In most cases such dual-purpose vehicles were based on a standard bus framework, though with a more elaborate exterior finish, and were often downgraded to normal full-time stage work after the first few years in service. The aim was to encourage the conversion to one-man operation, to improve the comfort of travel and to reduce the number of minor variations in design, which prevented manufacturers from stabilising their costs through longer production runs. The grant was increased to 50 per cent in 1971 and extended to include coaches, again to set specifications.

Just two new vehicles arrived in 1968; PTG 239F was a beefy-looking AEC Reliance 6MU4R with a Duple Commander 49-seat coach body which took the name Afan Commander. Meanwhile RTG 140F was a return to the old tried and trusted favourite for local bus work, a Leyland Tiger Cub with Marshall 45-seat bodywork. This had the sad significance of being the last vehicle delivered new in Thomas Bros. blue and primrose.

Two further additions to the fleet during 1968 were a pair of 1957 Leyland Tiger Cubs with Weymann 'Hermes' 44-seat bodies, similar to those which Thomas Bros. had delivered in the 1950s. OBX 780 and OBX 781 had been new to J. James & Sons Ltd. of Ammanford (nos. 225/6) and had latterly carried SWT fleet numbers 807 and 808.

A behind the scenes view of Thomas Bros. was available to members of the Omnibus Society over the weekend of 28th and 29th June. PTG 239F was one of several vehicles used on the tour and the vehicles already repainted in the new SWT-style red and cream livery were noted. Thomas Bros. opened its new booking office at Travel Corner, Bethany Square in July, closing the former office at 40A Station Road.

Some much-welcomed additional work arrived in October with the Sandfields to St. John's Colliery, Caerau service of W.L. Jones.

A cross section of the Thomas Bros. fleet parked in time-honoured fashion at Acacia Avenue during August 1968.
Roy Marshall, copyright The Bus Archive.

One of a pair of 1957 Leyland Tiger Cubs with Weymann 'Hermes' 44-seat bodies, similar to those delivered to Thomas Bros. in the 1950s. It had originated with James of Ammanford and was transferred into the fleet by SWT in 1968.

Fare play!

Some sample adult fares from 1969:

Western Avenue to Bethany Square: 11d (5p) single, 1/8d (8p) return.

Western Avenue to Aberavon Beach: 6d (3p) single.

Bethany Square to Margam: 10d (4p) single.

Tonmawr to Aberavon Beach: 1/3d (6p) single, 2/3d (11p) return, 10/6d (53p) weekly.

Glyncorrwg to Aberavon Beach: 3/3d (16p) single, 5/9d (29p) return, 25/6d (£1.27) weekly.

By this time there was interavailability of tickets with SWT and/or United Welsh between Pontrhydyfen (Oakwood) and Abergwynfi and between Margam and Baglan.

On 28th October, BP announced what was then the largest single investment in new plant at that time in the BP Group, estimated at over £125million making Baglan Bay one of the biggest petrochemical manufacturing sites in Europe.

At the end of the year, General Manager Anthony Beetham announced that he would be leaving to join City of Oxford Motor Services. His successor from 1 January would be D.N. Flower who would oversee Thomas Bros. in addition to N&C Luxury Coaches Ltd. (N&C). The reasons for this would soon become apparent.

1969
Nationalisation and rationalisation

Following the formation of NBC at the start of the year, it was clear that there was much overlap between the activities of the Swansea and Port Talbot based operators. With passenger numbers in decline, car ownership and traffic congestion on the rise and the consequent need to make economies, rationalisation, higher fares and cost savings seemed inevitable. N&C and Thomas Bros. both now under common local management, transferred to SWT control in April 1969; United Welsh followed in September 1970.

Unreliability and increasing fares did little to inspire public confidence. During February 1969, Port Talbot Guardian weekly newspaper reporter David Roberts highlighted how schoolchildren at Cwmavon refused to board the bus to Dyffryn Comprehensive because not enough seats were being provided for the pupils.

In March 1969 an early morning commuter service from Baglan was run using an engineer to drive buses, with a second acting as a steward. No fares were charged.

Meanwhile, part of life at Thomas Bros. meant membership of the very active Sports and Social Club which ran the canteen and organised children's parties. In addition there was a darts club and a small bore shooting club which were quite successful.

The two Leyland Tiger Cubs delivered in 1969 — this is VTG 142G — carried the South Wales Transport red livery from new but with Thomas Bros. fleetnames in SWT style.

Deliveries of previously ordered new vehicles continued in 1969. TTX 141G was an AEC Reliance with Marshall 49-seat bodywork. It was delivered with bus seating, which was exchanged with the high backed seats from 126 SNY. These were then retrimmed by Western Welsh at Ely in their contemporary dual purpose specification blue tartan moquette, prior to being refitted into TTX 141G. The vehicle was of unique appearance, with a cream and blue colour scheme based on the coach livery. It had chrome bumpers and a rear luggage locker, which was very useful on its many visits to Butlin's at Minehead. The vehicle was to the new bus grant requirements (e.g. one-man operated, full destination display, folding doors), but its final specification meant that it was clearly purchased for longer distance 'luxury' work.

The final pair of Leyland Tiger Cubs to be delivered to Thomas Bros. came in June. they were VTG 142G and VTG 143G and were among the last built for use in the UK. They had Marshall 45 seat bodies and were delivered in SWT red and cream livery but with Thomas Bros. fleet names. The pair had a somewhat ungainly appearance, having standard Marshall 8ft 3in bodies on the Tiger Cub's 8ft axles, Marshall having by now standardised on the wider bodies for Leyland Leopards by the time they were built.

A further piece of work arrived late in the company's history when it received the contract to run the rail replacement service for the closed Rhondda Tunnel on the remaining section of the Rhondda & Swansea Bay Railway. In 1967, severe distortion was observed in the tunnel around a third of the way through from the west end, close to a geological fault. The British Railways engineer closed the tunnel on safety grounds on 26th February 1968. This was supposedly a temporary measure whilst a decision was made on the future of the line. Initially, the contract for the replacement bus service went to N&C Luxury Coaches but this work was transferred to Thomas Bros. on formation of the NBC.

On 23rd December there was an industrial dispute when crews walked out at 5pm over the poor heating in buses. This was quickly resolved and services ran normally the following day.

At the end of 1969, Thomas Bros. operated 1,905,289 miles with miles per blameworthy accidents averaging 70,566.

The date of 13th January 1970 was certainly unlucky for some. Recently repainted Tiger Cub PTX 198, heading towards Port Talbot was in collision with a lorry near Pantdu, Cwmavon. The lorry driver had to be released by firemen and was taken to Neath General Hospital. The bus driver was uninjured and the conductress sustained minor injuries, as did six passengers aboard the bus.

1970-1971
The end game

The year 1970 started badly with a continuing 'flu epidemic which left the company seriously understaffed. One third of drivers and a quarter of conductors were off sick. Generally, a figure of 45 per cent under the normal requirement was reported which resulted in some services being suspended amid many complaints received.

Additionally, changes to drivers' hours regulations exacerbated a shortage of drivers and by July 16 conductresses were being trained as drivers.

This was seen as something of a novelty in its day. The women, aged from their early twenties to early forties, were given lessons in single-deck vehicle, SARO bodied Tiger Cub NNY 70, outside normal working hours. The move was also part of the plan to convert all services to one-person operation within two years, the elimination of conductors by then being seen as the way forward in the cash-strapped bus industry.

The first woman to pass as a driver was Joyce Warren who passed her PSV driving test on 24th November 1970, having been taught by Driver-Instructor Arnold Cooke. Joyce had joined the company in May 1958 and worked as a conductress. Her brother, Hywel Selway remembers the publicity it attracted:

"My sister Joyce Warren was a conductress with Thomas Bros. When they were being made redundant she started to learn how to drive a bus. She had never driven a car before but she became the first female bus driver in the company.

I can remember sitting around the television watching her being interviewed on the news. Joyce still met up with old colleagues until she passed away in 2013. Both my parents

The final coach to carry the Thomas Bros. name was delivered in 1970. AEC Reliance UWN 67H had Duple 41 seat bodywork and carried SWT red and cream coach livery. It wasn't long before the rest of the Thomas Bros. coach fleet was repainted in these colours.

Western Avenue was the main terminus at Sandfields Estate where several services met. In July 1969, AEC Reliances MNY 135E and DNY 134C wait to return towards Port Talbot.
Roy Marshall, copyright The Bus Archive.

worked for Thomas Bros. My father was a driver and mother a conductress."

It wasn't too long before a second conductress, Ann Hodges, attained her driving licence. Others soon followed.

A final new coach was delivered in 1970; UWN 67H arrived finished in standard SWT red and cream coach livery but with Thomas Bros. fleetnames. This was an AEC Reliance 6MU4R model with a Duple body and 41 seats. A final Thomas Bros. flourish was that the coach bore the name Afan Commander.

In September, United Welsh Services Ltd. was transferred to SWT control. Along with N&C and Thomas Bros. it would be completely absorbed from January 1971. On 19th November 1970, staff were issued with a notice confirming the merger of the local companies under the SWT banner.

In November 1970, all buses were given South Wales vinyl fleet names on a red background, irrespective of the vehicle's livery, with SWT legal lettering and renumbered into one common

Three 30 foot AEC Reliances with Willowbrook bodywork were ordered by Thomas Bros. but delivered in 1971, after SWT takeover. These were YWN 553/5/6J and carried the smart new SWT single deck livery favoured at that time.

series; this was the first time most Thomas Bros. vehicles had carried fleet numbers. Tiger Cubs were numbered from 301 upwards; 36 ft Reliances were renumbered in the 400 series and coaches became the 100 series. All future repaints were into the new SWT bright red and cream livery.

In December, amid concerns about early morning bus services, it was announced that the 40-year old practice of stabling a bus at Glyncorrwg overnight would cease.

In 1971, a trio of brand new AEC Reliances joined the expanded SWT fleet at Port Talbot; YWN 553J, YWN 555J and YWN 556J with Willowbrook 45 seat bodywork finished in a new livery which SWT was using on single deck deliveries at that time. These, however, were a modification of Thomas Bros. final vehicle order and it was the first time that Willowbrook bodywork had been specified during the company's entire history. But the Thomas Bros. story itself had come to an end.

Leyland Tiger Cub NNY 70 in use as a driver training bus during the period when conductors were being retrained as drivers.

'Regular crews became your friends. Clippies gave you a ticket and a smile with it, despite their heavy machines.'

A 1956 trade advertisement proclaiming the benefits for operators of the Bell Punch 'Ultimate' ticket machine.

There is always much more to the day to day life of any bus company than simply the vehicles that carry its passengers and on this count Thomas Bros. was no different. The company's front line road staff in particular always played a leading role in making things work.

Drivers and conductresses were ambassadors for the company and their friendly faces became familiar to regular passengers and were often a welcome sight. The road staff got to know their regular passengers and many of them became firm friends.

While the drivers knew their routes the company's conductresses were never short of social skills in getting to know their passengers, but they needed strength too.

For many years the Bell Punch 'Ultimate' ticket machine was used by these hard working frontliners. They were heavy to wear and use even though they only issued small square tickets, each value having a different colour.

Hard working road staff kept the wheels turning

Conductress Vera Howells works her way up the aisle of one of the SNY batch of AEC Reliances dating from 1963, collecting fares and dispensing tickets from her Bell Punch 'Ultimate' ticket machine. *Gilbert Ball*

A driver and conductress prepare to set off on their next shift.

Driver Vic Passmore in front of TTG 6.

One of the buses converted for one-man operation in 1966 for the Flat Fare experiment on service 12 was 12 CNY.
Roy Marshall, copyright The Bus Archive.

A longer route might require the issue of several tickets to the total value of the journey being made. It was effectively a mechanical version of the old Bell Punch ticket racks used in the early days of the industry and served the company for many years. These machines with their familiar sound became as much a part of travel on the company's vehicles as the crews themselves.

But times were changing and the advent of single crew operation eventually reached Port Talbot and Thomas Bros. A first foray into one person operation came on 19th June 1966 with the conversion of the Velindre to Afan Lido via Port Talbot General Station and Fairfield route. Appropriately for service 12, bus 12 CNY was suitably adapted with two seats removed and a passenger-operated Bell Punch Autoslot II ticket machine fitted along with price points for a flat fare scheme. Boarding passengers were reminded to insert 6d (3p) adult or 3d (1p) child into the machine using combinations of sixpenny or threepenny pieces. Return tickets were not available on the pay-as-you-enter service.

Although the exact fare was required, change was available from the driver. Initially, its two regular operators were Alf Hanson and Ernie Elward. Later, a Leyland Panther Cub, HTG 181D was also equipped with the ticket issuing system.

As a passenger Angela Warlow remembered the time well: "I recall the buses from the Afan Lido to Fairfield with the first ticket machines where you bought your own ticket, with 3d and 6d coins. I was in St Joseph's Comprehensive in the early 1970s. Ernie and Alf were always the drivers."

The Autoslot ticket machine fitted to 12 CNY. Alongside are images of pre-decimal threepenny and sixpenny coins.

THOMAS BROS. (Port Talbot) LTD.

SANDFIELDS (Fairfield) – GENERAL STATION CIRCULAR SERVICE

NEW EXPERIMENTAL SERVICE

As from the 22nd May, 1966, a new experimental timetable was introduced on the Fairfield service (Service 12). The service now operates between Port Talbot (General Station) and Fairfield, with certain journeys extended from Fairfield to Aberavon Beach. Full details of the timetable are shown overleaf.

Passengers should please note that on journeys from General Station to Fairfield and Aberavon Beach, the bus starts from the Plaza, and should board the bus at the bus stop outside the Plaza Cinema. The bus then operates via Talcennau Road, Danybryn Road, and Forge Road, thereby avoiding the traffic congestion of Station Road and also at the same time providing a service for residents of the Danybryn Road area to enable them to travel to and from Bethany Square, Aberavon Market, Fairfield and Aberavon Beach. On journeys extended to Aberavon Beach, the terminal point is the Afan Lido entrance.

As from the 19th June, this service will be operated with a pay-as-you-enter bus equipped with a new type of ticket machine. The flat single fare for the journey will be 6d. adult (3d. child), irrespective of how far you travel. On boarding the bus, passengers are requested to obtain their ticket by inserting the appropriate coin in the ticket machines, which are mounted on the right-hand side of the entrance. Please insert the correct fare of 6d. adult (one sixpenny piece or two threepenny pieces) or 3d. child (one threepenny piece) in the correct machine. To ensure the operation of this service without delay, passengers are requested to ensure that they have the correct coins available when they board the bus. If they do not have the correct coins available, they should ask the driver for change.

Passengers are asked to retain their tickets for inspection. Return tickets are not issued or available on this service.

DWJ 130897/L

Smiling conductresses with their ticket machines and money satchels. Among them Sarah Thomas, second from left and Betty King far right. *Steph Evans*

The growth of one person operation can be judged from a fleet list dated June 1968 which reveals that by then 10 of the Tiger Cubs had been fitted for one man operation. These used Setright ticket machines operated by the driver. The gradual phasing out of conductresses was seen as a negative step by regular passengers who welcomed their cheery demeanour, something which gave a human face to local bus services.

There is no doubt that for many it changed the experience of local bus travel and perhaps reduced the connection between the company and its valued passengers.

Memory Makers

Memories of Thomas Bros. conductresses abound with no shortage of tales of the many different characters and personalities — and sometimes their strictness too.

Linda Banks is among many with fond recollections. Her friend's mother, Marian Randall, was one of those who worked as a Thomas Bros. conductress. "One of her regular driver's was Vic Passmore. I even remember the registration of his regular bus. It was TTG 6," said Linda. "Sadly Marian passed away just after Christmas in 2020 a victim of the Covid virus. Marian's uncle had owned Davies Brothers buses, one of the companies which was sold to Thomas Bros."

Thomas Bros. driver Bill James and conductress May Willis with her heavy Bell Punch ticket machine enjoy a break during their shift.

Wendy Betts recalled that her aunt Kath worked on Thomas Bros. buses for years. "Somewhere I've got a photo of her retirement party. I've still got a Thomas

To page 124

The driving

When buses ruled the road, the driver was king, and when it comes to Thomas Bros. a great many live on in the memories of the passengers they regularly carried.

A group of drivers and conductresses await their next turn of duty up the Afan Valley at Bethany Square, Port Talbot, early 1960s.

Long serving driver Frank Jones seen with NNY 57 at Danycoed, Pontrhydyfen.

Drivers were proud of their professional role in the everyday life of the company and the majority could boast of being accident free.

Each year for decades a presentation took place at the annual dinner often held at the Globe Inn, Newton, Porthcawl around November or December time where safe driving certificates and badges were handed out and received with that same pride.

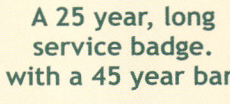

A 25 year, long service badge, with a 45 year bar.

But there was a different side to these drivers too. Many were characters and revelled in their familiarity with their grateful passengers. Lots of them haven't forgotten those drivers from an altogether different age of passenger transport. Many recall anecdotes that have stayed in their memories with the passing of time.

Christine Lane remembers Hughie and Harry, who were regular local drivers in Cwmavon, Port Talbot. "There was often a policeman on point duty directing traffic at the junction of High Street and Upper Water Street, just outside the Walnut Tree Hotel," she recalled. "There was one that didn't like Hughie and he would keep him waiting for ages before calling him out. Hughie would be cursing. We all thought it was hilarious."

Colin Thomson's father Alec known as 'Jock' drove with the company for many years. "His regular conductress was called Josie," said

A civic salute to the professionalism of Thomas Bros. road staff as a Port Talbot mayor hands out safe driving awards at one of the company's annual presentation events.

force

Rennie Richards, conductress Thelma O'Callaghan and driver Harry Pike alongside Saro-bodied NNY 66.

Colin. "I still have a couple of road safety medals that he was awarded. To my knowledge he never had a bump in his entire driving career."

Siân Louise Boxall recalled that her grandad Hughie Thomas and his brother Alan were both drivers for Thomas Bros and often talked of their experiences. Meanwhile, Howard Williams was another long time driver for the company. His son Alan recalled: "My dad Howard was a driver with Thomas bros from the early 1960s. He stayed until he retired with ill health at 58."

Drivers, from left: Sid Thomas, Mal Davies, Terry Davies, B. J. Hibbard, Private Hire; and Herbert Dodd.

Long term driverrs Harland Richards, left, and Vic Passmore with AEC Reliance 11 CNY.

David Williams highlighted the kindness that could often be demonstrated by drivers. "I remember one day when I was down the beach with my friends and we were catching the bus back to Fairfield," he said.
"I got on and had lost my money and the driver told the conductress to let me on anyway. They were both lovely people."

Stanley Williams recalled a scary moment though. "I remember cycling home from The Sec, which was the grammar school in Talcennau Road with my sister and as we arrived in front of the Walnut Tree Hotel, a Thomas Bros. bus passed us and turned left into Water Street.

"Fortunately my sister who was in front of me managed to stop in time otherwise she would have been under the back wheels of the bus. It was a very scary moment."

From page 121

Bros. badge. Her sister-in-law Brenda worked for them too," she said.

When Sharon Corcoran's dad Clayton Routliff was driving Thomas Bros. buses Marion Randall from Margam was his regular conductress. She recalled a time when it was her birthday and her father had taken her for a ride on one of his bus routes.

"Marion asked my dad to stop by a shop. She went in and bought me the biggest box of chocolates I had ever seen. I will always remember her, she was a lovely lady with pretty blonde hair.

"My dad also drove a coach on the regular Blackpool trips. Like many I have lots of happy memories," she added.

David Davies remembered his mother Frances working on Thomas Bros. buses for many years in the late 1950s as a conductress. She stayed until she took redundancy, at the time when single person operation came into being.

Iris Whitworth, left, in her original Thomas Bros conductress uniform, shortly after she started with the company and above, conductress Eluned McNeill in a post 1971 lightweight summer version.

Edna's new job was the route to her future!

Edna Wilkinson knew that her new job was just the ticket. From earning just £3 a week as a shop assistant she had boosted her pay packet three times over by becoming a bus conductress with Thomas Bros.

"I loved every minute of it from the moment I started in 1956 to the time I finished in 1960 to start a family. My surname was Davies at the time and I even met my future husband on one of our regular routes," recalled Edna fondly.

"We used to work mornings one week and then afternoons the next. The only drawback was that on morning shifts we had to get up at 5am for the worker's buses.
The passengers were lovely in those days, whichever route you worked. They went from the beach to Margam and to Cwmavon. My favourite run was the one to Cwmavon, perhaps because that's where I lived.

"I was only 18 when I started and looking back it was the best job I ever had.

More people travelled on the buses back then. It was like working in the community. You got to know the regulars and their habits. Best of all in those early days was that I had plenty of offers of dates!

"My husband spotted me on one occasion and when he realised that I regularly worked a particular route, he chased after the bus one day until he caught up and eventually jumped aboard."

Edna recalls that when she was employed by the company most of the female crew members were conductresses, but by the time that she left things were changing and

"There used to be a canteen in a shack next to the RAFA club in Victoria Road, near Aberavon Beach," he recalled. "Like many she said they were a great company to work for and good to their staff. The Margam terminus originally ended at Groes near the former site of the round chapel and the other end was in Fairway."

Thelma Callaghan, Mary Maund, Betty Turner, Kathleen Potter are just a few names of conductresses that Lillian Davies recalled.

"My gran Betty Downey was one too," she said. "Hughie Thomas was her driver for many years."

Cath Evans was another whose grandmother Rose Slade was a conductress. Cath said: "She later became a traffic warden and then a store detective. Everyone knew her and many a person left the town's Woolworths store on the end of her boot!"

Siân Holmes mother Anne Herman was also a Thomas Bros conductress. "I can remember the first clippies becoming bus drivers," she said. "My mother still remembers which buses go down which routes. We test her and tease her, She'll be 90 soon and still has a love of the buses."

Norma Hopkins recalled the first Thomas Bros bus that went up to Brynbryddan in Cwmavon. It was a welcome service.

"I remember a driver by the name of Hughie and the conductress called Margaret. They were on that first bus and often seemed to be together on that run.," she said. "It was a long time ago, but as children we loved Hughie, though were a little afraid of the conductress because she always kept us in line. Thinking about it now she must have had a hard time with us."

Hughie was Sian Louise Boxall's grandad: "Lots of people remember him driving. Sadly he passed away in 1982," she said.

women were encouraged to get behind the wheel.

"They were a marvellous company to work for in those days. They really looked after their staff.

"I'm sure many will remember the adventures on the annual staff trip. There was also a café at Aberavon beach just for Thomas Bros staff. That was welcome in summer when the passenger loads were greater as people headed to the beach."

Like Edna, most of her colleagues are now in their mid-80s. They all remember the bottlenecks of the old town, particularly Maypole Corner, narrow Water Street and the railway level crossing gates in Station Road, which regularly made time-keeping a challenge that was at best difficult. Crews regularly worked together and Willy Owen James was often Edna's regular driver.

Edna and fellow conductress Thelma Callaghan with Leyland Tiger Cub VTX 8, in the background.
Ann Matthews

Tickets for travelling

From the earliest times passengers on buses had to be issued with tickets. In Port Talbot these took many forms as can be seen from the array of those shown alongside.

1 Early Williamson Willebrew tickets. When issued the ticket would be trimmed at the fare paid.

2 A Bell Punch weekly return ticket.

3 This Williamson Willebrew ticket was issued for travel on Afan Valley services only.

4 A ticket that was valid for six return journeys in 28 days.

5 Workers' Weekly tickets for Abbey Works services only, Monday to Saturday.

6 A newspaper or parcel ticket.

7 This Setright Speed ticket, was issued on the company's one-man-operated services.

8 A selection of Bell Punch 'Ultimate' tickets. These were common, particularly amongst municipal operators during the 1960s. Each ticket had a separate colour and multiple tickets would be issued for higher fares.

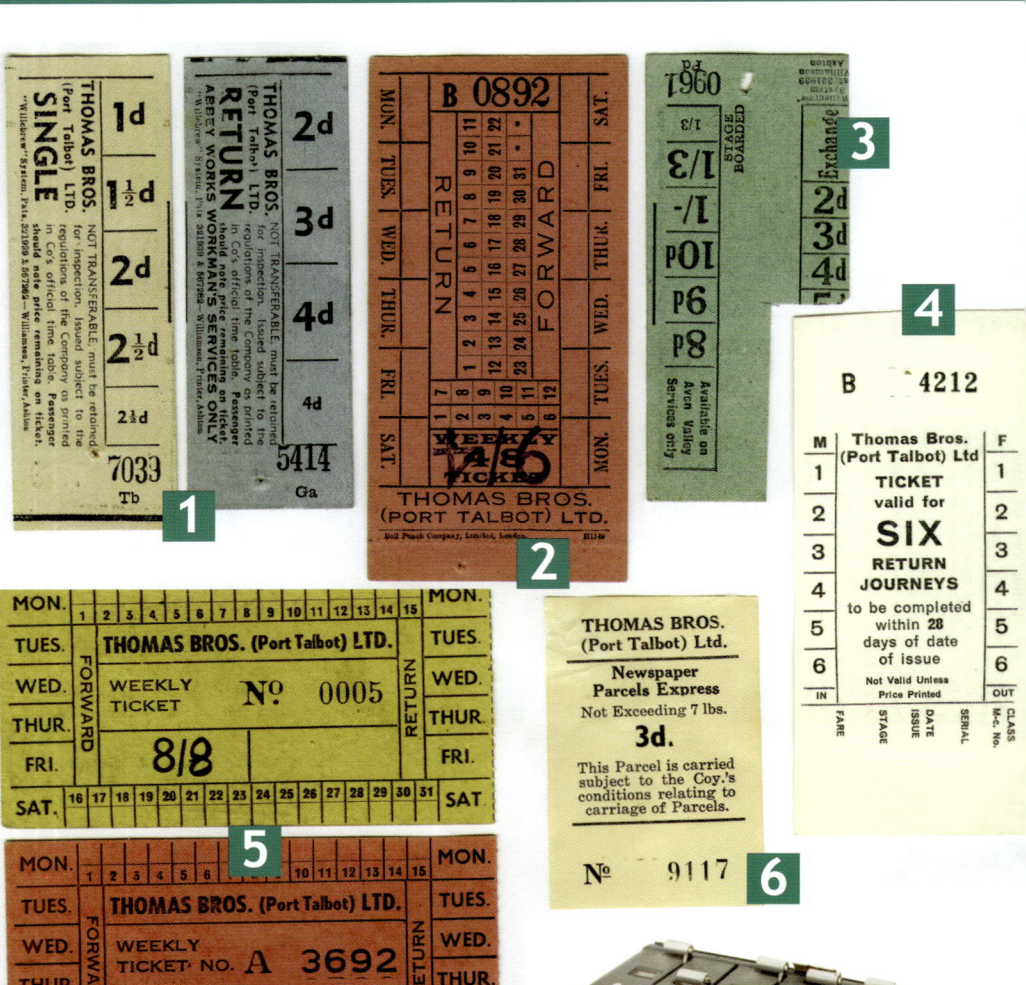

126

Rhiannon Jones told of how her sister and brother-in-law both worked for the company. "Joyce Warren was originally a conductress for Ralph Warren. Later, she became the company's first female bus driver. They both received awards for their safety records," she said.

Raymond Larkman's mother Audrey worked as a Thomas Bros. conductress for many years. "I used to wait for her bus, usually 14 HTG, to turn up on the bus stop opposite Madam Rene's shop in Water Street, to get a free lift home. They were happy days," he recalled..

Three Thomas Bros. conductresses on a staff trip to Malvern, 1957 — Betty downey, Betty Penhale and Edna Wilkinson. *Ann Matthews*

Joy Cross remembered Raymond's mother on the bus as she had to catch it to Tywyn School because the closer Tirmorfa School was overloaded at one time. "She used to give me free rides too," said Joy.

Christine Lawrence was another with family links to the company. "My auntie Muriel Lawrence was a conductress and I think her driver's name was Sid," she said. "I loved going on her bus; she used to let me turn the handle of the ticket machine and give passengers tickets. I felt so important doing that!"

Margaret Matthewman was another who loved travelling on Thomas Bros. buses. "My mother, Joan Thomas, was a bus conductress for a good few years. She loved it — always up early to take the Abbey workers in for their shift. Great memories and good times. I won't forget them ever, she said fondly."

"Thelma Callaghan was the best bus conductress ever," recalled Caron Morgan. "She was fabulous with all us kids — such a kind hearted lady."

Linda John Noble remembers Thelma in the 1960s too, when her dad Charlie Lambert drove for Thomas Bros.

Eileen Reynish regularly caught a No. 2 to get off in Sandown Rd.

"One of the conductresses who used to be on the bus I caught to work in the morning was a friend of my mother's, a lovely lady. Her name was Betty Penhale."

Diane Sambruck thought it was romantic that her mother had first met her father while giving out tickets as a conductress on the Goytre route.

Gerald Tucker knows that conductresses were not always friendly and smiley when performing their duties however.

"I got told off by a Thomas Bros. conductress for shooting her with my

To page 130

Memories in miniature

Mention of names such as Dinky Toys, Corgi, Spot-On or Matchbox to people of a certain age and you are certain to invoke a wave of nostalgia.

Memories of the diecast models made by those manufacturers are often accompanied by a tinge of regret that people no longer have a particular item. Many will have had that 'I had one of those' moment.

The number of toy fairs held each year and the variety of models available in online auction sites is proof enough that there is a buoyant market in vintage models, with buses being particularly popular.

There is also a large market for new collectable diecast models, with Exclusive First Editions (EFE), Oxford Models and Corgi being popular. The most popular scale is 1/76th, although the Corgi Classics 1/50th scale models also have a large following. Some manufacturers, for example Oxford Diecast, Base Toys and Classix have also been producing model ranges suitable for use with OO scale model railways. While many of the models are targeted at followers of the larger or more popular bus operators;

London Transport, Ribble or Southdown, 'niche' operators also get a look in. To date, only two proprietary models of Thomas Bros. vehicles have been produced. In October 2004, EFE released their model No. 12117, a 1961 AEC Reliance/Harrington Cavalier coach, 119 LNY 'Port Talbot Cavalier'. While generally true to its scale, one criticism has always been that the Danube Blue used on the model is a little too light. The other model is that of Thomas Bros. AEC Regent open top vehicle OD 7497 'The Margam Belle', released by Corgi (catalogue No. 97050) in 1993 as part of the 1/64th scale model range in a set with itself in Devon General livery. It is actually based on Corgi's Regent III model, so is definitely not one for the purists.

It is also worth picking out Oxford Models 2012 release no. 76OWB002, a utility Bedford OWB in Ministry of Supply brown livery as supplied to Thomas Bros.

Model marvels

1. A hand built wooden model of Thomas Bros. half cab coach JNY 377 created by an enthusiast.
Jean Rupert
2. Oxford Models produced this Bedford OWB in Second World War Ministry of Supply brown livery.
3. For many years this model occupied the window of the company's Station Road office.
4. Built from kits by Steve Davies. FWN633 hass Longwell Green body while NNY 71 is of Saro heritage.
Steve Davies
5. AEC Regent open topper OD 7497 'The Margam Belle', released by Corgi in 1993.
6. One of the later Leyland Tiger Cubs created from a kit produced by the Westward company.
7. A pair of EFE's model of 1961 Harrington bodied AEC Reliance 119 LNY, Port Talbot Cavalier.

during the Second World War. There are many other model buses which can be adapted to resemble Thomas Bros. vehicles, depending on the livery of the donor model and the ability of the modeller. To take things a stage further, there are a number of kits available which can be assembled and then painted in Thomas Bros. livery.

From page 127

pea shooter on the bus from Madam Rene's." David Davies also suffered the same fate. "I dropped stink bombs on the step of the bus. No smiles then!" he revealed.

Barbara Williams was a clippie with Thomas Bros. from 1960 to 1963. "I loved every minute of it and remember bus TTG 3."

Donald Barrett added: "I remember that registration number well too. When my father was there I can remember him driving it and I would stand at the front," said Donald.

"A story which did the rounds when I was an apprentice involved one of the older drivers who retired shortly after I started. He was Reg Williams or Reggie Bara as he was popularly known. He was a Cwmavon Road driver and was heading through Cwmavon one day when he pulled out in front of a car driven by the local doctor, causing the car to swerve and mount the pavement. The doctor got out in a rage and shouted at Reg: "Williams, you made a mistake then." to which Reg replied, "Yes doctor I did, but we all make mistakes, and most of yours are in Cwmavon Churchyard!"

"Then there was Ron Jenkins, a local chap who wasn't employed as such, but came along to the depot to help out. For his efforts he was given a 'wage' out of canteen funds. Ron become involved as far back as Sandfields Road days as various photos will testify. He would work a full day, sweeping the canteen, stocking its larder, running errands and just being everywhere. One story involving Ron, was that my colleague Tom Warmington asked him to run over to the shops and get him a

A group of driver recipients of Thomas Bros. long service awards, with Bernard Griffiths, company chairman; Mr FJ Woodworth, General manager. In the centre of the group is conductress Kathleen Williams.

Thomas Bros. was a real family affair

Forget all the modern digital and online methods of meeting a partner — you wouldn't have needed them if you worked for Thomas Bros.

The firm was a family affair without doubt and countless couples met up with one another during their daily duties and ended up getting married. In some cases generations were proud to say they worked for the seaside firm.

Karl Jones recalled that his wife's parents met each other when they both worked for Thomas Bros. They were Joe and Phyllis Patterson. Some may remember her by her maiden name which was Williams," he said.

Both Len Llewellyn's parents worked for Thomas Bros. for many years. "Dad was a bus driver and my mother was a conductress," he recalled.

Vicky Smith's parents were also both employed by the company. "My father Eric Edwards was a bus driver and my mother Gladys Edwards was a conductress with Thomas Bros."

Some of those who kept Thomas Bros. running smoothly take time out for a photograph in 1962
Back row from left: Inspector Vic Passmore, Inspector Glyn Morris, Transport Manager Bob Raymond, Chief Clerk Ken Watkins, General Manager Mr Hornblow, Chief Engineer Ernie Lewis, Inspector Dan Phillips, Inspector Killick and Stores Manager Dave Lewis. Front row from left: Clerk Megan Morley, Wages Clerk Brenda Wood, Clerk Jac Davies, Typist Anita Williams, Clerk Sandra Price, Secretary Diane Hooper, Telephonist Gill Matthews and Cash clerk Nell Wallace.

packet of 10 Woodbine cigarettes. "If they haven't got Woodbine, get anything." Tom told him. About 15 minutes later Ron returned and said to Tom: "They didn't have Woodbine, so I bought this." and handed Tom a custard slice!

Myra Mizen had even more family links: "My mother Esther Davies was a conductress. My dad Ralph Davies was a mechanic. My father's twin brother Graham was a driver and my cousin Les was a fitter," she said, adding that she spent many a time down at the depot and on the bus and particularly loved the Thomas Bros. Christmas parties.

Debra Lewis's aunt and uncle Bill and Jeannie Eldridge from Acacia Avenue also both worked there. "They even lived close by in Acacia Avenue," she said.

There is no doubt that Thomas Bros. was one of those companies that had a family feel about it.

Conductress Val Mort and driver Harland Richards with KNY 418, a 1950 Tilling-Stevens vehicle taken over from Davies Bros. Harland served the bus industry for 60 years, starting on horse drawn vehicles in Cwmavon. He became a bus driver in 1923, joining Thomas Bros. in 1931 before finally retiring in 1970.

'Staff had to service buses without proper facilities with bus wash water coming from a nearby stream in summer'

An aerial view of Port Talbot showing the mixed collection of buildings that made up the old depot around 1950.

As the Thomas Bros. company developed so too did not only its vehicles but also its properties including its garage and office facilities. Staff also progressed from one role to another and like many similar small companies families were often their lifeblood with grandparents, parents and children regularly involved.

Memories abound of people who at some point worked for the company as will have been seen with the fond recollections of road crews but there were others behind the scenes who played an equally important part in keeping the town of Port Talbot on the move.

Among these were the mechanics and maintenance staff as well as the administrative workers. They were all part of the team that made things work, kept the wheels turning and the passengers happy.

On the engineering side that wasn't always an easy task. The early garaging facilities were nothing if not primitive, yet the staff still managed to keep what were often ageing, well used vehicles on the road.

Modern premises that made life easier for staff

The view from the washing plant at Acacia Avenue shortly after opening. The former Rhondda and Swansea Bay Railway line alongside is now the busy A4241 Afan Way peripheral distributor road.

Driver Ralph Davies with a company colleague.
Myra Mizen

The primitive workshop area of the old Sandfields Road depot, far different to the improved working area in the new depot built at Acacia Avenue.

When BET took over at Thomas Bros. in 1951, buses were being maintained in an outdated 6,000 sq. ft. corrugated iron and timber facility in Sandfields Road, Aberavon. This was a legacy of the fact that the company had been built up from a disparate collection of small operators.

Lack of depot space meant that buses needed to be stored outside on an ash surface. A second overspill site was used occasionally, in the Port Talbot Docks area. Staff had the unenviable task of maintaining buses without adequate facilities with virtually all engineering work being tackled in cramped accommodation. In summer, if there was a hosepipe ban, water for cleaning buses had to be brought from a local stream.

Gilbert Ball has good reason to remember the early Thomas Bros garage. "It used to be on the old Fairfield at the top end of Sandfields Road. It was constructed from black painted corrugated sheets. I once had the task of climbing up onto the roof to recover my football. Unfortunately I fell off during the attempt and knocked myself out."

Les Davies recalled the camaraderie at the Acacia Avenue depot. "I was an apprentice there from 1963 with some great friends and colleagues," he said. "Apprenticeship covered all aspects of engine maintenance and rebuilds and also the preparation and inspection vehicles for their MOT test, as well as day to day maintenance.

"Sadly, everything changed when South Wales Transport took over and all the technical work was taken across to the company's main Ravenhill depot in Swansea.

"My father was a bus driver for Thomas Bros from the 1950s while my uncle, his twin brother, was a fitter in the garage right up until his retirement.

Raymond Dowrick also remembered when the old garage was on the former Fairfield

'Oi, Gerourofit!' came the shout

When the author . . .

Back in 1969 as naïve 12 year olds attending Dynevor School in Swansea, a few friends who were 'bus spotters' formed a club, ambitiously called the 'Swansea & District Omnibus Club'. Meetings were held at the back of geography lessons and a newsletter was handwritten on paper ripped from an exercise book. Eventually, we amassed the grand total of nine members, a couple of whom had no idea why they had joined, but admitted it seemed like a good idea.

One cold Saturday morning in February, armed with what were then called 'Runabout' tickets, two hardy souls – myself and Howard Williams – took it upon ourselves to visit Acacia Avenue depot. Naturally, of course, no prior permission from the company had been sought for the visit; it probably never even entered our heads. In those days, 'Health' meant you didn't have to see a doctor and 'Safety' was one of those funny pins you sometimes needed to hold your trousers up.

The newsletter later reported:

"After a while we found the Thomas Bros. garage at Acacia Avenue. It is not a big garage and quite a few vehicles have to be parked outside.

"We saw the two open toppers (GHT 127 & CAP 205) in the garage, both looking rather dusty. We were also fortunate enough to see PTG 239F, the new Duple Commander bodied Reliance.

"Whilst examining a Leyland Panther outside, a dirty old mechanic in an equally dirty old pair of dungarees shouted at us. So needless to say, we beat a hasty retreat!

"We had some unusual finds, including Great Yarmouth Setright tickets and part of an Aldershot & District timetable."

Happy, carefree days, without doubt!

Leyland Tiger NNY 56 about to get a wash and brush up at the Sandfields Road garage. Armed for the operation are, from left: D Amphlett, M Davies, Mrs Jones and R Richards.
Clare James

near the Aberavon Quins RFC clubhouse off Sandfields Road. "I remember there was a bus strike in the 1950s and I used to walk through the Fairfield garage on my way to school. There were so many buses parked up it was like a maze and I was lucky to get through, but it did make me late for school."

Meanwhile Tom Edwards actually worked there. "My first job after leaving school was as assistant storekeeper at the garage from 1950 to 1953," he said. "They were great times with fitters and apprentices driving buses around the garage yard. Then after National Service I came back as a wages clerk at the top office near the railway gates in Station Road, from 1955 to 1959."

Pat Harrington recalled where some of the company's worn tyres went: "As a child I was brought up in Fairfield. Thomas Bros. had their garage alongside the Fairfield where Harlequin Road was later built.

"Half of our huge bonfire for Bonfire Night was old tyres which they used to give us to burn. The fire would last for days.
There would be no chance of that happening today though."

Joanne Roberts' grandfather Gilbert Bish worked for them, along with Ron James Gilbert the coachbuilder. The other two coachbuilders were Sid Williams from Briton Ferry and Billy Routecliff from Sandfields."

Eventually Thomas Bros. moved its operations to a newly built state of the art garage at Acacia Avenue, Sandfields.

Ron James served his apprenticeship with Thomas Bros. starting in the old garage at the bottom end of Sandfields Road before moving to the new premises in Acacia Avenue.

"It was very modern for that time with central heating and sunken workshops," he recalled. "The garage opened in 1958. My father also worked there."

Alan Evans was another apprentice. "I served my time as an apprentice fitter from 1963 to 1967 when Tom Warmington was foreman and Mr Beetham was the manager," he said.

Anita James recalled her father Doug Amphlett working in the garage and driving the buses. "He had the distinction of driving the first bus into the new Acacia Avenue garage and also drove the company's first automatic bus," she said. "Times have changed especially with the advent of what they called 'one man-ers' with no conductresses."

Cathy Llewellyn lived alongside the bus depot in Acacia Avenue. "The noise and smell of diesel at 6am every morning wasn't a great

The original Thomas Bros. booking office at 40A Station Road, Port Talbot.

memory, but I loved growing up there," she recalled fondly.

"My mother was a conductress for a little while and I used to stand up at the front of the bus and sing when we got on the bus my mother was working on."

Lorraine Stevenson was another for whom the smell of diesel lingered long. "We lived just down the road from the bus depot in Acacia Avenue. I still remember the smell of the diesel when we played near there."

Diane Whittaker lived close by in Southville Road and used to go to the canteen window to buy bags of chips, while Susan Sullivan's mother used to clean the buses. They both have happy memories of the busy garage.

Peter Willment worked for them when they were being taken over by South Wales Transport. "The cooks in the Sandfields depot were a Mrs. Davies from Baglan, and a woman named Stella."

Most of all he recalled the buses: "Those Leyland Tiger Cubs were great to drive, he said."

The hunt for a site on which to build a new depot had begun almost immediately after the BET takeover. Surprisingly, in an industrial town such as Port Talbot where ample space for a new structure might be expected, great difficulty was experienced in finding one.

The site eventually selected was in residential Sandfields Estate and as a result plans met with much opposition which further hindered progress in. Because of this, it wasn't until 25th April 1957 that construction of Thomas Bros. much-needed new facility began.

In due course, a bright, new building was constructed at Acacia Avenue alongside the track of the Rhondda and Swansea Bay Railway line. This was on what would now be called a greenfield site and measured three acres. The smart new structure which incorporated a spacious head office, opened in June 1958. Thomas Bros. was now self-sufficient in engineering terms apart from any fibreglass body parts which were sourced from Western Welsh. Tenders for the demolition of the old garage were issued by Port Talbot Borough Council in September that year.

Dai Morris, eventually an engineer for the company, joined as an apprentice in 1964, working as a fitter until 1969 when he went to SWT. He recalled the names of many he worked with in the early days of his career:

"Garage staff in 1964 included Chief Engineer, Ernie Lewis; Stores Manager, Dave Thomas; Garage Foreman, L A (Tom) Warmington; Fitters Ralph Davies, Percy Croucher, Geoff Chapple and John Floyd; Coachbuilders Sid Williams and Gilbert Bish; Painter, Jeff (Dougie) Foulgar; Greaser Arthur Gardner; Fueler/Cleaners, Jim (The Milk) Thomas, Will Hale, Harland Richards (Ex-senior coach driver, leading up to retirement) There were two women day cleaners and apprentices, Dennis Richards, Ron James, Alan Evans, Colin Thomas, Les Davies, Wayne Jolley, and of course myself!

The new depot and head office at Acacia Avenue, Sandfields, Port Talbot which was opened with much ceremony on June 6th 1958. The lunch menu at the Walnut Tree Hotel included Mock Turtle Soup that day!

The Travel Corner agency at Bethany Square, Port Talbot with, below, B. Hibberd and Valerie Hughes at the front desk.

"Tom Warmington would normally be responsible for unit rebuilds and everything else, Ralph Davies normally manned the fuel pump shop and Percy Croucher would deal with electrics.

"As apprentices we would spend our first year working in the stores with Dave Thomas, or in the paint shop with Dougie. We would then progress to spending time with Tom on unit rebuilds and some time with Ralph in the pump room, before being let loose on the pits with the shift fitters. Saturday mornings saw us on workshop cleaning duties which was compulsory for all apprentices. Two apprentices worked Sunday mornings on a rota basis, one topping batteries, the other changing Plaza cinema stickers which were stuck to bus side windows advertising what was being shown at the local Plaza cinema the following week. Incidentally, Bob Raymond, who was Thomas Bros. Traffic Manager, was at the same time manager of the Plaza!"

The new offices at Acacia Avenue were a far cry from the first public office which was opened at 129 Station Road in December 1931. The later office for tours and tickets was at 40A Station Road while Thomas Bros. opened a new, enlarged tours and holiday booking office at Travel Corner, Bethany Square in July 1968, which brought closure of the former office at 40A Station Road.

Scattered each tell

Although Thomas Bros. as a company has long vanished from the transport scene, a handful of its vehicles fortunately live on in preservation. The known survivors can be seen on these pages.

1 One of the AEC Regals purchased soon after the BET group took over, DOD 474 is at the West of England Transport collection in Devon where it is being restored to its original Devon General condition. it is seen still with traces of the paint applied by Thomas Bros.

2 This - believe it or not - is the heavily rebuilt Thomas Bros. vehicle GNY 764. The new body was constructed by Debono and it is believed that the bus still exists in Malta. The original vehicle is pictured on page 152.

3 The only surviving Thomas Bros. Leyland Tiger Cub, OBX 781, was a former James, Ammanford vehicle which joined the Port Talbot fleet in 1968 as part of the BET/NBC re-organisation. It never carried the blue livery, but was instead painted in the standard red colours. It was last heard of being used as a traveller's home near Bristol.

survivors their tale

4 Bristol K5G GHT 127, formerly 'The Sandfields Belle' restored to its former Brighton, Hove & District cream and black livery and is pictured at the Bristol Harbourside bus rally on 22nd May 2005. *Richard Field*

5 CAP 205 Another Bristol K5G, it is seen here derelict at the premises of Seeboyers, Agricultural Engineers, Havelock, Ontario, Canada in 2012.

6 AEC Regent OD 7497 is pictured at the Devon General centenary celebration which took place at Newton Abbot racecourse on 4th August, 2019. Now restored to its former Devon General livery, the bus proudly carried the name 'The Margam Belle' during its distant days with the Thomas Bros operation. *Richard Field*

7 Nowadays in store at Barry, Vale of Glamorgan, AEC Regal IV coach MTG 172 awaits restoration and is seen at the Swansea Bus Museum, on 3rd August, 2014. *Richard Field*

8 The one that got away. For a time, SARO bodied Tiger Cub NNY 70 languished at Port Talbot and there was a scheme to restore it. Alas, this wasn't to be and the bus was eventually and sadly, scrapped.

New beginnings

The opening of the new buildings at Acacia Avenue in June 1958 must have been welcomed universally by all the staff. The building was certainly an improvement on everything that had gone before and lived up to its role as Head Office.

The staff who populated the spacious offices had an equally important part to play as the glue which held the whole operation together. Among them was Dawn Margetson who recalled her pride in the part she played. "My first job after leaving school was working in the bus office above the chemist store in High Street, alongside the River Afan and right by the bridge. There was a bay window on the first floor directly over the river and believe it or not that was my desk.

"The conductors and conductresses used to come in to pay in their takings and I had to tally the money with their ticket numbers and then give them receipts. At 14, I was so proud of myself then."

Thomas Bros apprentices Wayne Jolly, Ron James, John Aubrey and Dennis Richards in the early 1960s.
Dai Morris

Caroline Haimes started her first job as a telephonist and receptionist at the depot in Acacia Avenue. "It was a fun place to work and I loved every minute," she said.

Gillian Davison also worked there. "I got on well with the office staff, garage staff and the bus crews," she said. "It was a real friendly place in which to work."

Rob Duncan recalled that his mother Anne contributed to the firm by doing part of the wages. "She worked from home during the late 1950s and I remember her using a small adding machine," he said.

Apprentices Colin Thomas and Gary Gardner decided the engine cover of open topper GHT 127 was the place to be for this break time snapshot while in front, from the left are: Tom Warmington, foreman; Percy Croucher, fitter; Peter Jones, coachbuilder, along with apprentices Viv Evans, Ronnie Jenkins, Brian Skerry, Les Davies and Dai Morris.
Dai Morris

Fitters at work in the service bays of the newly opened Acacia Avenue depot in 1958.

A Dawson washing plant at Acacia Avenue made cleaners' lives much easier, as is seen here.

Bernard Jones told of how his mother Madge Jones was a cook in the Thomas Bros. canteen in Forge Road, just opposite the Odeon Cinema, before transferring to be a conductress in the early 1960s."

Frank Berni has a different reason for recalling the Acacia Avenue offices though:

"As children living in Southdown View we would go to the Thomas Bros. depot at the crossroads of Southdown Road and Acacia Avenue and buy sweets, ice cream and best of all caps for our cap guns. Also, from 1962 I started catching the bus from the bus stop between Southville Road and Longview Road to Tywyn School. I have lots of happy memories linked to the company," he said.

The building, which is still in use as a bus depot, stands on a rectangular site and is a steel-framed structure supporting a light steel trussed roof. The external elevations and roof are clad with cement sheeting, with the roof incorporating glazed panels to provide excellent natural lighting to the workshop. The building is entered via roller shutter doors at each end, providing clear, open space and is fitted with a number of full length vehicle servicing pits, body shop, paint shop, machine shop and stores.

The ultimate challenge

L. 'Ernie' Lewis, AMIRTE.

The man with the ultimate challenge of keeping the fleet in good order and calming the high spirits of the apprentices was Chief Engineer L. 'Ernie' Lewis. Ernie was born at Bargoed on 23rd January 1920. After he had served a five year apprenticeship with the Glamorgan and Monmouthshire Motor Co., he joined Reliance Motors in 1939 as a chargehand leading fitter. Following service in the Second World War he was appointed foreman with Thomas Bros. in 1947, being promoted to the role of chief engineer when the company became part of the BET Group in 1951.

'Nationalisation meant that slowly, but surely the Thomas Bros. operation was absorbed into SWT oblivion'

Having imposed its identity in the 1970s, National Bus back tracked a decade later. The Market Analysis Project schemes sought to revive local brands as SWT Leyland National 777 illustrates.

In the years after nationalisation, Port Talbot depot, its staff and the local bus services became fully integrated into the SWT network. The coach fleet became part of SWT's enlarged coaching activity, initially based at Singleton Street, Swansea, while Travel Corner at Bethany Square became part of SWT's booking office network, eventually becoming a fully functioning travel agency.

From 1973, new vehicles allocated to Port Talbot included the ubiquitous Leyland Nationals and lightweight Ford R1014s, all in the standard National Bus 'poppy' red livery. Former Thomas Bros. vehicles moved out to other SWT depots; the SNY AEC Reliances went to Brunswick Street depot, Swansea. More notably, Leyland Tiger Cubs RTG 140F, VTG 142G and VTG 143G were transferred to the company's westernmost outpost at Haverfordwest. Here, they joined the mainly Leyland fleet which was a remnant of the depot's former Western Welsh ownership. VTG 142G later became SWT's last operational Tiger Cub.

A change of colour and what might have been

At the time of the takeover VTX 7 became the first Thomas Bros vehicle to be painted red. It had been in a serious collision with a road tanker in Station Road, Port Talbot in 1963. *Roy Marshall, copyright The Bus Archive.*

A group of staff at Acacia Avenue depot during the time SWT was taking over Thomas Bros which will explain the red buses along with the mix of uniforms. Back Row, from left: Dai Haymer, George Lloyd, Margi Fox, Tudor Griffiths and Denzil Henwood. Front: Edna Jones, unidentified, Nancy Miller and Gwyneth Allsopp with what looks to be a new Setright ticket machine.

Thomas Bros. Lineage

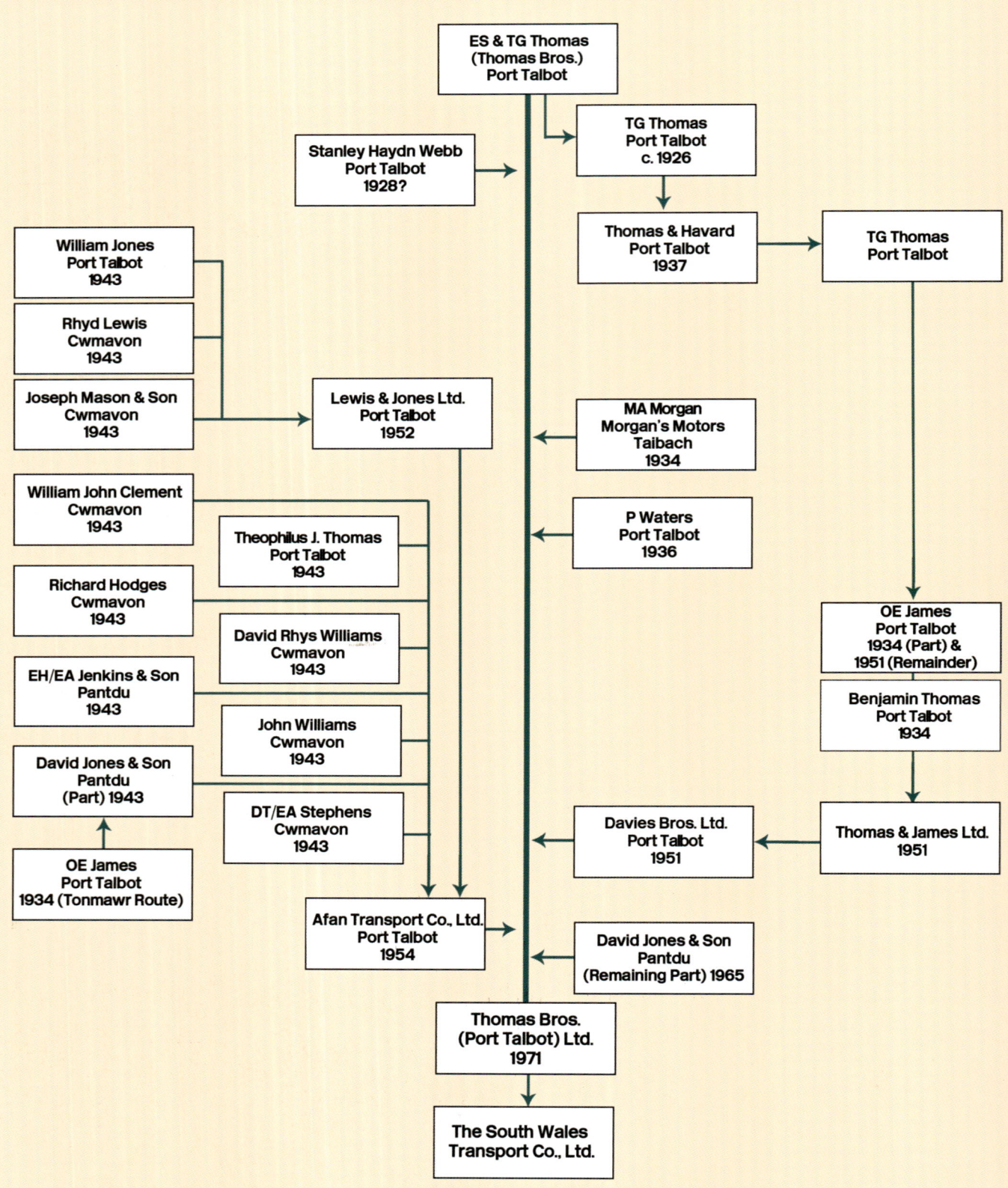

In SWT's dual purpose livery and carrying fleet number 421, DNY 131C has a good load as it returns to Sandfields Estate.

Meanwhile, 16 HTG and 123 NTX soldiered on as towing vehicles for a few years.

The final Thomas Bros. bus to be taken out of regular service was AEC Reliance MNY 135E which was withdrawn in the autumn of 1981. At this time, Port Talbot depot became the storage point — some would say dumping ground — for withdrawn SWT vehicles. The vandalised remains of many buses were gathered there prior to dispatch, usually to one of the several breaking yards in Barnsley.

Service revisions in connection with a National Bus 'Marketing Analysis Project' took place in June 1980. At this time, Port Talbot area services were rebranded under the 'Afanway' name. This was a recognition perhaps that large, anonymous bus operators are not always favoured by local bus users and local government. It is a conundrum which the larger bus operators wrestle with to this day.

On 26th October 1986 the Transport Act 1985 was implemented which deregulated local bus services. With the new legislation came a return to the 1920s with any operator free to register a bus service. SWT faced competition from the likes of Jervis and Margam Cabs in the Port Talbot area, initially using vehicles which were not really suited to local bus operation.

SWT of course continued as a National Bus Company until privatisation in a management buy-out in 1987. Within a year SWT had bought long established operator AE & FR Brewer of Caerau. That company was then enlarged to operate SWT's eastern area services, including those at Port Talbot. SWT and Brewers were in turn sold to Badgerline in 1990 and became part of the emerging FirstGroup in 1995. The separate company identities were abandoned and changed to the present First Cymru Buses Ltd., in 1999.

But what would have happened if Thomas Bros. hadn't sold out to BET in the 1950s? Port Talbot's population was growing at that time so it should have become a successful local independent company. The nearest comparisons we can make are with Llynfi of Maesteg and Brewers of Caerau. These were self-contained operators with a mixed bag of mainly secondhand vehicles. Eventually they sold out to SWT and their names disappeared from the scene. Probably, given the changes in the bus industry in the 1980s, declining patronage, increasing car use and rising costs it's fair to assume that Thomas Bros. would have gone the same way. It's all speculation, of course, but that seems the most likely scenario. The end result would have been a situation very similar to that which prevails today.

A time of transition brought a mixture of red and blue liveried buses at the Acacia Avenue depot.

Firms in Thomas Bros.

Name & Legal Address	Started	Ended	Routes	AVBOA Member
William John Clement, 5, David's Row (1925), 15, Sea View, Aberavon (1927), 21, Ynysygwas, Cwmavon (1931), 70, Sandfields Road, Aberavon (1939).	Jun-23	Aug-43	Aberavon - Cwmavon & Pontrhydyfen/ Tonmawr	Yes
Richard Hodges, 10, Tymaen Street (1923), 1, Salem Street (1931), 31, Salem Road 1933-39) Cwmavon.	Aug-23	Dec-41	Aberavon - Cwmavon & Pontrhydyfen/Tonmawr	Yes
Owen Elias James, 65, Velindre Street, Port Talbot.	1932?	Mar-34	Aberavon Beach - Margam (Groes). Aberavon - Dyffryn Rhondda Colliery. Cwmavon - Cefn Coed Colliery.	
Elizabeth Ann Jenkins (Formerly E.H. Jenkins & Son), 47, Pantdu, Aberavon.	Oct-21	8/43?	Pwllglaw - Glenhafod Colliery.	Yes
David Jones & Son, Avon Hill House, Pantdu, Port Talbot.	Apr-24	Sep-65	Aberavon - Cwmavon & Pontrhydyfen/Tonmawr. Cwmavon - Dyffryn Rhondda Colliery. Cymmer - Cefn Coed Colliery. Cwmavon - Taibach (Steelworks).	Yes
William Jones, 12, Glyndwr Street, Port Talbot.	1923?	1944	Aberavon - Cwmavon & Pontrhydyfen/Tonmawr. Port Talbot - Bryn Colliery.	Yes
Rhyd Lewis, Gadlys Depot Garage, Depot Road, Cwmavon.	Sep-28	1944	Aberavon - Cwmavon & Pontrhydyfen/Tonmawr.	Yes
Joseph Mason & Son, 13, Tymaen Street, Cwmavon.	Jul-21	1944	Aberavon - Cwmavon & Pontrhydyfen/Tonmawr.	Yes
Lewis & Jones, 12, Glyndwr Street, Port Talbot.	1944	Feb-52	Aberavon - Cwmavon & Pontrhydyfen/Tonmawr. Port Talbot - Bryn Colliery.	
Mary Anne Morgan/Rhys Morgan (t/a Morgan's Motors), 17, High Street, Taibach.	Jan-28	Sep-34	Goytre - Bethany Square and Goytre - Aberavon Beach	Yes
David Thomas Stephens/Elizabeth Anne Stephens, 68, Gower Street, Cwmavon.	Sep-24	Aug-43	Aberavon - Cwmavon & Pontrhydyfen/Tonmawr.	Yes
Benjamin Thomas, 17, Margam Terrace, Port Talbot.	Oct-21	Mar-34	Aberavon Beach - Margam (Groes).	Yes
Theophilus J. Thomas, 20, Glyndwr Street, Port Talbot.	May-21	Aug-43	Aberavon - Cwmavon & Pontrhydyfen/Tonmawr	Yes
P. Waters, 14, Blodwen Street, Port Talbot.	1933?	Apr-36		
Stanley Haydn Webb, 15, Tymaen Street, Port Talbot.	Aug-22	Sep-28	Aberavon Beach - Cwmavon	Yes
David Rhys Williams, Arfon Cottage, Cunard Row, Cwmavon/18, Johns Terrace, Tonmawr.	Feb-23	Jul-39	Aberavon - Cwmavon & Pontrhydyfen/Tonmawr.	Yes
John Williams, 4, Salem Road, Cwmavon.	Mar-33	Aug-43	Aberavon - Cwmavon & Pontrhydyfen/Tonmawr.	Yes
E.S. & T.G. Thomas (1920), 1, Alfred Street, Aberavon. Thomas Bros. (Formed 1931), Thomas Bros. (Port Talbot) Ltd. (1933) 2, Talbot Street, Aberavon	1920	Dec-70	Aberavon Beach - Taibach - Goytre. Aberavon Beach - Margam (Groes). Port Talbot - Pontrhydyfen. Pwllyglaw to Cefn Coed Colliery (1934).	
Thomas Gwyn Thomas, 1, Alfred Street, Aberavon.	1934	1934?		
Thomas & Havard, 1, Alfred Street, 81, Sandfields Road, Aberavon.	1934	1937		
Afan Transport Co., Ltd., Port Talbot.	1943	Nov-54	Aberavon - Cwmavon & Pontrhydyfen. Contract services.	
Davies Bros. Ltd./Richard Selway Davies, 2, Grugoes Terrace, Port Talbot.	Mar-34	Jun-51	Aberavon Beach - Margam. Margam - Elba Tinplate Works.	
Thomas & James Ltd., 4, High Street, Aberavon.	Mar-34	Jun-51	Aberavon Beach - Margam (Groes). Cwmavon - Cefn Coed Colliery. Aberavon Beach to Maudlam refused in 1934.	

genealogy

Notes

Acquired by Afan Transport Co. Ltd.

AVBOA. Acquired by Thomas Bros (Port Talbot) Ltd.

Sold to Davies Bros. in 1934, who bought B. Thomas at the same time to form Thomas & James. Set up again in 1936 for private hire until 1951.

Acquired by Afan Transport Co., Ltd.

Took over Jenkins, Pantdu and B. Thomas, Port Talbot. Services only were acquired by Afan Transport in 1952. Continued with private hire and contract work until sold to Thomas Bros. (Port Talbot) Ltd. in 1965.

These three were merged to form Lewis & Jones in 1944, selling out to Afan Transport in 1952.

An amalgamation of Rhyd Lewis, William Jones and Joseph Mason. Acquired by Thomas Bros. (Port Talbot) Ltd. subsidiary Afan Transport Co., Ltd. in 1952.
Acquired by Thomas Bros (Port Talbot) Ltd. Continued as private hire operator called Red Triangle until 1938.

Acquired by Afan Transport Co. Ltd.

Sold to Davies Bros. in 1934, who bought O. E. James at the same time to form Thomas & James.

Acquired by Afan Transport Co. Ltd.

Acquired by Thomas Bros (Port Talbot) Ltd.

Acquired by Afan Transport Co. Ltd.

Acquired by Afan Transport Co. Ltd.
The founding business of what later became Thomas Bros. (Port Talbot) Ltd. E.S. Thomas died c.1926 and T.G. Thomas operated alone and later with H.T. Havard. Bought out by O.E. James. Formed subsidiary Afan Transport Co., Ltd. in 1943 to consolidate AVBOA operators on the Aberavon - Cwmavon & Pontrhydyfen corridor. Acquired by BET June 1951.

T.G. Thomas operated in his own name, later forming a partnership with H.T. Havard (Thomas & Havard) until 1937. He then returned to being a sole trader until bought out by O.E. James.
Ended 1937 when T.G. Thomas applied for the licences in his own name. Taken over by Owen E James.
Set up by Thomas Bros. (Port Talbot) Ltd. in 1943. Absorbed R. Hodges, J. Williams, W. Clement, T.Thomas, D. R. Williams, Thomas (Brynbryddan). Afan Transport Co., Ltd. was wound up and combined with Thomas Bros. in 1954.

Set up Thomas & James Ltd. when they acquired Benjamin Thomas and Owen Elias James in 1934.

Set up by Davies Bros. to acquire B. Thomas and O.E.James on formation in 1934. O.E.James set up again in 1936 for private hire, continuing until 1951.

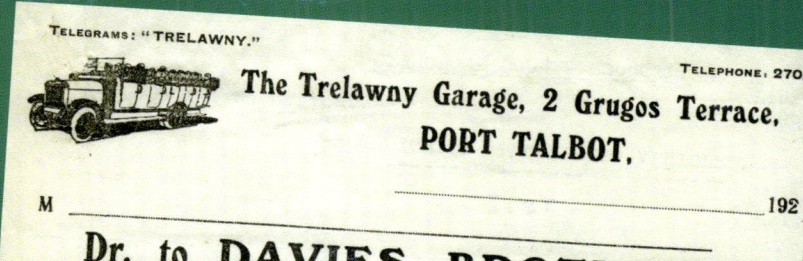

Davies Bros' 1931 Morris Dictator saloon TH 1511 creates a wave in the floodwaters near Port Talbot General railway station as it passes a Western Welsh AEC Renown double decker.

This 1948 AEC Regal III was operated by Jones of Pantdu. The Longwell Green 39-seat bus bodied vehicle had previously carried a coach body built by Longford.

On 17 July 1951 guests arrive for the opening of the new hot strip mill at the Abbey Works. The coach is a neatly turned out Crossley SD42/6 of 1949 JTG 63 with its original D.J.Davies 33 seat body belonging to David Jones & Son, Pantdu.

147

A day in the life

The following is a partial crew and vehicle allocation list from 5th December 1958, unearthed by former SWT manager Peter Heath. Of interest are the duties which particular individuals were working that day, together with the vehicles which were being used.

The low numbers in the right hand column refer to the registrations of the Leyland Tiger Cub fleet, but the list also shows the last of the ageing pre-BET vehicles, being used for works and schools services.

377: A 1948 Leyland PS1, registered HNY 377.

415: A 1948 Leyland PS1, registered HNY 415.

418: A 1950 TSM K6LA7, registered KNY 418.

480: A 1946 AEC Regal, registered HTT 480.

549: A 1949 Dennis Lancet J3, registered JTG 549.

633: A 1949 AEC Regal III, registered FWN 633.

675: A 1949 AEC Regal III, registered JNY 675.

764: A 1948 AEC Regal III, registered GNY 764.

More information about these vehicles can be found in the fleet list.

Driver Harland Richards with AEC Regal JNY 675, 1949. The record shows that on 5th December 1958, 675 worked the 4.30pm service from the Abbey Works to Tonmawr. Meanwhile Harland had started his day on an early shift, working a contract from Tonmawr before going on to work local services between Sandfields and Port Talbot.

CONDUCTORS	DETAILS FOR **FRIDAY 5TH DECEMBER 1958**		DRIVER/BUS (Reg No.)
	Garage... 5.00 a.m. H. Richards, R. Richards, D. Mort, V. Davies.		
	Station to Maudlam Bridge	7.00 a.m.}	R.Richards/65
	Station to Mc Alpine	7.35 a.m.}	ditto
N. Jones	Brynbryddan to Talbot Square	8.30 a.m.}	ditto
	Bethany Square to Abbey Works (via Margam)	8.40 a.m.}	ditto
	Margam to Beach	9.00 a.m.}	ditto
	Brynbryddan to Talbot Square (FRIDAY ONLY)	9.15 a.m.}	ditto
	Southdown Road Roundabout to Station	3.30 p.m.}	M.Stephens/549
	Central School to Goytre	3.45 p.m.}	ditto
	N.T.O. to Bethany Square	4.40 p.m.}	ditto
	Abbey Works Offices to Estate 1	5.10 p.m.}	ditto
	Tonmawr to Abbey (CONTRACT)	7.15 a.m.}	H.Richards/764
	Estate 2 to Market	8.30 a.m.}	H.Richards/62
K. Williams	Market to Abbey Works (via Margam)	8.40 a.m.}	ditto
	Margam to Estate 1	9.05 a.m.}	ditto
	Southdown Road Roundabout to Market	3.30 p.m.}	Terry Davies/6
	Catholic School to Margam	3.45 p.m.}	ditto
	Cold Mill to N.T.O.	4.30 p.m.}	ditto
	N.T.O. to Goytre (Also pick up at Talbot Arms Taibach via Margam)	4.40 p.m.}	ditto
	N.T.O. to Estate 2...to leave N.T.O.	5.05 p.m.}	ditto
	and to run via South Road and leave Staff Offices	5.10 p.m.}	ditto

# of buses and drivers

V.Mort	Cash Clerk Duty	7.30 a.m.}	A.Gardner/61
	Station to McAlpine	7.35 a.m.}	ditto
	Pontrhydyfen to Camavon School	8.35 a.m.}	ditto
	MEAL BREAK - PICK UP BUS AT GARAGE		
	Estate 1 to Groes	4.16 p.m.}	V.Davies/67
	Groes to Beach	4.44 p.m.}	ditto
	Beach to Groes	5.09 p.m.}	ditto
	Groes to Estate 1	5.30 p.m.}	ditto

USE DUTY 18.A. VEHICLE AND WORK FOLLOWING JOURNEYS:-

L.Webb	Estate 1 to Market	4.05 p.m.}	D. Nichols
	Market to Estate 2	4.20 p.m.}	ditto
	Market to Estate 1	4.50 p.m.}	ditto
	Estate 1 to Market	5.06 p.m.}	ditto
	Market to Estate 2	5.20 p.m.}	ditto
	Estate 2 to Market	5.36 p.m.}	ditto
	Market to Estate 1	5.50 p.m.}	ditto

R.Feehely	Estate 2 to Station	8.03 a.m.}	**P.Croucher/54**
	Estate 1 to Station	8.35 a.m.}	ditto
	Central Schools to Goytre via Park School	4.00 p.m.}	**C.Lambert/764**
	Cold Mill to N.T.O.	4.30 p.m.}	ditto
	N.T.O. to Estate 2 (Put PRIVATE on destination board after		
	Leaving A.Works/Parry's 1st Stop)	4.40 p.m.}	ditto
	Dry Docks to Groes (Pick up on service)	5.00 p.m.}	ditto
	Groes to Estate 2	5.30 p.m.}	ditto

M.Parr	Southdown Road Roundabout to Market	3.30 p.m.}	A.Wilson/68
	Catholic School (Bailey Street) to Estate 2	3.45 p.m.}	ditto
	C.R. Shop to Estate 2	4.35 p.m.}	ditto
	Estate 1 to Talbot Arms, Taibach	5.05 p.m.}	ditto
	Taibach to Estate 1	5.25 p.m.}	ditto
	Estate 1 to N.T.O.	9.25 p.m.}	ditto
	N.T.O. to Cold Mill and Main Canteen	9.45 p.m.}	ditto
	Main Canteen and Cold Mill to N.T.O.	10.05 p.m.}	ditto
	N.T.O. to Estate 1	10.10 p.m.}	ditto

J.Hill	TO TAKE DUTY 14.A. BUS AT TERMINUS AND DO THE FOLLOWING JOURNEYS:-		
	Estate 2 to Velindre	4.41 p.m.}	R.Warren
	Velindre to Estate 2	5.05 p.m.}	ditto

Myra Evans	Southdown Road Roundabout to Market	3.30 p.m.}	B. Harrington/62
	Catholic School (Bailey Street) to Estate 1	3.45 p.m.}	ditto
	Central Repair Shop to Market	4.35 p.m.}	ditto
	Abbey Works to Estate 2 (Staff)	5.10 p.m.}	ditto
	Aberavon to Brynbryddan & Tabor	9.05 p.m.}	ditto
	Tabor & Brynbryddan to Aberavon	9.15 p.m.}	ditto
	Market to N.T.O.	9.30 p.m.}	ditto
	N.T.O. to Cold Mill (2 Journeys)	9.45 p.m.}	ditto
	Cold Mill to N.T.O. (2 Journeys)	10.07 p.m.}	ditto
	N.T.O. to Estate 1	10.10 p.m.}	ditto
G. Davies	Southdown Road Roundabout to Groes	3.25 p.m.}	V. Passmore/64
	Groes School Children to Taibach (Wern Road)	3.45 p.m.}	ditto
	Eastern School Children to Groes (via Shopping Centre)	4.00 p.m.}	ditto
	Brick Stores to Estate 2 (via West Road)	4.35 p.m.}	ditto
	Estate 1 to N.T.O.	9.25 p.m.}	ditto
	N.T.O. to Cold Mill	9.45 p.m.}	ditto
	Cold Mill to N.T.O.	10.07 p.m.}	ditto
	N.T.O. to Estate 2.	10.10 p.m.}	ditto
	Abbey Works Bus Park to Tonmawr	4.30 p.m.}	W.H. Pike/415
	Margam to Wern Works	9.30 p.m.}	ditto
	Wern Works to Margam	10.05 p.m.}	ditto
M. Bevan	STANDBY AT GARAGE	5.00 a.m. to 9.00 a.m.	59
	Estate 2 to Groes	4.06 p.m.}	G. Morris/61
	Groes to Beach	4.34 p.m.}	ditto
	Beach to Goytre	4.59 p.m.}	ditto
	Goytre to Estate 2	5.20 p.m.}	ditto
	Wm. Press Yard and No.4 Bridge to Station	4.30 p.m.	B. Lukins/480
	Wern Works FRIDAY ONLY	4.00 p.m.}	G. Davies/377
	McAlpines to Station	4.25 p.m.}	ditto
	Wern Works to Margam	5.00 p.m.}	ditto
	McAlpines to Station	4.30 p.m.}	A.R. Edwards/418
	Maudlam Bridge to Station	5.00 p.m.}	ditto
	Abbey Works Bus Park to Tonmawr	4.30 p.m.	I. Howells/675
	Beach to Wern Works	9.35 p.m.}	56
	Wern Works to Beach		A. Thomas
J. Selway	Duty 17.M.		Terry Davies
M. Roberts	Duty 17.A.		G. Ward
S. Thomas	Duty 11.A.		D. Gosling
N. Crocker	Duty 20.M.		D. Morgans
	Duty 7.A.		H. Jenkins

N.T.O. - New Temporary Offices, in front of the main canteen.

Something of a rarity locally, KNY 418 was a 1950 Tilling Stevens Motors K6LA7 which came with the Davies Bros. fleet in 1951 and saw service until 1960.

When the fleet of Jones, Pantdu was taken over in 1965, Thomas Bros. quickly disposed of a number of buses which had no place in the modern fleet. One such vehicle was this Crossley SD42 with Duple body, KTD 7, which had been new in 1949 to Robinson, of Great Harwood, near Blackburn, Lancashire.

THOMAS BROS. (PORT TALBOT) LIMITED
WEEKLY ANALYSIS OF TRAFFIC AND OTHER RECEIPTS
TO BE SENT TO THE SECRETARY EVERY MONDAY

For the Week ended 21st June 1968			ROUTE	For the Week ended 21st June 1969				
Car Miles Run	Receipts			Receipts			Car Miles Run	
TOTAL	TOTAL	Per Car Mile		Per Car Mile	TOTAL	+ Increase/-Decrease	TOTAL	+ Increase/-Decrease
	£	d.	**STAGE CARRIAGE**	d.	£	£		
1,769	300	40.70	Beach - Margam	37.20	290	-10	1,871	+102
6,587	1,251	45.58	Housing Est. - Margam	47.53	1,269	+18	6,408	-179
2,932	555	45.43	Housing Est. - Goytre via Beach	48.22	576	+21	2,867	-65
2,553	385	36.19	Baglan Est. - Velindre via Housing Est./Beach	37.91	405	+20	2,564	+11
1,237	130	25.22	Baglan Est. - Margam via Main Road	27.94	149	+19	1,280	+43
2,928	499	24.30	Abbey Works Services	40.22	518	+19	3,091	+163
158	14	21.27	Open Top Decker Services	11.01	5	-9	109	-49
2,022	223	26.47	Aberavon - Tonmawr	21.56	199	-24	2,215	+193
4,512	670	35.64	Sandfields Est./Beach - Brynbryddan/Tabor	38.52	705	+35	4,392	-120
969	85	21.05	Station - Fairfield - Beach	25.26	110	+25	1,045	+76
4,475	509	27.30	Port Talbot - Abergwynfi & Glyncorrwg	26.98	503	-6	4,475	0
n/a	21	n/a	Proportion SWT Co. Routes 6 & 7	n/a	21	n/a	n/a	n/a
30, 142	4,642	36.96		37.60	4,750	+108	30,317	+175

'Examination of the types of vehicles used reveal much about how the company drove itself forward to success.'

This 1948 ex-Rhondda AEC Regal III originally had a Longwell Green B34R body, but GNY 764 later found its way to Malta, where it was heavily and unrecognisably rebuilt.

As with many bus operators whose origins are deep rooted in the distant past or who owe their birth to the merger of a number of different operators the Thomas Bros. fleet list provides an interesting read.

The further back down the decades one looks the more diverse and unusual the vehicles employed for passenger transport with the company becomes.

Close examination of the list offers clues as to the development of vehicles from basic First World War lorry conversions to the more sophisticated vehicles which appeared in the 1960s. The early fleet included several makes which will be unfamiliar to modern bus watchers.

Information here is as complete as it has been possible to determine at the date of publication. Lack of space prevents listing where buses ended up after service with Thomas Bros.

As the years passed bus building developed and like many other operators Thomas Bros. settled on their favourite builders. The firm's later vehicle buying policy reflected the preferences of its parent BET group resulting in a fleet consisting of Leylands and AECs.

Facts and figures about the fleet

A pair of Leyland Tiger Cubs representing an everyday scene at Victoria Road, Port Talbot in the 1960s.

Noted for its breathtakingly poor fuel consumption, KTX 476 was a 1951 Bedford SB/Duple C33F acquired via the Afan Transport wing with the business of Lewis & Jones Ltd, Port Talbot in 1952. It later passed to Hastelow, Malvern.

Looking as if it had recently been repainted, former Sheffield 1937 AEC Regal, DWE 606 in Sandfields Road, opposite the old depot with Chief Engineer, Ernie Lewis.

Reg No.	Built	Chassis	Body	Origin (If not new)	In	Out	Notes
Vehicles Acquired 1920-1951							
1920							
L 6454		Garner 2ton 30hp Ch28		Former WD lorry	6/20		
L 6455		Leyland 36hp (2164) Ch30		Former WD lorry	6/20	1930	
1921							
L 9544		Daimler 35hp (3346)	Ch26		5/21	1926	
L 9972		Ford T 1ton 22.4hp (451435677)	Lorry, 14 seats	Adapted for passengers and goods.			
CY 3829					4/21		
1922							
NY1554	1922	Ford (4618603)	14 Seats	W.J. Tunningley	7/22	5/24	
1923							
NY 3458	1915	Daimler W or Y 22hp (3962)	Norman Ch26		6/23	1932	
L 3655	1915	Overland 25.3hp (11173)	Car, 6 seats	Private Owner	1/23		
1924							
NY 5835	1917	AEC YA (9655)	B26-		6/24	Dec-28	
NY 2193	1922	Lancia 35hp (Z4239)	B14-	Jones & Morgan, Bryncethin	4/24	7/26	
1925							
No known vehicle acquisitions.							
1926							
TX 581		AEC 204 (204038)	United B20-		4/26	12/32	
1927							
NY 5669	1924	Ford 1 ton (9153234)	Lorry, 14 seats	Alfred Jones, Neath	11/27	1928	
1928, 1929							
No known vehicle acquisitions.							
1930							
VM 7247	1929	Halley CS2 (3359)	B32R	Copwood, Manchester	10/30	12/42	
1931							
DJ 5030		Bedford WLG (112055)	B20		5/31		
1932							
KO 8824	1928	Bean 14hp (1018/11)	Willowbrook B14F	Darenth Bus Service/East Surrey Traction	1931		
YX 7518	1928	Bean (1569/11)	Holbrook B14F	Newlands & District/ East Surrey Traction	1931	6/38	
1933							
WN 5834	1933	Bedford WLB (109175)	Duple B20F		7/33	1938	
TG 2296	1931	Bean (2440/11)	B14-	R. Hodges, Cwmavon.	7/33	12/33	

Reg No.	Built	Chassis	Body	Origin (If not new)	In	Out	Notes
TX 5583	1928	Graham Dodge 24hp (D171356)	B14-	E.A. Jenkins & Son, Port Talbot	10/33	12/36	
VX 8830	1930	Dennis Dart (75718)	Thurgood B20F	Hicks, Felstead/ Hodge, Erith	11/33	9/39	
SC 2944	1928	Leyland Lion LSC3 (47761)	Midland B31F	Scottish Motor Traction, Edinburgh (694/G4)	12/33	5/38	

1934

Reg No.	Built	Chassis	Body	Origin (If not new)	In	Out	Notes
VR 770	1929	Halley (3417)	B32R	W. Jones, Brynhyfryd, Swansea	5/34	6/37	
DT 1299	1928	Thornycroft A6/YB6 (16422)	B24-	Morgan's Motor Services, Taibach	1934		

1935

No known vehicle acquisitions

1936

Reg No.	Built	Chassis	Body	Origin (If not new)	In	Out	Notes
TX 2704	1927	Oldsmobile (2505)	14 seats	P. Waters, Port Talbot	4/36	1936	
WN 1867	1929	Dennis ES (17709)	SWT B32R	South Wales Transport (199)	6/36	12/38	
TG 2296	1931	Bean (2440/11W)	14 seats	R. Hodges, Cwmavon	7/36	6/37	
TH 4096	1934	Bedford WLB (109373)	Duple B20F	Davies Bros., Pencader	10/36	1943	

1937

Reg No.	Built	Chassis	Body	Origin (If not new)	In	Out	Notes
CNY 940	1937	Bedford WTB (111558)	26 seats		7/37	1943	
CTG 176	1937	Bedford WTB (111680)	Duple B26F		7/37	1943	
JJ 9749	1933	Leyland Cub KP5 (1182)	Duple C24F	Manny's Luxury Coaches, SW9	1/37	3/43	
OT 9062 or 9350	1928	Dennis H (H90011/12)	Strachan & Brown H56ROS	Aldershot & District	1937	1937	
ATD 500	1935	Leyland Cheetah LZ1 (8977)	Leyland B26F	Leyland Motors (Demonstrator)	12/37	1940	

1938

Reg No.	Built	Chassis	Body	Origin (If not new)	In	Out	Notes
WN 2496	1929	Dennis EV (17850)	SWT B32R	South Wales Transport (203)	6/38		
AVT 773	1934	Leyland Lion LT5A (5120)	Duple DP38F	Milton Bus Service, Hanley (3)	6/51	3/51	
AVT 774	1934	Leyland Lion LT5A (5120)	Duple DP38F	Milton Bus Service, Hanley (4)	6/51	9/49	

1939

Reg No.	Built	Chassis	Body	Origin (If not new)	In	Out	Notes
VH 3812	1931	AEC Regal (6621079)	Craven B32R	Hudderfield J.O.C. (84)	5/39	12/42	

1940

Reg No.	Built	Chassis	Body	Origin (If not new)	In	Out	Notes
BBU 748	1939	Bedford WTB (9315)	Plaxton C26F	Ralph Renton (Broadway Coaches)	5/40	6/40	
BBU 765	1939	Bedford WTB (9680)	Plaxton C26F	Ralph Renton (Broadway Coaches)	5/40	6/40	
TH 8647	1937	Albion PV141 (44011H)	Thomas C32F & Thomas	Sage, Burry Port	7/40	1944	

Reg No.	Built	Chassis	Body	Origin (If not new)	In	Out	Notes
1941							
TG 4862	1933	Guy ONDF (9846)	B20F	R. Hodges, Cwmavon	2/41	12/42	
DV 8504	1931	Leyland Lion LT2 (51278)	Jeffreys B32F Notes	Devon General (19)	1941	12/50	*1*
1942							
ETX 998	1942	Bedford OWB (8923)	Duple B32F		8/42	2/52	
DNC 182	1942	Dodge			1942	10/43	
1943							
FNY 179	1943	Bedford OWB (12250)	Duple B32F		1943	5/44	
FNY 192	1943	Bedford OWB (12450)	Duple B32F		3/43	1950	
FNY 193	1943	Bedford OWB (12434)	Duple B32F		2/43	1950	
FNY 194	1943	Bedford OWB (12421)	Duple B32F		2/43	2/52	
FNY 350	1943	Bedford OWB (14315)	Duple B32F		6/43	1/52	
FNY 470	1943	Bedford OWB (15501)	Duple B32F		8/43	1/52	
1944							
FNY 672	1944	Bedford OWB (18909)	Duple B32F		3/44	3/52	
FNY 684	1944	Bedford OWB (19932)	Duple B32F		5/44	1944	
FNY 872	1944	Bedford OWB (22947)	Duple B32F		10/44	1952	
FNY 903	1944	Bedford OWB (23306)	Duple B32F		12/44	1951	
AG 6022	1931	AEC Regal (662481)	Burlingham B36F	Ayr & District/ David Jones & Son, Pantdu	5/44		
DV 8508	1931	Leyland Lion LT2 (51437)	Park Royal C31F	Western Welsh (10)	5/44	1948	
OD 1833	1932	Leyland Lion LT5 (51437)	Weymann B31F	Western Welsh	5/44	1948	
1945							
FTG 247	1945	Bedford OWB (30280)	Duple B32F		9/45	1/52	
FTG 248	1945	Bedford OWB (30282)	Duple B32F		11/45	1/52	
OD 1834	1932	Leyland Lion LT5 (572)	Weymann B31F	Devon General/ Jones, Pantdu	12/45	12/45	
1946							
BBU 748	1939	Bedford WTB (9315)	Plaxton C26F	Ralph Renton (Broadway Coaches)	7/46	10/48	
1947							
GNY 647	1947	Leyland Tiger PS1	Whitson C33F		1947	3/52	
GNY 699	1947	Leyland Tiger PS1/1 (462156)	Whitson C33F		3/47	11/58	
GTX 3	1947	Bedford OB (52720)	Mulliner B32F		7/47	1/52	
HNY 80	1947	Maudslay Marathon III (70058)	Whitson C33F		11/47	1950	
BBU 765	1939	Bedford WTB (9680)	Plaxton C26F		3/47		

Reg No.	Built	Chassis	Body	Origin (If not new)	In	Out	Notes
HG 2298	1933	Leyland Titan TD3 (3268)	English Electric H29/23R	Burnley, Colne & Nelson ()	7/47	9/49	
HG 2935	1934	Leyland Titan TD3c (4804)	English Electric H29/23R	Burnley, Colne & Nelson (89)	7/47	3/51	
HG 2961	1934	Leyland Titan TD3c (4811)	English Electric H29/23R	Burnley, Colne & Nelson (96)	7/47	2/51	
HG 2301	1934	Leyland. Titan TD3 (3264)	Park Royal H29/23R	Burnley, Colne & Nelson ()	9/47	4/48	

1948

Reg No.	Built	Chassis	Body	Origin (If not new)	In	Out	Notes
HNY 377	1948	Leyland Tiger PS1/1 (471965)	D.J. Davies C33F		1/48	2/59	
HNY 415	1948	Leyland Tiger PS1/1 (472596)	Burlingham C33F		1/48	4/60	
HNY 566	1948	Bedford OB (55604)	Jeffreys B32F		2/48	9/52	
HTG 986	1948	Bedford OB (83262)	Mulliner B31F		8/48	8/52	
HG 2303	1933	Leyland Titan TD3 (3267)	Park Royal H29/23R	Burnley, Colne & Nelson (58)	3/48	12/48	
HG 2306	1934	Leyland Titan TD3 (3271)	Park Royal H29/23R	Burnley, Colne & Nelson (61)	11/48		
HG 2962	1934	Leyland Titan TD3c (4812)	English Electric H29/22R	Burnley, Colne & Nelson (97)	12/48	6/49	
HG 4038	1936	Leyland Lion LT7c (9601)	English Electric B38R	Burnley, Colne & Nelson (139)	12/48	7/52	
HG 4476	1936	Leyland Lion LT7c (10670)	English Electric B38R	Burnley, Colne & Nelson (143)	12/48	10/51	
JX 1912	1934	AEC Regent (O6612693)	Roe H28/26R	Halifax Corporation (12)	4/48	9/51	
JX 1913	1934	AEC Regent (O6612695)	Roe H28/26R	Halifax Corporation (13)	4/48	9/51	
JX 2038	1934	AEC Regent (O6612712)	English Electric H30/24R	Halifax Corporation (15)	4/48	9/51	
JX 2305	1935	AEC Regent (O6612902)	Roberts H28/26R	Halifax Corporation (20)	6/48	9/51	

1949

Reg No.	Built	Chassis	Body	Origin (If not new)	In	Out	Notes
JNY 200	1949	Bedford OB (102520)	Mulliner B31F		2/49	3/52	
JNY 675	1949	AEC Regal III (9621A723)	Burlingham C33F		5/49	1960	
JTG 954	1949	Bedford OB (119433)	Mulliner B31F		10/49	3/52	

1950

Reg No.	Built	Chassis	Body	Origin (If not new)	In	Out	Notes
JTX 676	1950	AEC Regal III (9621E1072)	Burlingham C33F		3/50	by 1964	**11**
BBN 182	1940	Leyland Titan TD7c (303236)	Massey H30/26R	Bolton Corporation (224)	4/50	5/52	
BBN 194	1940	Leyland Titan TD7c (303248)	Massey H30/26R	Bolton Corporation (236)	4/50	5/52	

Reg No.	Built	Chassis	Body	Origin (If not new)	In	Out	Notes
1951							
BOL 36	1936	Daimler COG5 (8196)	MCCW B34F	Birmingham City Transport (36)	1/51	9/52	
BOL 40	1936	Daimler COG5 (8193)	MCCW B34F	Birmingham City Transport (40)	1/51	11/53	
EOG 275	1939	Leyland Titan TD6c (300583)	MCCW H28/24R	Birmingham City Transport (275)	1/51	5/52	
CVP 237	1937	Daimler COG5 (10099)	MCCW H30/24R	Birmingham City Transport (1137)	3/51	11/53	
Unknown Dates							
EL 8466	1923	Vulcan (53559)	20 Seats			3/30	
OD 3?38		Leyland LT					

Vehicles taken over under B.E.T control in June 1951
From Davies Bros Ltd / Thomas & James Ltd., Port Talbot

Thomas and James was a subsidiary of Davies Bros., formed to operate works and contract services of its parent company. It is known that vehicles moved between the two fleets.

Reg No.	Built	Chassis	Body	Origin (If not new)	In	Out	Notes
HB 5776	1939	Bedford WTB (16223)	Jeffreys C26F		6/51	1952	
HB 6472	1947	Dennis Lancet J3 (311J3)	D.J.Davies C35F	D.J.Davies, Merthyr	6/51	by 1956	2
AOP 47	1935	Daimler COG5 (8131)	MCCW B34F	Birmingham City Transport (47)	6/51	1953	
AOP 72	1935	Daimler COG5 (8155)	Strachans B34F	Birmingham City Transport (72)	6/51	1952	
DNY 204	1938	Bedford WTB (111969)	Jeffreys C26F		6/51	1952	
DWE 606	1937	AEC Regal (06622123)	Cravens B32R	Sheffield Corporation (A206)	6/51	1954	
FNY 184	1943	Bedford OWB (12240)	Duple B30F		6/51	1952	**3, 4**
FNY 191	1943	Bedford OWB (12450)	Duple B30F		6/51	1952	**3, 4**
FNY 563	1943	Bedford OWB (17671)	Duple B30F		6/51	1952	**3, 4**
FNY 564	1943	Bedford OWB (17674)	Duple B30F		6/51	1952	**3, 4**
FNY 873	1943	Bedford OWB (22319)	Duple B30F		6/51	1954	**5**
FTG 336	1945	Bedford OWB (32146)	Duple B32F		6/51	1952	
FTG 628	1946	Bedford OB (18757)	Duple B32F		6/51	by 1952	
HNY 941	1948	Bedford OB (76101)	Duple C29F		6/51	1954	
JNY 336	1949	Dennis Lancet J3 (529J3)	D.J.Davies C35F		6/51	by 1959	
JTG 549	1949	Dennis Lancet J3 (660J3)	D.J.Davies C35F		6/51	1960	
JTX 650	1949	Seddon Mk IV (3537)	Seddon B31F		6/51	1957	
KNY 418	1950	TSM K6LA7 (9576)	Dutfield C33F		6/51	1960	

Reg No.	Built	Chassis	Body	Origin (If not new)	In	Out	Notes
HG 2935	1934	Leyland Titan TD3c (4804)	English Electric H29/23R	Burnley Colne & Nelson (89)	6/51	1951	**6**
HG 2961	1934	Leyland Titan TD3c (4811)	English Electric H29/23R	Burnley Colne & Nelson (96)	6/51	1951	**6**
HG 4038	1936	Leyland Lion LT7c (9601)	English Electric B38R	Burnley Colne & Nelson (139)	6/51	1952	
HG 4476	1936	Leyland Lion LT7c (10670)	English Electric B38R	Burnley Colne & Nelson (143)	6/51	1951	
JX 1912	1948	AEC Regent (O6612693)	Roe H28/26R	Halifax Corporation	6/51	1951	
JX 1913	1948	AEC Regent (O6612695)	Roe H28/26R	Halifax Corporation	6/51	1951	**7**
JX 2038	1948	AEC Regent (O6612712)	English Electric H30/24R	Halifax Corporation	6/51	1951	**8**
JX 2305	1948	AEC Regent (O6612902)	Roberts H28/26R	Halifax Corporation	6/51	1951	**6**
AVT 773	1934	Leyland Lion LT5A (5120)	Duple DP38F	Milton Bus Service, Hanley	6/51	1951	**9**
BBN 182	1941	Leyland Titan TD7c (303236)	Massey H30/26R	Bolton Corporation (224)	6/51	1952	
BBN 194	1941	Leyland Titan TD7c (303248)	Massey H30/26R	Bolton Corporation (236)	6/51	1952	
BOL 36	1936	Daimler COG5 (8196)	MCCW B34F	Birmingham City Transport (36)	6/51	1952	
BOL 40	1936	Daimler COG5 (8193)	MCCW B34F	Birmingham City Transport (40)	6/51	1953	
CVP 237	1937	Daimler COG5 (10099)	MCCW H30/24R	Birmingham City Transport (1137)	6/51	1953	**9**
EOG 275	1939	Leyland Titan TD6c (300583)	MCCW H28/24R	Birmingham City Transport (275)	6/51	1952	
ETX 998	1942	Bedford OB (8923)	Duple B30F		6/51	1952	**3, 4**
FNY 194	1943	Bedford OWB (12421)	Duple B32F		6/51	1952	**4**
FNY 350	1943	Bedford OWB (14315)	Duple B30F		6/51	1952	**3, 4**
FNY 470	1943	Bedford OWB (15501)	Duple B30F		6/51	1952	**3, 4**
FNY 672	1943	Bedford OWB (18909)	Duple B30F		6/51	1951	**3**
FNY 903	1943	Bedford OWB (23306)	Duple B30F		6/51	1951	**3**
FTG 247	1945	Bedford OWB (30280)	Duple B30F		6/51	1952	**4**
FTG 248	1945	Bedford OWB (30282)	Duple B30F		6/51	1952	**4**
GNY 699	1947	Leyland Tiger PS2 (462156)	Whitson C33F		6/51	1958	
GTX 3	1947	Bedford OB (52720)	Mulliner B30F		6/51	1952	

From Thomas Brothers Ltd., Port Talbot / Afan Transport Ltd., Port Talbot

Afan Transport was a subsidiary of Thomas Bros., formed in 1944 to operate works and contract services of its parent company. It is known that vehicles moved between the two fleets.

159

Reg No.	Built	Chassis	Body	Origin (If not new)	In	Out	Notes
HNY 377	1948	Leyland PS1 (471965)	Whitson C33F		6/51	1955	
HNY 415	1948	Leyland PS1 (472596)	Burlingham C33F		6/51	1960	**11**
HNY 566	1948	Bedford OB (61497)	Jeffreys B32F		6/51	1952	
HNY 941	1948	Bedford OB (76101)	Duple C29F		6/51	1952	
HTG 986	1948	Bedford OB	Duple B31F		6/51	1952	
JNY 200	1949	Bedford OB (102520)	Mulliner B31F		6/51	1952	
JNY 675	1949	AEC Regal III (9621A723)	Burlingham C33F		6/51	1960-?	
JTG 954	1949	Bedford OB (119433)	Mulliner B31F		6/51	1952	
JTX 676	1950	AEC Regal III (9621E1072)	Burlingham FC33F		6/51	by 1964	**12**

Notes

1 Acquired as a fire damaged wreck for £60 and rebodied.

2 Vehicle fitted with bus seats in 1953.

3 Wartime utility body. The 32 wooden slatted seats were replaced with 30 upholstered seats, postwar.

4 Each was part of a batch of ten Bedfords sold to a dealer for £2000 in 1952.

5 Had been rebodied in 1949 after a fire.

6 Dismantled by the company in 1952.

7 Dismantled by the company in 1951.

8 Later used as a storage shed by the company.

9 Had been rebodied with a wartime utility body. Used as a staff canteen at the depot and later at Aberavon Beach.

10 This was carrying its third body when it arrived at Thomas Bros. Birmingham had transferred the original to Daimler COG5 COX 970 (970) in 1947. In its place, CVP 237 had been fitted with that from Daimler COG5 COX 987 (987). On withdrawal, CVP 237 was stored and then passed to dealer Bird's Commercial motors, Stratford-upon-Avon. There it was fitted with the body from sister CVP 115.

11 Radio fitted from new.

12 Vehicle destroyed by fire on its first trip in May 1949. Chassis rebuilt by AEC at Southall and rebodied by Burlingham, Blackpool.

Vehicles purchased after BET takeover, 1951-1971

1951

Reg No.	Built	Chassis	Body	Origin (If not new)	In	Out	Notes
BCY 578	1938	Leyland TD5 (16669)	Weymann L27/26R	South Wales Transport (510/78)	11/51	5/53	
EFC 287	1937	AEC Regal (O6622107)	Weymann B35F	City of Oxford Motor Services (JD10)	7/51	10/53	
EFC 290	1937	AEC Regal (O6622110)	Weymann B35F	City of Oxford Motor Services (JD99)	7/51	12/52	
EFC 292	1937	AEC Regal (O6622112)	Weymann B35F	City of Oxford Motor Services (JD104)	7/51	12/53	
FWL 633	1938	AEC Regent (O6615440)	Park Royal H28/24R	City of Oxford Motor services (H134)	6/51	6/53	
FWL 636	1938	AEC Regent (O6615443)	Park Royal H28/24R	City of Oxford Motor services (H141)	7/51	12/53	
FWL 645	1938	AEC Regent (O6615394)	Park Royal H28/24R	City of Oxford Motor Services (H120)	6/51	12/53	

Reg No.	Built	Chassis	Body	Origin (If not new)	In	Out	Notes
FWL 647	1938	AEC Regent (O6615396)	Park Royal H28/24R	City of Oxford Motor Services (H122)	6/51	12/53	

1952

Reg No.	Built	Chassis	Body	Origin (If not new)	In	Out	Notes
AOP 52	1935	Daimler COG5 (8148)	MCCW B34F	David Jones & Son/ Birmingham C.T. (52)	2/52	2/52	**13**
BOL 35	1936	Daimler COG5 (8192)	MCCW B34F	David Jones & Son/ Birmingham C.T. (35)	2/52	2/52	**13**
DDV 429	1939	AEC Regal (O6623309)	Harrington B35F	Devon General (SR429)	2/52	7/54	
DDV 430	1939	AEC Regal (O6623310)	Harrington B35F	Devon General (SR430)	6/52	5/56	
DDV 431	1939	AEC Regal (O6623311)	Harrington B35F	Devon General (SR431)	6/52	5/56	
DDV 432	1939	AEC Regal (O6623312)	Harrington B35F	Devon General (SR432)	1/52	10/56	
DDV 435	1939	AEC Regal (O6623315)	Harrington B35F	Devon General (SR435)	2/52	8/56	
DDV 438	1939	AEC Regal (O6623318)	Harrington B35F	Devon General (SR438)	2/52	4/54	
DDV 439	1939	AEC Regal (O6623319)	Harrington B35F	Devon General (SR439)	2/52	8/56	
DDV 440	1939	AEC Regal (O6623320)	Harrington B35F	Devon General (SR440)	2/52	3/55	
DDV 443	1939	AEC Regal (O6623323)	Harrington B35F	Devon General (SR443)	1/52	7/54	
DOD 458	1940	AEC Regal (O6623436)	Weymann B35F	Devon General (SR458)	6/52	4/56	
DOD 459	1940	AEC Regal (O6623437)	Weymann B35F	Devon General (SR459)	6/52	6/55	
DOD 465	1940	AEC Regal (O6623443)	Weymann B35F	Devon General (SR465)	6/52	4/55	
DOD 466	1940	AEC Regal (O6623444)	Weymann B35F	Devon General (SR466)	2/52	7/54	
DOD 474	1940	AEC Regal (O6623452)	Weymann B35F	Devon General (SR 474)	2/52	7/54	**14**
DOD 477	1940	AEC Regal (O6623455)	Weymann B35F	Devon General (SR477)	2/52	1/54	
KTX 476	1951	Bedford SB (1626)	Duple C33F	Lewis & Jones Ltd.	2/52	1954	**15**

Notes

General: The fleet of ex-Devon General AEC Regals and vehicles from Oxford and SWT in 1951 were transferrred to Thomas Bros. by BET at the time of takeover in line with the group's policy of replacing older, non-standard less robust vehicles. There was the added safety benefit of eliminating the risk from running vehicles for which a full service history might not have been known. The first ten vehicles were given a notional value of £100 each, plus tyres and all were serviced and repainted by Devon General at Torquay before being sent to Port Talbot.

13 Not used by Thomas Bros. Described as 'mechanically deplorable'.

14 Purchased for preservation in 1964 and it is currently a long term restoration project at The West of England Transport Collection, Winkleigh.

15 Coach style body, but fitted with bus seats.

Reg No.	Built	Chassis	Body	Origin (If not new)	In	Out	Notes
1953							
HTT 480	1946	AEC Regal (O6624806)	Weymann B35F	Devon General (SR480)	4/53	9/59	**16**
HTT 500	1946	AEC Regal (O6624826)	Weymann B35F	Devon General (SR500)	4/53	2/59	**16**
HTT 501	1946	AEC Regal (O6624827)	Weymann B35F	Devon General (SR501)	4/53	9/59	**16**
JTT 708	1946	AEC Regal (O6624833)	Weymann B35F	Devon General (SR508)	4/53	9/59	**16**
MTG 172	1953	AEC Regal IV (9822S211)	Burlingham C41C		3/53	5/64	**17**
NNY 54	1953	Leyland Tiger Cub PSUC1/1 (534015)	Weymann B44F		11/53	6/63	
NNY 55	1953	Leyland Tiger Cub PSUC1/1 (534024)	Weymann B44F		11/53	6/63	
NNY 56	1953	Leyland Tiger Cub PSUC1/1 (534060)	Weymann B44F		11/53	?/64	
NNY 57	1953	Leyland Tiger Cub PSUC1/1 (534047)	Weymann B44F		12/53	11/67	
NNY 58	1953	Leyland Tiger Cub PSUC1/1 (534075)	Weymann B44F		11/53	1/71	**18**
NNY 59	1953	Leyland Tiger Cub PSUC1/1 (534207)	Weymann B44F		12/53	9/67	
NNY 60	1953	Leyland Tiger Cub PSUC1/1 (534208)	Weymann B44F		12/53	8/65	
NNY 61	1953	Leyland Tiger Cub PSUC1/1 (534206)	Weymann B44F		12/53	2/67	
NNY 62	1953	Leyland Tiger Cub PSUC1/1 (534209)	Weymann B44F		12/53	9/67	

Notes

16 *Repainted into Thomas Bros livery by DG at Torquay.*

17 *Named Port Talbot Monarch*

18 *NNY 58 lasted longer than any of the first batch of Tiger Cubs as for many years it was fitted with a removable rear panel and a towing bracket, doubling up as the depot towing vehicle.*

1954

Reg No.	Built	Chassis	Body	Origin (If not new)	In	Out	Notes
NNY 63	1954	Leyland Tiger Cub PSUC1/1 (534216)	Saunders-Roe B44F		5/54	12/67	
NNY 64	1954	Leyland Tiger Cub PSUC1/1 (534281)	Saunders-Roe B44F		5/54	7/65	**19**
NNY 65	1954	Leyland Tiger Cub	Saunders-Roe B44F		5/54	?/68	
NNY 66	1954	Leyland Tiger Cub PSUC1/1 (542504)	Saunders-Roe B44F		5/54	1/66	
NNY 67	1954	Leyland Tiger Cub PSUC1/1 (535279)	Saunders-Roe B44F		5/54	?/64	

Reg No.	Built	Chassis	Body	Origin (If not new)	In	Out	Notes
NNY 68	1954	Leyland Tiger Cub PSUC1/1 (542902)	Saunders-Roe B44F		5/54	?/64	
NNY 69	1954	Leyland Tiger Cub PSUC1/1 (542906)	Saunders-Roe B44F		5/54	7/68	**19**
NNY 70	1954	Leyland Tiger Cub PSUC1/1 (542907)	Saunders-Roe B44F		6/54	1/71	**20**
NNY 71	1954	Leyland Tiger Cub PSUC1/1 (542908)	Saunders-Roe B44F		6/54	?/70	

Notes

19 *After withdrawal, NNY 64 was converted to a mobile shop for use in the Port Talbot area. A second also was converted and this seems likely to have been NNY 69.*

20 *Converted to a training bus 1969 and fitted with coach seats. It was later stored in a vandalised state at Acacia Avenue depot pending possible preservation but this never materialised and it was eventually scrapped. This was the last vehicle to carry Thomas Bros. blue livery.*

1955

Reg No.	Built	Chassis	Body	Origin (If not new)	In	Out	Notes
PTX 197	1955	Leyland Tiger Cub PSUC1/1 (545541)	Weymann B44F		3/55	1/71	
PTX 198	1955	Leyland Tiger Cub PSUC1/1 (545386)	Weymann B44F		3/55	?	
PTX 199	1955	Leyland Tiger Cub PSUC1/1 (545387)	Weymann B44F		3/55	1/71	
PTX 202	1955	Leyland Tiger Cub PSUC1/1 (545542)	Weymann B44F		3/55	1/71	
PTX 203	1955	AEC Reliance (MU3RA071)	Burlingham C41C		3/55	?/66	**21**

Notes

21 *Named Pride of Port Talbot*

1956

Reg No.	Built	Chassis	Body	Origin (If not new)	In	Out	Notes
BBO 893	1939	Leyland Tiger TS8 (300729)	Brush B32F	Western Welsh (312)	4/56	12/58	**21**
BUH 55	1939	Leyland Tiger TS8 (302942)	ECW B35F	Western Welsh (705)	4/56	12/58	**21**
GCY 432	1950	AEC Regal III (9621A1043)	Windover C33F	South Wales Transport (1005)	1/56	?/61	
TG 2	1956	AEC Reliance (MU3RA499)	Burlingham C41C		3/56		**22**
TG 3	1956	Leyland Tiger Cub PSUC1/1	Weymann B44F		8/56	1/71	
TG 4	1956	Leyland Tiger Cub PSUC1/1	Weymann B44F		8/56	1/71	
TG 5	1956	Leyland Tiger Cub PSUC1/1	Weymann B44F		8/56	1/71	
TG 6	1956	Leyland Tiger Cub PSUC1/1	Weymann B44F		8/56	1/71	

Reg No.	Built	Chassis	Body	Origin (If not new)	In	Out	Notes

Notes

21 Purchased as a stop-gap until the delivery of further Leyland PSUC1/1s

22 Named Port Talbot Princess

1957

Reg No.	Built	Chassis	Body	Origin (If not new)	In	Out	Notes
GCY 435	1950	AEC Regal III (9621A1046)	Windover C33F	South Wales Transport (1008)	4/57	?/62	
VTX 7	1957	Leyland Tiger Cub PSUC1/1 (574850)	Weymann B44F		6/57	1/71	**24, 25**
VTX 8	1957	Leyland Tiger Cub PSUC1/1 (574851)	Weymann B44F		6/57	1/71	**24**

Notes

24 VTX 7, VTX 8, XNY 9 and XNY 10 all featured a destination box over the door when new. They were in use when new but were all covered over by 1964/5

25 VTX 7 was involved in a serious head on collision with a road tanker in 1963, the front end being rebuilt in house.

1958

Reg No.	Built	Chassis	Body	Origin (If not new)	In	Out	Notes
FWN 633	1949	AEC Regal III (6821A270)	Longwell Green B34F	South Wales Transport (104)	11/58	?/60	
GCY 436	1950	AEC Regal III (9621A1047)	Windover C33F	South Wales Transport (1009)	4/58	?/60	
GCY 438	1950	AEC Regal III (9621A1049)	Windover C33F	South Wales Transport (1011)	4/58	?/60	
GNY 764	1948	AEC Regal III (O962184)	Longwell Green B34R	Rhondda Transport (64)	7/58	9/60	**26**
XNY 9	1958	Leyland Tiger Cub PSUC1/1 (577845)	Weymann B44F		9/58	1/71	**24**
XNY 10	1958	Leyland Tiger Cub PSUC1/1 (577846)	Weymann B44F		9/58	1/71	**24**

Notes

24 VTX 7, VTX 8, XNY 9 and XNY 10 all featured a destination box over the door when new. They were in use when new but were all covered over by 1964/5

26 Exported to Malta after withdrawal (Re-registered DBY312 and then EBY484). Rebodied Debono B40F, 1963. Believed to be still in existence, 2020.

1959

Reg No.	Built	Chassis	Body	Origin (If not new)	In	Out	Notes
11 CNY	1959	AEC Reliance (2MU3RA2110)	Burlingham C41F		5/59	?/69	**27**
12 CNY	1959	Leyland Tiger Cub PSUC1/1 (594220)	Park Royal B45F		7/59	1/71	**28**
13 CNY	1959	Leyland Tiger Cub PSUC1/1 (594221)	Park Royal B45F		7/59	1/71	

Notes

27 Named Port Talbot Crusader. This was a comparatively rare example of the unsuccessful Mk VII version of the Burlingham Seagull body. It ended its days as a mobile uniform store with SWT and suffered fire damage in 1969.

28 12 CNY became Thomas Bros. first attempt at one person operation on the route from Velindre to Afan Lido via Port Talbot General and Fairfield. It had two seats removed in 1967 and was fitted with an Autoslot ticket machine. There were two regular drivers, Alf Hanson and Ernie Elward.

Reg No.	Built	Chassis	Body	Origin (If not new)	In	Out	Notes
1960							
CAP 205	1940	Bristol K5G (55.068)	ECW CO33/26R	Brighton, Hove & District (351)	6/60	?/70	**29**
CAP 237	1940	Bristol K5G (55.076)	ECW CO33/26R	Brighton, Hove & District (359)	8/60	9/60	
14 HTG	1960	Leyland Tiger Cub PSUC1/1 (604694)	MCCW B45F		8/60	1/71	
15 HTG	1960	Leyland Tiger Cub PSUC1/1 (604715)	MCCW B45F		8/60	1/71	
16 HTG	1960	Leyland Tiger Cub PSUC1/1 (604716)	MCCW B45F		8/60	1/71	

Notes

29 Named The Afan Belle. CAP 205 & 237 were rebuilt to convertible open top form by BH&D in 1951 and 1952 respectively. CAP 205 was later exported to to Canada, initially to Derrick Arnold, of Cobourg, Ontario then Seeboyers, Agricultural Engineers, Havelock. It is believed that it still exists in derelict form.

1961

Reg No.	Built	Chassis	Body	Origin (If not new)	In	Out	Notes
OD 7497	1934	AEC Regent (O6612445)	Short O31/24R	Devon General (DR210)	3/61	10/65	**30**
JK 7431	1938	AEC Regent (6616132)	Northern Counties O30/26R	Eastbourne Corporation (10)	?/61	?/65	**31**
117 LNY	1961	Leyland Tiger Cub PSUC1/1 (614584)	Park Royal B45F		7/61	1/71	**32**
118 LNY	1961	Leyland Tiger Cub PSUC1/1 (614585)	Park Royal B45F		7/61	1/71	**33**
119 LNY	1961	AEC Reliance (2MU3RA3213)	Harrington C41F		7/61	1/71	**34**
120 LNY	1961	AEC Reliance (2MU3RA3214)	Harrington C41F		7/61	1/71	**35**

Notes

30 Named The Margam Belle. Converted to open top by Longwell Green in April 1955. Bought as a replacement for CAP 237. Vehicle preserved.

31 Named Sandfields Belle. When new it had Northern Counties H24/24R bodywork and was one of the last AEC Regents delivered new with a petrol engine. It was re-engined and rebuilt in 1956 to Open Top O28/24R and named The White Knight. Eastbourne sold it in 1960 to Thomas Bros. (Port Talbot) Ltd. for seafront services where it was renamed. It was due to be replaced in 1962, but the lack of a suitable alternative meant that it was overhauled and ran with Thomas Bros. until 1965. It was withdrawn in 1965 and sold to Way's scrapyard in Splott, Cardiff. It was still there 10 years later! It then passed to the West of England Transport Museum, Winkleigh in 1978. By 1985 it had moved on to the Chalk Pits Museum, Amberley, Sussex. It then moved back home to Eastbourne and was stored in a shed at Wenhams. The shed was destroyed in the great storm of 1987 and it is believed that JK 7431 was scrapped after that...unless someone knows different!

32 117 LNY was the subject of a livery exercise in 1964 an attempt to brighten-up the fleet appearance. Whilst the standard livery layout was retained, the main 'Thomas Bros Blue' colour was replaced by the lighter 'Danube Blue' as used on the coaches. It was later returned to standard livery, 117 LNY was also painted into reverse coach livery in an another attempt to brighten up the fleet livery. When first painted in this livery it featured a cream 'V' on the front but the 'V' was painted out before it left the paint shop.

33 118 LNY was given a livery variation utilising the standard colours with the addition of a deep frontal 'V', similar to that carried by contemporary City of Oxford vehicles. The exercise wasn't deemed a success and

Reg No.	Built	Chassis	Body	Origin (If not new)	In	Out	Notes

118 was soon returned to the usual livery style. Also worthy of mention is that the fleetname was repositioned using a 'bold extended' font, which became the norm thereafter. It replaced the previous version that was in Gill Sans font and centrally fixed on the body sides. The bus also pioneered roof mounted illuminated advert panels which were developed between the General Manager and Park Royal. The panels were lit by fluorescent tubes which also lit the inside of the bus - a feature which became widespread in the UK in later years.

34 Named Port Talbot Cavalier.

35 Named Maid of Port Talbot.

1962

Reg No.	Built	Chassis	Body	Origin	In	Out	Notes
121 NTX	1962	AEC Reliance (2MU3RA4067)	Harrington C41F		4/62	1/71	**36**
122 NTX	1962	Leyland Tiger Cub PSUC1/1 (624751)	Alexander B45F		6/62	1/71	
123 NTX	1962	Leyland Tiger Cub PSUC1/1 (624750)	Alexander B45F		8/62	1/71	

Notes

36 Named Afan Star.

1963

Reg No.	Built	Chassis	Body	Origin	In	Out	Notes
124 SNY	1963	AEC Reliance (4MU4RA4703)	Marshall B53F		6/63	1/71	
125 SNY	1963	AEC Reliance (4MU4RA4704)	Marshall B53F		6/63	1/71	
126 SNY	1963	AEC Reliance (4MU4RA4705)	Marshall DP49F		6/63	1/71	**37**

Notes

37 126 SNY was a 49-seat semi-coach, which wore a livery incorporating Thomas Bros Blue and Danube Blue, with the customary Primrose relief. When TTX 141G was delivered with bus seating in 1969, these were exchanged with the DP seats from 126 SNY. These were then retrimmed by Western Welsh at Ely in their DP specification blue tartan moquette, prior to being refitted into TTX 141G.

1964

Reg No.	Built	Chassis	Body	Origin	In	Out	Notes
127 WNY	1964	AEC Reliance (4MU4RA5028)	Harrington C49F		1/64	1/71	**38**
128 WNY	1964	AEC Reliance (4MU4RA5066)	Marshall B53F		5/64	1/71	
129 WNY	1964	AEC Reliance (4MU4RA5067)	Marshall B53F		5/64	1/71	
130 WNY	1964	AEC Reliance (4MU4RA5068)	Marshall B53F		5/64	1/71	

Notes

38 Named Afan Venturer.

Reg No.	Built	Chassis	Body	Origin (If not new)	In	Out	Notes

1965

From David Jones & Son (Port Talbot) Ltd., Pantdu, Port Talbot.

These vehicles were delicensed when acquired and were quickly disposed of by Thomas Bros; none are known to have been operated.

Reg No.	Built	Chassis	Body	Origin (If not new)	In	Out	Notes
EM 4687	1950	AEC Regal III (9621E882)	Burlingham FC37F	Lawrenson, Bootle	9/65	9/65	**39**
HTG 294	1948	AEC Regal III (O962325)	Longwell Green B39F		9/65	9/65	**40**
JOD 611	1949	AEC Regal III (9621A332)	Duple C32F	Devon General (TCR611)/ Western Welsh (524)	9/65	9/65	
JOD 615	1949	AEC Regal III (9621A336)	Duple C31F	Devon General (TCR 615)/ Western Welsh (528)	9/65	9/65	
JTG 63	1949	Crossley SD42/6 (98077)	Burlingham FC37F		9/65	9/65	**41**
KTD 7	1949	Crossley SD42 (97683)	Duple C33F	Robinson, Great Harwood	9/65	9/65	
LNY 231	1951	AEC Regal III (9621A1004)	Plaxton Consort FC37F		9/65	9/65	**42**
MTG 172	1953	AEC Regal IV (9822S211)	Burlingham C41C		9/65	9/65	
OTG 529	1954	AEC Reliance (MU3RV174)	oe C41C		9/65	9/65	
PDE 40	1951	Albion Victor (73113C)	Duple C31F	Gough, Milford Haven	9/65	9/65	
GHT 127	1941	Bristol K5G (53.001)	ECW O33/26R	Bristol Tramways (3315)/ Brighton, Hove & Dist. (992)	3/65	8/69	**43**
DNY 131C	1965	AEC Reliance (4MU3RA5529)	Weymann DP49F		5/65	1/71	
DNY 132C	1965	AEC Reliance (4MU3RA5526)	Weymann B53F		5/65	1/71	
DNY 133C	1965	AEC Reliance (4MU3RA5527)	Weymann B53F		5/65	1/71	
DNY 134C	1965	AEC Reliance (4MU3RA5528)	Weymann B53F		5/65	1/71	

Notes

39 *Originally Harrington C33F, rebodied in 1958.*

40 *Originally Longford C33F, rebodied in 1956.*

41 *Originally Davies C33F, rebodied in 1957.*

42 *Originally Strachan FC37C, rebodied in 1960.*

43 *Named The Sandfields Belle. Converted to open top by Brighton, Hove & District in 1956.*

1966

Reg No.	Built	Chassis	Body	Origin (If not new)	In	Out	Notes
HTG 179D	1966	AEC Reliance (2MU4RA6221)	Duple Northern C41F		2/66	1/71	**44**
HTG 180D	1966	Leyland Panther Cub PSRC1/1 (L53726)	Strachan B47F		8/66	1/71	

No.	Built	Chassis	Body	Origin (If not new)	In	Out	Notes
HTG 181D	1966	Leyland Panther Cub PSRC1/1 (L53727)	Strachan B47F		8/66	1/71	
HTG 182D	1966	Leyland Panther Cub PSRC1/1 (L53476)	Strachan B47F		8/66	1/71	**45**

Notes

44 *Named Afan Highwayman.*

45 *The three Leyland Panther cubs were notoriously underpowered and tended to overheat. Later in its life, HTG 182D had the engine radiator moved from the front to the back, resulting in a 'bulge' beneath the rear window. This failed to cure the problem. This bus was fitted for one person operation by Thomas Bros.*

1967

No.	Built	Chassis	Body	Origin (If not new)	In	Out	Notes
MNY 135E	1967	AEC Reliance (6MU3RA6546)	Marshall DP49F		?/67	1/71	
OTX 136F	1967	AEC Reliance (6MU3RA6543)	Marshall B51F		11/67	1/71	
OTX 137F	1967	AEC Reliance (6MU3RA6544)	Marshall B51F		11/67	1/71	
OTX 138F	1967	AEC Reliance (6MU3RA6545)	Marshall B51F		11/67	1/71	

1968

No.	Built	Chassis	Body	Origin (If not new)	In	Out	Notes
OBX 780	1957	Leyland Tiger Cub PSUC1/1 (576299)	Weymann B44F	James, Ammanford (225)	7/57	1/71	
OBX 781	1957	Leyland Tiger Cub PSUC1/1 (576300)	Weymann B44F	James, Ammanford (226)	7/57	1/71	
PTG 239F	1968	AEC Reliance (6MU4R6863)	Duple (N) Commander III C49F		2/69	1/71	**46**
RTG 140F	1968	Leyland Tiger Cub PSUC1/2 (850723)	Marshall B45F		?/68	1/71	

Notes

46 *Named Afan Commander.*

1969

No.	Built	Chassis	Body	Origin (If not new)	In	Out	Notes
TTX 141G	1969	AEC Reliance (6MU3R877)	Marshall DP49F		4/69	1/71	**47**
VTG 142G	1969	Leyland Tiger Cub PSUC1/12 (950458)	Marshall B45F		6/69	1/71	**48**
VTG 143G	1969	Leyland Tiger Cub PSUC1/12 (950459)	Marshall B45F		6/69	1/71	**48**

Notes

47 *TTX 141G was delivered with bus seating which was exchanged with the DP seats from 126 SNY. These were then retrimmed by Western Welsh at Ely in their DP specification blue tartan moquette, prior to being refitted into TTX 141G. This was the sole semi-coach to be specified with chrome bumpers and a rear luggage locker and saw use on the tours to Minehead.*

48 *Delivered in SWT red and cream livery, but with Thomas Bros. fleetnames.*

Reg No.	Built	Chassis	Body	Origin (If not new)	In	Out	Notes
1970							
UWN 67H	1970	AEC Reliance 6MU4R7289	Duple Northern C41F		3/70	1/71	**49**

Notes

49 Due to be named Afan Crusader but appeared with Afan Commander nameplates. Delivered in SWT cream and red coach livery.

1971

Reg No.	Built	Chassis	Body	Origin (If not new)	In	Out	Notes
YWN 553J	1971	AEC Reliance (6MU2R7388)	Willowbrook B45F		5/71		**50**
YWN 555J	1971	AEC Reliance (6MU2R7390)	Willowbrook B45F		5/71		**50**
YWN 556J	1971	AEC Reliance (6MU2R7389)	Willowbrook B45F		5/71		**50, 51**

Notes

50 Ordered by Thomas Bros. but delivered after SWT takeover in full SWT livery and numbered 261/3/2 respectively.

51 Delivered as UWN 674H but entered service registered YWN 556J.

Ancilliary Vehicles

Reg No.	Built	Chassis	Body	Origin (If not new)	In	Out
L 9972		Ford T 1 ton 22.4hp	Lorry	Previously a lorry-bus, used only as a lorry after 1925.	1921	4/30
NY 5669	1924	Ford T 1 ton	Lorry	Ex-Alfred Jones, Neath. Previously a lorry-bus, used only as a lorry after 1928.	11/27	3/29
NY 8082	1925	Morris Cowley	Van	Subject to a legal case in 1934 after Thomas Gwyn Thomas had used the same registration plate on a car, while still running the van.	5/25	1934
TG 2062		Morris Minor	Van	Ex-Ben Embling, Porthcawl		5/42
?		Ford AA	Lorry			
CTG 585			Car			4/53
DNY 835			Car			4/53
MTG 919		Austin A40	Car			1955
MTX 407		Bedford	Van			
NNY 70	1954	Leyland Tiger Cub/ SARO B44F	Driver Training Vehicle		6/54	1/71
NWN 917		Ford Consul	Car			
SWN 538		Ford 5 cwt	Van			
953 FNY		Ford Consul	Staff Car			
?		Ford Thames 7cwt	Van		10/58	
850 GCY		Ford Zephyr 6	Car			
104 SNY		Austin	Van			1965
KNY 690D		Morris Commercial	Van			
MCY 806F		Ford Zephyr 6	Car			

'The almost ghost bus fleet that ferried those who responded to the demands of town's giant steel plant'.

There was one bus company in Port Talbot's past that was travelled on by so many, yet rarely rates a mention when conversation turns to the town's many bus operators.

Most of those latter day operators and their vehicles have figured somewhere as the Thomas Bros. story unfolded, but there was one exception that, because of its size was surprisingly difficult to miss — the Steel Company of Wales. For many decades the town's main employer the company operated a fleet of vehicles.

These were used mainly for transporting staff around what was once Europe's largest steel plant covering many square miles. On occasions they could be seen on the town's streets ferrying in and out of the sprawling plant key personnel.

These easily recognisable vehicles might on occasions have been used for conveying workers on staff outings. Given their role in life it is not surprising perhaps that they were utilitarian in many aspects.

This, almost ghost fleet comprised a small number of Davies-bodied Austin K8 14 seaters with only three forward gears, plus some Dennis Falcon 37-seaters, also with Davies bodywork.

Dennis 5/D, MTX 298, on its way through the giant steelworks site during November 1961.

The dragon that ran a bus fleet of its own

The fleet lined up at the steelworks. The darker vehicles, right, were Austin K type vans used to distribute hot meals prepared in the main canteen for the various smaller canteens around the sprawling works.

With the destination showing 'Main Canteen' this was Dennis 9/D, MNY 551, when fairly new. Bodywork was by D.J. Davies, Merthyr.

Visitors on a tour of the steelworks guided by senior blast furnace staff. One each of the Austin and Dennis buses was used on the tour. Interestingly while the majority of the men are wearing safety helmets the women are carrying theirs.

The SCoW fleet

Fleet no.	Reg.	Chassis no.	Year	Make/Body
1/D	MNY 551	174L6	1952	Dennis Falcon II Davies B37F
2/D	MNY 638	175L6	1952	Dennis Falcon II Davies B37F
3/D	MTX 110	179L6	1953	Dennis Falcon II Davies B37F
4/D	MTX 259	178L6	1953	Dennis Falcon II Davies B37F
5/D	MTX 298	181L6	1953	Dennis Falcon II Davies B37F
6/D	MTX 433	182L6	1953	Dennis Falcon II Davies B37F
7/D	MTX 665	183L6	1953	Dennis Falcon II Davies B37F
8/D	MTX 726	184L6	1953	Dennis Falcon II Davies B37F
9/D	NTX 217	185L6	1953	Dennis Falcon II Davies B37F
	NTG 415	25648	1953	Austin K8/CVC Davies B14F
	NTG 557	25649	1953	Austin K8/CVC Davies B14F
	NTG 720	25646	1953	Austin K8/CVC Davies B14F
	NTG 797	26201	1953	Austin K8/CVC Davies B14F
15B	NTX 17	26296	1953	Austin K8/CVC Davies B14F
BD11	656 PTG	90498	1962	Bedford SB5 Duple Midland B42F
BD14	657 PTG	90560	1962	Bedford SB5 Duple Midland B42F
BD13	658 PTG	90563	1962	Bedford SB5 Duple Midland B42F
BD12	659 PTG	90554	1962	Bedford SB5 Duple Midland B42F
BD15	660 PTG	90590	1962	Bedford SB5 Duple Midland B42F

There is a possibility that there was one additional Dennis Falcon II; chassis no.176L6 is shown simply as being intended for a steelworks, but no registration or body type has yet been identified.

Since they were intended mainly for short internal journeys at the plant, they were fitted with utility-type wooden seats and on the works roads, they were not the most comfortable of vehicles.

In 1962 they were joined by five Bedford SB5s with Duple 42-seat bodies, which presumably replaced the Austins.

A contemporary photograph shows one of the K8s looking extremely 'tired' in later life and it is possible also that by 1965 at least one of them had migrated across to Velindre Tinplate Works, Swansea.

The livery of the Austin K8s and Dennises was principally maroon, a similar shade to the plant's steam locomotives. The Bedford SB5s and the later Ford Transits and Ford As were painted in BSC blue and white livery.

The bus fleet, also known as brakes — a legacy from the days of horse drawn transport — had a number of SCoW Austin K canteen vans allocated to the same department. The brake drivers' office and rest room was at the rear of the main canteen. At the time there were only four cooking canteens and the brakes delivered food and serving staff to the smaller canteens dotted around the sprawling works.

This unique fleet even laid claim to its own maintenance and engineering department.

Austin K8 15B (NTX 17) has its fuel tank topped up at the pumps.

In what, by then, was a fresh blue and white livery 1962 Bedford SB5 BD15, 660 PTG, is seen at the Abbey Works bus station.

The fleet and, no doubt, some of the regulars who drove these vehicles around Port Talbot and the steel plant proudly lined up with them, and among them the Austin K vans.

Apart from the buses themselves, one of the most important aspects of public transport for the passengers at least is bus stops and shelters to protect them in wet and windy Wales! The bus stop and shelter above was typical of those that abounded in Thomas Bros. territory while one of a different design, offering more protection was the aim of the build crew to the left seen outside Cymmer council offices around the end of the 1950s. They are from the left: Edgar Edwards, Billy Jones and David Townsend.

Abbreviations

Abbreviations used in this book:

AEC	Associated Equipment Company
AVBOA	Avon Valley Bus Owners Association
BBC	British Broadcasting Corporation
BET	British Electric Traction Co., Ltd.
BR	British Rail(ways)
BTC	British Transport Commission
GKB	Guest, Keen, Baldwin.
GKN	Guest, Keen & Nettlefolds
GWR	Great Western Railway
KC	King's Counsel
MoWT	Ministry of War Transport
N&C	Neath & Cardiff Luxury Coaches Ltd.
NCB	National Coal Board
NTO	New Temporary Offices
PC	Police Constable
PR	Public Relations
PTMPA	Port Talbot Motor Proprietors Ass.
PTR&D	Port Talbot Railway and Docks Co.
SARO	Saunders Roe
SCoW	Steel Company of Wales
SLF	Super Low Floor
SWT	The South Wales Transport Co., Ltd.
TBAT	Tilling & British Automobile Traction Ltd.
TC	Traffic Commissioner
TWW	Television Wales and the West
UK	United Kingdom
WW	Western Welsh Omnibus Co., Ltd.

Body and Seating Codes

Standard PSV seating codes when describing the body and seating arrangements for double and single deck buses and coaches as detailed below:

The seating capacity of a double deck vehicle is expressed as the number of seats in the upper saloon over the number of seats in the lower saloon highbridge and lowbridge refer to the body layout and not the overall height of the vehicle (i.e. lowbridge has a sunken gangway on the upper deck).

Letters placed before the seating capacity:

B	Single-deck bus
C	Single-deck coach
CO	Convertible open top vehicle
Ch	Charabanc
DP	Single-deck dual-purpose vehicle
F	Full fronted vehicle (where not normally fitted)
H	Double-deck highbridge bus
L	Double-deck lowbridge bus
O	Permanent open top vehicle

Letters placed after the seating capacity:

C	Centre entrance (if there are two or more pairs of seats in front of the entrance)
D	Dual entrance/exit (or more than two)
F	Front entrance
R	Rear entrance

Bibliography

Anon., Changes in South Wales in Vintage Roadscene Archive No.5 (Kelsey Publishing, 2019).

Barrie, D.S.M., A Regional History of the Railways of Great Britain, Volume 12, South Wales (David & Charles, 1980).

Bett, W.H., Gillham, J.C., Price J.H., The Tramways of South Wales. (Light Rail Transit Association, 1993).

Brewster, D. E., Motor Buses in Wales 1898-1932 (Oakwood Press, 1975).

Cummings, John, Railway Motor Buses and Bus Services in the British Isles 1902-1933. (Oxford Publishing Co., 1980).

Fulford, Roger, Five Decades of B.E.T. 1896-1946 (B.E.T., 1946).

Fulford, Roger, The Sixth Decade 1946-1956 (Blackmore Press, 1956).

Gardiner, F. & Hilliard, F., British Bus Fleets No. 18 South Wales (Ian Allan, 1963).

Gardiner, F. & Hilliard, F., British Bus Fleets No. 18 South Wales (Ian Allan, 1966).

Hale, Michael, Steam in South Wales Volume Six, The General Scene (The Welsh Railways Research Circle, 1999).

Holding, David & Moyes, Tony, History of British Bus Services: South Wales (Ian Allan, 1986).

J.M.A., Planning and Building Up an Open-top Service in Bus and Coach magazine (Iliffe & Sons, Ltd. October 1961).

Jones, Brian, Port Talbot – A History of Past Personalities Volume 2 (Brian Jones, 1990).

Lambden, William, Serving a Thriving and Growing Steel Town in Bus and Coach magazine. (Iliffe & Sons, Ltd. February 1958).

McCloy, Robert Travels in the Valleys (Historical Association, Swansea Branch, 2012).

Mercer, Neville, A Flock of Seagulls (Local Transport History Library, 2019).

Mingay, G.E., Fifteen Years On. The B.E.T. Group 1956-1971 (B.E.T., 1973).

Morgan, H., South Wales Branch Lines. (Ian Allan, 1984).

Morgan, Kenneth O., The People's Peace. British History 1945-1990. (Oxford University Press, 1990).

Mulley, Corinne and Higginson, Martin, Companion to Road Passenger Transport History. (R&RTHA, 2013).

Parry, Stephen, History of the Steel Industry in the Port Talbot Area 1900-1988 (University of Leeds -School of History, 2011).

Secombe, Harry, Welsh Fargo. (Robson Books, 1981).

Simmonds, Robin G., A History of the Port Talbot Railway & Docks Company and the South Wales Mineral Railway Company, Volumes 1 and 2 (Lightmoor Press, 2012 and 2013).

Truran, Gerald, Blackpool, South Wales in Classic Bus magazine, October-November 1997 (Classic Bus Publishing, 1997).

Truran, Gerald, Saunders-Roe Anglesey Ltd., (Bryngold Books, 2009).

Various, A Fleet History of Devon General Omnibus and Touring Company Ltd. (PSV Circle, 2015).

Various, Old Port Talbot & District in Photographs, Volume 1 (The Port Talbot Historical Society, 1979).

Woodhams, John, The Bedford OB and OWB (D.P.R. Marketing 1986).

The last Thomas Bros. vehicle in service, MNY 135E, at Cwmavon. It was withdrawn in 1981.

A big thank you!

On a social media site the people of Port Talbot were invited to share their memories of Thomas Bros. A small number of replies at best was anticipated, but instead hundreds were received!

It is clear that this small company meant a great deal to the community. In the process of reaching out some old friends appear to have been re-united so the results go beyond what appears on these pages.
A really big 'Thank You' is owed to everyone who responded. They all helped formulate the memories that make this book.

There are many others who have contributed to the information contained in these pages. Jeff Johnson and David Beilby who provided information relating to the early fleet and Andrew Porter for his assistance in unravelling some of the many mysteries of the company's antecedents. I am especially indebted to the late Byron Westlake and Dai Morris who were particularly helpful in clarifying details relating to vehicle specifications and engineering matters.
Alan Williams kindly donated a photograph album and information relating to the Acacia Avenue depot from his late father, driver John Howard Williams. Mike Taylor kindly permitted access to the files and information collected by his late father, Chris Taylor. Notes made by the late Gerald Truran were also consulted, courtesy of Helen Truran.

Peter Hale, John Weager and the team at the Bus Archive assisted greatly with company service applications and other details, while Peter Heath miraculously uncovered a staff and vehicle rota from 1958. I am also grateful to Stacy O'Sullivan and the team at the Richard Burton Archives in Swansea University for allowing me to peruse the Thomas Bros. financial records and ledgers which they hold.

Other photographs are mainly from the author's or publisher's collections and we have attempted to track down the photographers, who have given permission to include their work. We hope that anyone finding their uncredited work here will approve of their inclusion.

Thanks are also due to Richard Field, Vernon Morgan, David Wita, Huw Morgans, James Shortland, Jeff Phillips and Damian Owen for permitting access to the Port Talbot Historical Society's photographic archive.

Publisher David Roberts, who I have known for many years, had the unenviable task of trying to understand exactly what I was on about as I tried to impose my views on how the tale should be told and the book should appear! Finally, but not least my wife Fran who tolerated the mess I made with papers and the frequent need to be 'left alone'.

Phil Trotter, 2023.

A brief reprise of the Thomas Bros. name and livery came in 2014 when First Cymru Transbus Dart SLF 42694, CU03 BHW, was one of four buses chosen to carry a heritage livery as part of the SWT Centenary celebration. The vehicle is pictured at Heol Camlas, Cwmavon on 30th August, 2017; the bus was later scrapped by the company.
Richard Field